PENGUIN BOOKS

WAIN

Hunter Davies was born in Renfrew educated at Durham University, an half in the Lake District. As a journalist he worked on the *Sunday Times,* where he was chief features writer and then editor of the magazine. He wrote regular columns for *Punch* and currently writes interviews for the *Independent* and the *Daily Mail.* For three years he presented *Bookshelf* on BBC Radio 4. He is the author of over thirty books, including biographies of Wordsworth, Columbus, the Beatles, Beatrix Potter and Robert Louis Stevenson. He has written several books about Lakeland, including *A Walk around the Lakes,* and publishes his own bestselling guide, *The Good Guide to the Lakes.* He is married to the novelist and biographer Margaret Forster.

WAINWRIGHT

The Biography

HUNTER DAVIES

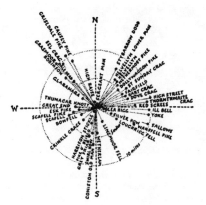

PENGUIN BOOKS

PENGUIN BOOKS

Published by the Penguin Group
Penguin Books Ltd, 27 Wrights Lane, London W8 5TZ, England
Penguin Putnam Inc., 375 Hudson Street, New York, New York 10014, USA
Penguin Books Australia Ltd, Ringwood, Victoria, Australia
Penguin Books Canada Ltd, 10 Alcorn Avenue, Toronto, Ontario, Canada M4V 3B2
Penguin Books (NZ) Ltd, 182–190 Wairau Road, Auckland 10, New Zealand

Penguin Books Ltd, Registered Offices: Harmondsworth, Middlesex, England

First published by Michael Joseph 1995
Published in Penguin Books 1998
1 3 5 7 9 10 8 6 4 2

Printed in England by Clays Ltd, St Ives plc

Contents

Apart from those listed below, all the photographs in this book have been provided by the family, and I would like to thank Betty Wainwright, Peter Wainwright, Jack Fish and Linda Collinge: 10 Bob Alker; 14 Ken Shepherd; 15 Gillian Murphy; 21 Jack Woods; 22 Newcastle University; 23 Lancashire Evening Post; 24–7 Richard Else; 28 Westmorland Gazette; 37 Sheila Richardson.

List of Illustrations

Acknowledgements

First and foremost, thanks to Betty Wainwright without whom none of this could have been possible. Then to Peter and Doreen Wainwright. Also to Jack Fish (AW's nephew), Sheila Dobson (AW's niece), Linda Collinge (AW's great niece), and Jane King (Betty's daughter).

In Blackburn, I would like to thank Lawrence Wolstenholme, Clifford Singleton, Richard Slater. Also Bob Alker in Garstang, Roy Wallis in Chorley, Margaret Ainley in Brighouse, Bill Mitchell in Giggleswick, George Haworth in Carnforth, and Donald Haigh of Chadderton for the Len Chadwick letters.

In Kendal, particular thanks to Percy Duff, Harry Firth, Andrew Nichol, Harry Griffin, Beryl Williams, Ken Shepherd, John Marsh, Donald James, Bill Tate, John Estensen, Richard Rogers, Carol Davies, and Jimmy Richardson

Elsewhere in Cumbria – Mary Burkett, Molly Lefebure, Sheila Richardson, Eric Robson, Eric Wallace, Chris Jesty, Michael Moon, Bernard Oakley, and Bruce Hanson.

Also many thanks to Gillian Murphy (daughter of Henry Marshall), Hazel Maudsley (widow of Eric), Richard Else, Derry Brabbs, Frank Nash, David Pegg, Valerie Malam. Not forgetting Jenny Dereham, of course.

Introduction

I've always been a Wainwright fan. If you think a fan should not be let loose on a biography, that they should always be written by cold, clear-headed detached outsiders, able and willing to expose and examine every wart and blemish, then hard luck, this has been a labour of love. I've enjoyed every moment tracking down his life, talking to his family and friends, following his footsteps, on paper and on fell, and being ever careful, as he always advised, about where I put my feet. Along the way, I have stumbled across the odd wart and the minor blemish, and discovered a more complex and passionate character than any reader of his books could ever have imagined, but then this is the modern age, unquote, not nineteenth-century hagiography. Readers of today's biographies expect inner turmoils and sexual longings to be revealed. We want to know it all, because to know all is to understand, so we like to think.

I became a fan some twenty-five years ago when I first picked up Book Five, *The Northern Fells*, to climb my local Caldbeck Fells, and was astonished to find there were seven books in the series, all hand drawn, hand written. My next reaction was jealousy. Why hadn't I thought of such a book? Then it was utter admiration. How did he do it? How come one person has so many skills? Who is he anyway? And is he dead or what?

I later had the pleasure of meeting him, in 1978, before he came out and achieved national recognition through his books published by Michael Joseph and his TV series. At the time, I was never sure about this exposure, suspecting him of selling out, not realising the altruistic reason for his acceptance of media fame so late in life.

It didn't make me less of a fan. I still consider his *Seven Pictorial Guides to the Lakeland Fells* to be works of art. I'll go further. I think they are masterpieces. Why not use that word? Why should poems and plays, novels and paintings be allowed such accolades and not little guide books which you can slip into your pocket, slip into your life? Wainwright has become a household god, a term of reference, for millions of people. Two million, I reckon. That's my estimate of the total sales so far of those seven little books.

What sparked me off, to ask to do the biography, was reading *Memoirs of a Fellwanderer* (published 1993) when I was a judge for the Lakeland Book of the Year competition. (It wasn't eligible for the award, by the way, being a composite of two earlier books.) I thought, once again, how few and meagre were the personal details he ever gave away, despite the word 'Memoirs', and despite dropping hints of certain important events in his life, without ever explaining them. He had died in 1991, so I wondered who was doing his biography. I made enquiries and found that his widow, whom I had met in 1978, had turned down all requests during the first year after he died. Too soon, too upsetting. Now she felt stronger, more able to cope with the thought of some sort of book about him. I persuaded her that a biography should be done. Why should the poets and painters have all the accolades?

But is his life story worth telling? Several people asked that. After all, his real career was pretty humdrum. (I won't mention his day job here, although all true fans know what it was, as in the book itself I take things chronologically, not revealing events ahead until they happen – the first rule, I always think, of any biography.) His personal papers proved so rich, people were so kind in providing me with letters he had written, relatives and friends were happy to share their memories, that one problem turned out to be too much material.

Having first go at anyone's life is always exciting, if worrying. Writing biographies of Wordsworth, Beatrix Potter, George Stephenson, Christopher Columbus or Robert Louis Stevenson means following a path which has been hacked by others, where gardens have been laid out, trees established. The aim then is to re-assess the old plantation, or approach it from a new direction. The first biographer has a different job. He has to carve out his own route, arrange the landscape in order, when in real life there was little order, or was part of several orders, all happening at the same time. There is a responsibility to the rough ground – not to soften or hide, yet not create unnecessary features.

Wasn't Wainwright a very private person, who hated even having his photograph taken? True. In his lifetime, he would probably not have allowed any of this material to be seen. Just as he might have hated any physical memorial to him in Lakeland. But he is not alive. We who are left who admired him must be allowed to remember him in our own way, as long as his family do not object. His creative work came out of his life, as you will see, and we can better understand what drove him on if we know from whence he came. That's my excuse. Oh, and if he is watching, from over there, up on Haystacks, I must apologise for calling him Alfred in the early chapters. He would have really hated that. It just seemed so cold and impersonal to call a boy or a young man by his surname. After that, I do slip into Wainwright or AW. I did think of calling him Aloysius, but that was his joke.

Hunter Davies, Loweswater, 1995.

CHAPTER ONE

Birth in Blackburn, 1907

Alfred Wainwright was born on 17 January 1907 in Blackburn, Lancashire. Today, the town is quietly proud of Wainwright, in a careful, understated way, but there are plans afoot to create a Wainwright Trail, guiding you around the town to the various locations associated with his birth and early years. Very like the Trail they have already created for Kathleen Ferrier, Blackburn's only other distinguished personage of the twentieth century, unless you count the late Russell Harty, the popular TV personality. Kathleen Ferrier, born in 1912, later moved to Cumbria and, like Wainwright, it was in her adopted county that she first achieved national recognition.

The Ferrier Trail takes you to some interesting buildings, as her father was a headmaster and she went to a rather good school, but they are having trouble planning a similarly interesting route for future Wainwright pilgrims. His background was strictly working class, his homes humble, his schools unrenowned, but the main problem is that Blackburn is still in the throes of urban clearance. At present, there is a proposal to extend the inner ring road, known as Barbara Castle Way. (No, she was not a Blackburn girl, but she did give it thirty-four years as its MP.) It is possible that this extension could wipe out for ever vital traces of Wainwright's roots, hence the delay in marking up and colouring in his Town Trail. John Lennon gave Blackburn a mention in passing, drawing attention to its existence for those outside Britain who might never have heard of this Northern industrial town, with his reference to 'four thousand holes in Blackburn, Lancashire'. There could be more holes to come.

Blackburn had a big effect on Wainwright's life, his values and his attitudes, but he could in fact have been born anywhere, anywhere that is amongst a dozen or so towns across Lancashire and Yorkshire. His father, Albert, was a travelling stone mason whose work took him round the two counties. He was born in Penistone near Barnsley on 10 July 1870, the son of a builder, and in his early years he achieved some success, running a quarry in partnership with his brother.

He married Emily Woodcock on 9 August 1893, at Netherfield Congregational Church in Penistone. Emily was aged twenty at the time of the wedding, small and slight, the daughter of an ironmonger. Albert was twenty-three, tall and burly. They had met through the Church where they had both been Sunday School teachers. On their marriage, the other teachers gave them a Bible, suitably inscribed in copperplate handwriting: 'Presented to Mr and Mrs Albert Wainwright of Netherfield Congregational Sunday School on the occassion of their marriage as a small token of our appreciation of their service in the Sunday School, and wishing them long lives of usefulness and happines and all good things. Signed on behalf of the Teachers – A Glassey, Pastor.'

Their first child, Alice Mary, was born on 17 June 1894 in Penistone. Not long afterwards, things went wrong at the quarry and Albert took to the road as an itinerant stone mason, moving around, trying to find work. Their second child, a son called Frank, was born on 29 July 1896 in Barnsley. Their third, another daughter, Annie, was born in January 1900 in Morecambe.

Albert's trouble was drink. His beer-drinking exploits figure in every family memoir, although it is not clear if it was drink which caused the collapse of his quarry business, or whether he took to the bottle afterwards to make up for the disappointment. On the day of his second daughter's arrival in 1900, he decided to have a few drinks, on the way to register the birth. The Boer War was at its height and in the pub he heard talk of some battle at Pretoria. Arriving at the Registrar's Office, he decided to christen the new baby Annie Pretoria. Annie went through her childhood deeply embarrassed by what he had done. When Inspectors visited her school, the teacher always asked her to stand up and give out her full name.

It was the prospect of work on some railway arches which took Albert and his family to Blackburn in January 1901, settling there from then on. They rented a two-up-and-two-down terrace house at 331 Audley Range, about a mile from the centre of Blackburn, a long, straight, busy, dusty road. The rent was 4/6d a week. Opposite was a little brick works. All around were cotton mills and belching factory chimneys.

The history of textiles in Blackburn goes back to Elizabethan times. It was then a large village of some 2,000 which had grown up on the banks of the Blakewater, or black stream, which flows into the River Darwen. There was no sign of any Roman settlement, but a Roman road did cross the stream at the point where Blackburn eventually emerged. The first mention of 'Blackburne' as a place was in the Domesday Book. Wool was the first industry to be produced locally, woven in people's homes, and by 1650 there was a blue and white pattern known nationally as 'Blackburn checks'. In the eighteenth century, cotton took over from wool, and was at first still woven in the workers' homes. Then came a technological revolution which changed not just Blackburn but the whole of Lancashire and, in effect, the industrial world. James Hargreaves invented the spinning jenny in 1764 which enabled the spinners to keep pace with another Lancashire invention, John Kay's flying shuttle. Production moved out of the homes into factories, but not without opposition. Angry weavers marched on Blackburn factories in the 1820s, breaking up the new steam-powered looms. One of the early cotton factory owners in Blackburn was Robert Peel, grandfather of Sir Robert Peel.

People flocked to work in the new cotton factories from all over the north of England, and even from Scotland and Ireland. By 1844 the population of Blackburn was 40,000, many of whom, according to a Lancashire historian, were 'of the poorer sort of people, with pale and emaciated features'. There was a temporary halt to the industrial explosion in 1862 caused by the American Civil War which dried up the importation of raw cotton.

Blackburn, with a population which had jumped to 63,000, was the hardest hit town in Lancashire – twenty-five mills stopped production, 7,238 mill hands were out of work, 8,215 were on short time and only 7,127 were in full-time work.

By 1901, when the Wainwrights arrived in Blackburn, the population was 130,000. Children were still starting work in the mills as young as eight but the work force was largely women. Mothers would get their young children up before they went to work, at four-thirty in the morning, and take them to a grandma or a child minder's cottage. At dinner-time – midday – the older children would bring the babies to the mill to be breast-fed by the mother. She herself would probably have bread and dripping, sitting by her loom.

Most people lived in back-to-back, two-up-and-two-down terrace houses with no bathroom and no internal lavatory. In the back yard would be an outside closet or privy, freezing in winter, so a chamber pot was used, kept under the bed. The privy was basically a pail with a wooden board over it, emptied by a gang of what were called 'midnight mechanics'. By 1920, Blackburn still had 11,819 pail-and-slop closets waiting to be converted to running water.

Each morning, a knocker-up walked along every street at five o'clock, rattling the upstairs bedroom window with a long stick. Mill girls would hurry to the mill in their shawls and clogs, their footsteps echoing on the cobblestones. Five minutes late and you could be fined, or perhaps locked out, the mill gates closed in your face, so you lost a whole day's pay. Families without any bread-winner could end up in the Poor House. It was only after the Liberal Government's landslide victory in 1906, and the emergence of the first Labour MPs, that education and social conditions began slowly to improve, exploitation of child labour in the mills ceased and better schools were introduced, free up to the age of thirteen, with a midday meal provided.

Escape was provided by the church and by football. The Wainwrights were Congregationalists, even if Albert by this time was only notionally so, preferring to stay at home on Sundays. There being no pubs open, he would talk to his pigeons which he kept in the back yard. There were ten Congregational chapels to chose from and Emily Wainwright enrolled her family at Furthergate, one of the earliest, founded in 1852. She and her children went at least three times on a Sunday, to Sunday School classes and to services. Churches were social centres, where people enjoyed singing and meeting their friends. Sunday was considered the most enjoyable day of the week, the day of no work, dressing in your best and, with luck, having a proper meal at dinner-time.

Emily Wainwright was very religious and kept a commonplace book in which she copied down little biblical quotations and poems, sayings and moral stories which she had read or been told. It shows she was literate, and had good, plain handwriting.

Some go to church, just for a walk.
Some go there, to have a talk,
Some go there to gain a lover
Some go there, their faults to cover
Some go there for observation
Some go there for speculation
Some go there, to sleep and nod
But few go there, to worship God.

One or two of the entries do have a bit of humour to them, even when they are of a religious nature.

I am a threepenny bit. I am not on speaking terms with the butcher. I am too small to buy a pint of beer. I am not large enough to purchase a box of chocolates. A permanent wave won't look at me. They won't let me in at the pictures. I am hardly fit for a tip – but, believe me, when I go to Church on Sunday, I am considered 'some money'.

The word 'believe' obviously caused her some trouble. In the margin she has tried it out two ways in pencil, before committing herself to the correct spelling in ink.

Men followed football. Blackburn Rovers, the team which Alfred Wainwright followed all his life, founded in 1875, was one of the original members of the Football League – but in the early years, another Blackburn club was even more famous. This was

Blackburn Olympic which, in 1883, was the first non-southern, non-public school club to win the English F.A. Cup. They were always short of money and their first pitch, which was rented, was so narrow that their long-throw expert could hurl the ball out of play on the opposite side. When they did acquire a little grandstand, it got blown away by the wind.

But everything came together in the 1882–3 season. They got a crop of excellent players, devised the first 2–3–5 system, while everyone else was still playing 2–2–6, and in the semi-finals they thumped Old Carthusians. They then had to travel to London, to Kennington Oval, to play Old Etonians in the final. They beat them 2–1 and when their captain, a Blackburn plumber, went up to receive the cup, he led a team of four cotton millworkers, two iron foundry hands, a picture framer, a clerk, a publican and a dentist. It was Olympic's finest hour, and they were carried shoulder high by their supporters waiting for their return at Blackburn station. Alas, it was almost their final hour. Within six years, they had been forgotten – and Blackburn Rovers had taken over as the most successful club in England. They won the Cup in 1884 – and the next two years as well. The whole of Blackburn turned out to greet their triumphant return each time, blocking all the main streets.

A great many chips were consumed in Blackburn every Saturday, before and after each match, and during the week as well. Every corner had its own chip shop and families survived on bags of chips and fish costing a ha'penny, one penny or tuppence. There was a tradition, now gone, peculiar to the Blackburn area, of collecting your family's chips in a basin. You would join the queue, place your basin on the counter, then loll against the wall, talking to your friends whilst watching your basin travel along the cooking range, getting warm as it moved towards the head of the queue. Each basin was different, enamel or china, blue or striped, new or cracked, so you could watch for your basin getting near the top of the queue. Alfred Wainwright loved chips, all his life, just as much as he loved the Rovers.

CHAPTER TWO

Alice and Emily's Memoirs

Alice was aged twelve in 1907 when her little brother Alfred was born, the Wainwrights's youngest and final child. Frank was ten and Annie seven, which means they were all old enough to remember the birth, but Alice remembered it very clearly – and many years later, around 1941, she committed her memory to paper. She decided to sit down and write the story of her early life, a fascinating document which has been preserved by her son, Jack Fish. It mentions the 4/6d. a week rent when they moved into Audley Range in 1901 – which, forty years later, so she says, when her mother was still living in the same house, had risen to only 8/-. Ah, the decades of low or almost non-existent inflation.

> nothing more, but he turned
> on me like a wild man and
> told me to clear out, he would
> let me know he was boss, then
> he told me "I was just like
> my mother" and I said "I
> was proud of it", then of course

Alice's handwriting is immaculate, even neater than her mother's, her spelling correct and her language grammatical, even if now and then she misses out a capital letter at the beginning of a new sentence. She writes in green ink, which gives her little notebook even more of an artistic glow. 'I think I was about twelve years old when Father came into our bedroom one morning and told us we had got another brother. We all went into mother's room to see what he was like. I well remember looking under the bed clothes and saw what seemed to me such a tiny baby, his eyes dark and shiny and his hair was light, the only one in our family with that colour, though my grandad was very sandy. We all loved this new baby very much and perhaps spoilt him a bit, he was christened Alfred. I can picture him now, as we sat at the table for our meals, he on a high chair with his back to the fire between mother and father. When I look back I think "what a happy family we might have been if the cursed drink had never entered the home . . ."'

Alfred, in his own brief memoir of his early life, *Ex-Fellwanderer*, published in 1987, revealed that his father was a drunk: 'My father, a stonemason, was an alcoholic when he had any money . . .' but gives few details. Alice spells out exactly what it was like, in her own words, and own punctuation, living with such a father.

At a very early age I knew the tragedy & misery caused by drink. Mother told me I hadn't reached the age of 2 years when Father took his first glass of beer which was the beginning of a drunkards life. He didn't care for home, wife or children, or how we lived so long as he could get drink. He might have had rows of houses, he was left by his father with a grand building business & good prospects but it all went & misery came.

Here are a few incidents which happened, they are not very pleasant to recall. I wonder now, however Mother put up with it and always left so cheerful. Never once do I remember seeing her pull a long face, but, very often I saw her with a sad one when she didn't know I was watching. She had a smile & cheerful word for everyone she came in contact with, and helped many in trouble, though her own heart was breaking.

When very young I used to listen for father's footsteps coming up the pavement, and could always tell if he had been drinking, for then his steps would be unsteady, and directly I heard them like that I used to tremble and was very frightened, how awful to be afraid of ones own father.

I was never very strong and on one occasion the doctor told Mother to avoid any excitement for me. During the same week father came home drunk, and as soon as he entered the door, he looked like a mad man & sounded like one. Mother had been washing all day, since 5.30 in the morning. He started swearing and carrying on as soon as he entered the door. Mother didn't speak a word, so he went up to her to strike her, when my brother Frank, who was only very young went between them. Father then turned to him and took hold of him by the throat. I was on the couch and when I saw him, I jumped up, screamed, then dropped on the floor. It was a full week before I saw Father again, he avoided meeting me. Whenever I was coming home he would either go out or go to bed.

Mother used to say the home was happier when he wasn't working & he hadn't any money, and couldn't get hold of anything to pawn. He used to spend nearly all his earnings in drink. I used to go to the Queen Hotel at Saturday dinnertime and get some money which was never more than a few shillings if he had worked all week, but, if I hadn't gone he would have spent all. I had to go into the public house and look around for him, the place was always full of men. He was very cross if I went up to him and asked for some money. I had to stand at the door until he saw me, then he would come to me and give me what I had to have and then go back again. Often did I plead with him to come home, but no, he wouldn't. Then mother had to go and find the cheap chops, while I stayed at home to look after the other children. She washed and cleaned 5 days a week to earn a little to live on. She used to get up at 5 oclock in the morning and start washing and was still washing when I got home from school at tea-time. This happened on Mondays and Tuesdays, other days she went out washing and cleaning and I carried the key to school. She took Alfred with her when he was only a few weeks old, when she really ought to have been resting a while.

One morning she was making breakfast for all of us quietly. Father was grumbling as usual, he had been drunk the night before and had kept Mother wake nearly all night swearing and singing in turn, and now he wanted some money and she hadn't any for him, and as she knelt down to warm the butter, he cowardly struck her and make her eye very black. He was a giant besides her, being over 6 ft high, and yet he waited until she was down and couldn't defend herself before he struck her. Oh! the irony of it.

On one occasion I remember he was again carrying on, the language he used was terrible. I stood it as long as I could then said. *Oh! Dad do hush*, nothing more, but he turned on me like a wild man and told me to clear out, he would let me know he was boss. Then he told me 'I was just like my Mother' and I said 'I was proud of it', then of course I had to fly. I went over to Mrs Fish's and told her I had got turned out. I sat down trembling and presently my Mother came to see if I was there. She asked if I might stay for the night. When I went home the day after, there wasn't a word said about it. I used to wonder, if, when he came to his senses if he was sorry, and what his thoughts were. There were times when I had such a dread of him, that, quite unknown to my Mother, I would hide his razor. I was so afraid of him murdering us all in bed. It was awful. Even now I shudder when I think of it.

To get drink he would take and pawn anything. One day he went out with a new undervest on. When he got home he hadn't a vest on but a pawn ticket in his pocket for it.

I wonder now, how Mother used to feed us. Of course, the food was always very plain, but we never went short though she went hungry. She told me in later years how she used to put all she had on the table and didn't know where the next meal would come from but, somehow or other there was always something happened which provided us with another meal.

Why did Emily put up with it? The answer lies in her own note-book. On almost every page she has recorded a homily on the need to be dutiful, cheerful, and ever willing to put up with life's burdens.

There are sadder hearts than yours – go and comfort them and they will comfort you.
Don't be a fault finder – unless you are a fault mender.
One thing that improves the longer it is kept is your temper.
Live for others and you will never be lonely.
God does not comfort us to make us comfortable, but to make us comforters.

There is one slightly longer excerpt, more philosophical which has a rather resigned and pessimistic undertone to it.

At one time or another, as we journey through life, the essential solitariness of the soul is brought home to each of us, & in no way more forcibly than by the discovery of how astonishingly little the happenings which affect us most poignantly affect other people – even our nearest & dearest. A tidal wave convulses our own personal existence – swamping perhaps, the whole of life's happiness in its course – & they hardly realise it; or if, for a brief space, they seem to grip the immensity of one's loss, the impression quickly fades away, & very soon we are left to get on with life as best we can, single-handed.

On the whole, though, she was endlessly cheerful and optimistic, despite everything. Strangely enough, when Albert was off the drink, everyone spoke of his good temper, as Alice herself recalls at the end of her memoir.

When father wasn't drinking he could be one of the nicest men one could wish to meet & had such a lot of patience with children. often have I and my friends put curling pins in his hair and he never tired of amusing us. he would do almost anything we asked him, even stand or try to stand on his head or play games with us, but directly drink was in him, he was a changed man.

   Mother would go to chapel every Sunday night where she found such a lot of comfort and a lot of good friends who remained friends until she passed away. Two things I specifically remember about Mother. The peculiar radiance of her face, a light shining from within, and the fact that when she was in a room the whole atmosphere seemed beautifully uplifted.

From Alice's memoirs, and Emily's own choice of uplifting homilies, it can be seen that while Emily did believe that crosses in life were to be borne stoically, she herself still tried to be happy, two lessons she hoped to pass on to young Alfred. Not quite with total success.

CHAPTER THREE

Schooldays, 1914–20

Alfred's own first memories, as recalled in *Ex-Fellwanderer*, were of the sounds and sights which lodged in his mind from his early years in Audley Range – a withered aspidistra, mice and cockroaches crawling round the kitchen range, a sticky flycatcher black with casualties hanging from the gaslight, steaming clothes suspended from a pulley in the ceiling. These are images remembered by most people, from those days, in those sorts of conditions, but the dominant feature in that particular part of Lancashire was of course the mill.

I remember, as a child, lying in bed in the early mornings, the stillness of the night broken by the knocker-up on his rounds as he tapped on the bedroom windows along the street with a long stick. His visits were followed by a half-hour's silence and then came the first clatter of clogs on the pavement outside, this noise gathering momentum and growing in volume, rising to a crescendo for five minutes before dying away as suddenly with an occasional hurried scurrying by those late for work. Then the mill hooters sounded, like sirens calling the faithful to prayer, some whining, some whistling, some screaming, some tremulous, some thunderous and frightening in the darkness of a winter's morning. I came to know all the mills by the sound of their hooters, all distinctive; they signalled the start of work.

  Sundays were different. The mill hooters were silent; there was no clatter of clogs. Most people went to church or chapel, or, if they did not, respected those who did. My father, to his credit, never went drinking on Sundays and stayed indoors. People wore their best clothes, the men appearing in suits, often shiny with age; hats replaced caps, and a few even sported bowlers. But it was the womenfolk who transformed the scene. Many were unrecognisable on Sundays; during the week I had seen them shuffling along the pavements draped in long shawls, with thick black wrinkled stockings and clogs, like ghouls going to a funeral. On Sundays they became butterflies, with a lifespan as brief, wearing hats adorned with wax flowers and fruit, smart costumes and dresses, silk stockings covered legs that had seemed shapeless, and neat shoes took the place of heavy clogs. On Sundays women became ladies.

Alfred remembered his father being without any saving graces, a drunk, pure and simple, even if he did have to rest his drinking elbow on Sundays. This made the boy naturally full of sympathy for his mother.

I had great compassion and love for my mother, who had come from a good family. She had few comforts. To earn a few extra shillings she had to take in washing from rather more affluent neighbours, and I was often awakened during the night by the sound of the mangle downstairs in the kitchen. She always saw that her children had enough to eat, but I noticed at times that she went without herself. Every Friday evening a lady in a fur coat called for the rent of six shillings a week, and I cringed with shame on the occasions when my mother had to say that she could not manage to pay the rent that week but would settle the arrears as soon as she could.

I wished I was old enough to go to work to help my mother, or find a buried treasure. But there were no buried treasures in Blackburn in those days and none above ground either.

He didn't relate the story, still told amongst his Blackburn relations today, how his mother once served up a delicious rabbit stew which they all tucked into with gusto, until Alfred went out into the back yard – and found that his rabbit hutch was empty.

His first rabbit had been given to him by his father in December 1918 when Alfred was eleven, which shows some slight degree of paternal interest, but this died on 13 February 1919, and was buried the same day – so presumably not eaten. He did a drawing of it, and listed its food, as a piece of school work. The drawing is rather crude, the handwriting carefully printed, not joined up, and there is a bit of boasting going on, saying that 'the garden' was now going to be used as a rabbit run. They had no garden, of course, just a 15 feet by 15 feet enclosed concrete yard, like everyone else.

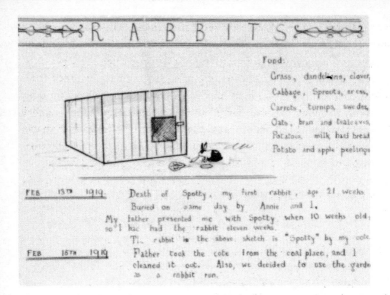

R A B B I T S

Food:

Grass, dandelions, clover,
Cabbage, Sprouts, cress,
Carrots, turnips, swedes,
Oats, bran and tealeaves,
Potatoes, milk, hard bread
Potato and apple peelings

FEB 13TH 1919. Death of Spotty, my first rabbit, age 21 weeks.
Buried on same day by Annie and I.
My father presented me with Spotty when 10 weeks old,
so I had had the rabbit eleven weeks.
The rabbit in the above sketch is "Spotty" by my cote.

FEB 15TH 1919 Father took the cote from the coal place, and I
cleaned it out. Also, we decided to use the garden
as a rabbit run.

Alfred went to the local Board school with the other boys and
girls of his age from the neighbourhood, playing marbles in the
gutters, collecting cigarette cards, hunting caterpillars and, when
he had any money, going to the cinema on Saturday afternoons.
He did a lot of drawings, copying famous sportsmen, or cartoons
from the comics of the times. Many others did this too, but he
moved on to do original work, sketching his school friends and
teachers.

Where he was slightly different was in his passion for making lists. 'On wet nights I stayed indoors, sitting by the window, keeping a census of all who passed in various categories: pedestrians, cyclists, horses and carts.' Possibly this interest stemmed from his love of maths and facts and figures. He also went off on long solitary walks, to local parks and beauty spots and then further afield to the local moors and hills. He fell in love with maps, studying them for hours, copying them out. He created his own maps of Lancashire and the North, using different coloured pens and various elaborate symbols. There were probably no maps at

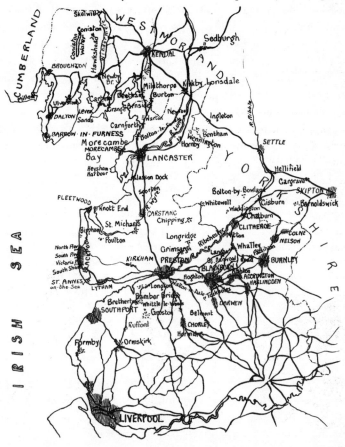

home, but at school he had to copy and create maps in Geography lessons – many of which he kept all his life.

National events hardly impinged on his life, although he was aware of the sinking of the *Titanic* in 1912, and of course the First World War. Blackburn was never a main target for German aeroplanes, but a few bombs and zeppelins flew around. His father went into a munitions factory and his brother Frank, aged eighteen in 1914, was called up for the Army. Alfred was terribly proud of Frank, the tall, handsome, older brother, especially when he strode home in his uniform as a lance corporal.

Alice and Annie as they grew up revealed slightly different temperaments. Alice was quiet, serious and rather ladylike, which shows in her autobiographical fragment, while Annie was noisier, jollier and made people laugh. Alice started work around the age of twelve, mornings only, in a little local sweat shop, supposedly to learn stocking knitting, but found herself running errands and winding wool instead.

Then when I was 13, someone adviced [sic] Mother to let me go into the mill and learn winding, so into the mill I went and liked it very much.

Well, do I remember the first week I earned 10/2 when I drew my wage, I received a gold half sovereign. I was very proud and hurried home, in fact, I went through all the backs, so I could run and keep looking at the brightness of it. I carried it in my hand all the way, and, oh! the joy of placing it in Mother's hand and the radiance of her face and the tears in her eyes, I can almost see her now when I think of it. She said she would try and give me a penny for every shilling I earned, but oftener than not she could only give me 1 penny a week. It was whilst I was at the same mill I had my first visit to Blackpool and my first glimpse of the sea (I never remembered the sea at Morecambe) The masters of the mill gave the workpeople a trip every year. I went, and what a thrill I got, it was the first time I had seen so much water, it seemed wonderful.

Alice didn't stay long at the mill, never liking it, and perhaps being too ladylike for such grim, noisy surroundings and the earthy companionship. She got a job with a tailoring firm in the middle of Blackburn, eventually becoming a seamstress.

Annie went straight into the mill at twelve – part time, then full time at thirteen – and loved it straightaway. She had apparently been considered good enough to go on from the Board school, Accrington Road Elementary, to the Higher Elementary, but she refused, preferring to stay with her girl friends and go into the mill. She remained a mill girl for the rest of her working life.

Alice got married in 1920 at the age of twenty-six to John Fish, a time clerk in an iron foundry, whom she'd met at Furthergate church – and they eventually moved into a house just a few doors away from her parents at 323 Audley Range.

Alfred turned twelve in 1919, time to think about leaving school and start work, in the normal way of things. Many boys went into the mills as well, sweeping up, doing unskilled work, then learning a skill.

I rather fancied myself as an office boy. Sitting at a desk seemed to me preferable to standing at a loom and although I didn't know anybody who worked in an office and had little idea of the nature of the duties I liked writing and was good at sums, attributes I thought would be necessary, and, besides, office work was considered superior, pay was higher and working hours shorter. My teachers too thought I shouldn't go into the mills and urged me to continue my education at a higher elementary school in the town centre. The prospect appalled me. This was a much posher school, standards were higher and I might be a dunce. I wouldn't know anybody there, the boys came from better homes, and the move would involve expenses of shoes, decent clothes and tram fares on wet days, expenses I knew my mother could not afford without further sacrifices. But although she would have welcomed another wage in the house, she wanted me to go. So I went in great trepidation, feeling I was cutting adrift from my pals and things familiar, and going into the unknown.

Alfred need not have worried. He'd been top in most subjects at his old school and turned out top in most things again at his new school. This was right in the middle of Blackburn, not far from the Town Hall, and was officially called the Higher Elementary School. It was built just before the war, so it was relatively new, and was usually known as Blakey Moor school, from its location in the street still called Blakey Moor. Originally, it had been a piece of leftover moorland, kept as waste ground for use for fairs or markets, but this had long since been built over.

Today, the school itself has gone, along with Accrington Road Elementary, Alfred's previous school. This had been a Board school where many kids were ragged, or dressed in handed-down clothes from older brothers, clogs on their feet, their noses often running. Blakey Moor was a definite step up, where pupils were meant to be a bit smarter and with luck would go into minor white collar jobs.

In the same year, in the same class with him was George Haworth. 'There were fifty in our class, boys and girls but mainly boys. I can still recall the names of thirty of the boys, but only ten girls. Shall I tell them you? I lie awake at night remembering them when I can't sleep. One of the girls in the class was Jessica Lofthouse, you know, who wrote those Lancashire books, but she wasn't as sound on her facts as Wainwright.

'I remember Alf very well. Very good results he always had. He was rather reserved and aloof, very tall with red hair. He didn't mix much. He went on a lot later about the Rovers, but I don't remember him going to matches at the time. He never discussed players with me. I did, all the time. I can tell you every team from the 1920s. Do you want to hear?'

George left school at sixteen, after his matriculation, going to work for a bleach firm in Manchester, then returned to Blackburn to run the Post Office in Furthergate. 'I knew his mother and sisters very well. Nice people. The way Alfred later described his sisters as just being mill girls was a bit unfair. They were, but you wouldn't have thought so. I've no memory of his father. I think they kept him quiet.'

In 1971, George retired and moved to Arnside, where he still lives, aged eighty-eight. He wrote to Wainwright when he became famous, recalling their time at Blakey Moor. 'He wrote back and said it wasn't a happy year. That's not my recollection. He seemed very happy to me at the time . . .'

Alfred was often teased about his fiery red hair at school – 'an embarrassment that led me to wear a cap when out of doors to avoid or minimise the shouts of "Carrots" that followed me along the street'. He was certainly pleased enough with his progress at Blakey Moor to have kept, all his life, a collection of school exercises, reports and essays. (Nothing, alas, has survived from his Accrington Road days.)

In his half-yearly report for 1920 he was top in the class with 90%. Almost all the comments, by the individual teachers, were 'excellent'. His English was particularly good, with 49 out of 50 for Grammar and Composition. For Maths he got 50 out of 50. Drawing was also pretty high – 47 out of 50 – but he wasn't so hot at French, coming only fourth in the class with 82 out of 100. It wasn't a subject he found much use for later in life, but it was a sign that Blakey Moor was quite a superior school, by teaching French at all. It was, of course, not in the same league as Blackburn's truly superior school, Queen Elizabeth's Grammar School, re-founded 1567, where the middle classes sent their sons, for relatively modest fees, preparing them for the professions. Still as grand today, now that it's independent once again, it boasts in its current advertisement that it gets twenty-one places a year at Oxbridge.

As well as keeping the maps of England which he drew for school work, Alfred also kept some of his essays. In one he wrote that the best stories are adventure stories, and noted that he'd just been reading *The Gorilla Hunters* and *The Children of the New Forest*. He also liked school stories – 'because they give us the idea of what "playing the game" is'. Sounds as if he should have been at Queen Elizabeth's. He also retained several of his Arithmetic tests, which is more unusual. Sums are sums, why keep them for ever, even if they were all correct.

Perhaps the most interesting item from his year at Blakey Moor is an essay entitled 'My Future', written on 8 March 1920, when he was aged thirteen.

CHAPTER FOUR

Work Days, 1920–31

On 19 October 1920, Alfred received a note from the Borough
Engineer's office inviting him for a job interview. He'd heard they
were looking for an office boy and had decided to apply. His
headmaster advised against it, saying he should stay on and sit his
matriculation exam, but Alfred was determined to leave. He wanted
to help his mother by bringing in some extra money, as his father
was still drinking heavily.

A job at the Town Hall was considered a sure sign of success
for a working-class boy, a job for life if you kept your nose clean,
and a job with social prestige. In Blackburn's Town Hall, you also
got to work in a rather distinguished building. The Town Hall
was built in 1856, at the beginning of Blackburn's industrial
greatness, so they had wanted something suitably impressive. For
£30,000, they got a large, Italianate edifice, built like a grand
palazzo. It's still today the handsomest building in Blackburn,
though rather ruined by a modern monstrosity next door, known
as the New Town Hall.

There used to be an equally famous landmark nearby called the
Market Hall Clock Tower, but it was destroyed by civic vandalism
in 1964. There was a golden ball on the top of the clock tower
which rose at noon each day, then descended at one o'clock when
a gun was sounded at the Town Hall, a practice which continued
until 1931. No wonder Town Hall employees felt pretty grand
themselves, even humble office boys.

Alfred got the job, and what seemed to him the magnificent
wage of 15 shillings a week. 'I ran all the way home to tell my
mother. My spending money increased from a penny to 1/3d a

week; a penny in the shilling being the customary reward for wage earners. I would now be able to go to a better cinema and attend Rovers' matches instead of having to stand outside the ground trying to assess the scoring from the shouts of the crowd instead. This was affluence indeed; I was beginning to feel like a man.'

Not quite. He was still in short trousers, despite being almost six feet tall, and on his first day at work he turned up in his school collar, a celluloid affair, fastened at the neck with a stud. He was taken aside by the head of the office and told that office workers wore ties. He got one next day from his big brother, but it was a couple of years before he took the plunge into long trousers.

There were remarks at work about his ginger hair, but nothing too annoying. More worrying was his eyesight. He'd noticed at elementary school that he'd had to sit in the front row to read the blackboard, and at the cinema if he wanted to read the captions to the silent films, and at Ewood Park if he wanted to make out Rovers' new signing, so he saved up until he had a guinea, enough to get his eyes tested and acquire a pair of spectacles. He chose rimless ones, thinking they would be less noticeable. 'There was a silly stigma about the wearing of glasses by young people; it was said that a boy who wore glasses would never get a girl, and vice versa even more so.'

After three years, he was transferred to the Borough Treasurer's Department where he was told the chances of advancement were better. This was a much smarter, more prestigious department with staff from middle-class families, many of whom had been to the Grammar School. Alfred felt rather inferior at first, both socially and intellectually, but he was very keen to get on, his ambition being to earn £5 a week. It was soon pointed out to him, however, that this was virtually impossible. Unless he had the proper professional qualifications, there would be no further promotion. All around him, young men of the same age were hard at it every evening, studying for exams. Alfred found out that his headmaster had been right, he should have stayed on and passed his matriculation.

To catch up with his colleagues, he had first of all to take what was called a preliminary examination – which they were exempt from, being grammar school cads. This meant going to night-school, returning to the sort of school lessons he thought he'd given up for ever, English, Maths, History and Geography. There was also a form of self-improvement involved. He became proud of his command of English, written English mostly, as his Lanca-shire accent was as strong as ever, and he found himself feeling superior to his old friends from school. They were now working in Blackburn's mills and factories, and ended all sentences with 'you know' and 'like' and massacred verbs by saying 'you was' and 'I were'. 'Gradually I withdrew from the company of old acquaint-ances and preferred to be solitary, no doubt earning a reputation as a snob.'

At work, he took a pride in his ledgers, believing they should not only be accurate but works of art in themselves.

I liked working with figures and proving them accurate by finding them all in balance at year end. There was satisfaction in preparing annual accounts that I knew to be absolutely correct in every detail. I had been taught at primary school to write legibly and keep my exercise books tidy, lessons I never forgot, and it was a fetish of mine, almost an obsession, to keep my ledgers neat, columns of figures being in strict alignment and written narratives as clear to read as typeset print. I took a great pride in my account books and conducted by example a personal rebellion against sloppy work, a prime cause of mistakes and wasted time.

After he'd passed his prelims, the real slog began if he was to qualify as a municipal accountant. This introduced new subjects like accountancy, auditing, economics and local government law. The exams cost money to take and were expensive to prepare for. He wrote around for the cheapest set of correspondence courses and found one at seven guineas which he could pay in monthly instalments. He prepared a work schedule for himself, all colour coded and beautifully laid out, setting himself so many hours work every evening.

I worked hard at this, denied the home comforts of my colleagues, studying in a cold bedroom under a flickering gas jet, and trying to concentrate despite the street noises and sounds from downstairs, which too often included the ravings of a drunken father. I sacrificed all my leisure time, except for weekly visits to the cinema and the Rovers, losing touch completely with former mates who still gathered at the street corner and had now added the pursuit of girls to their repertoire of pastimes.

Looking back later in his memory, the whole of the 1920s seemed to be totally devoted to study, which was technically true, as his various examinations did go on for almost ten years. He became a reclusive figure in his private life, but at work he soon began to make new friends.

Lawrence Wolstenholme, born in May 1909, was two years younger than Wainwright, and also went to Blakey Moor school but stayed until sixteen, joining the Borough Treasurer's office in 1925. He was an enthusiastic walker, and had been much further afield than Alfred who so far had only done local walks. 'When he heard I'd been to the Lakes', said Wolstenholme, 'we became friends. We found we talked the same language. We both loved books about climbing in the Alps and the Himalayas, especially by Frank Smyth. It was meat and drink to us. It was very romantic, to seventeen- and eighteen-year-old youths in Blackburn, to plan in our minds walks in the Himalayas.'

In idle moments at his desk, Alfred drew imaginary programmes of walks in the Himalayas. He also drew cartoons and drawings of footballers, the sort he'd done at school, but very soon he started on the people in the office, using words this time as well as pictures. They were done on small scraps of paper, then stapled together, like a little booklet. When he finished one, he would throw it across to Lawrence's desk, to amuse him or keep him back from his work.

Lawrence, who later became Borough Treasurer of Blackburn, and in 1995 was still living in the town, kept a large bundle of Wainwright drawings. One of them shows Alfred, Lawrence and another colleague, Fred Sellers, as footballers. 'The Ideal Half-back

Line – Skill, Speed, Beauty.' Fred Sellers was very small while both Lawrence and Alfred were tall, over six feet. Lawrence had big sticking-out ears and was classified as Speed while Alfred labelled himself 'Beauty'. Was this a joke, or did he fancy himself? 'He had his hair thick at the front and combed back. He thought he was the double of a film star of the time called Rod La Roque.'

The earliest surviving of the little booklets is dated August 1925 and entitled 'The Pictorial Gazette – the unofficial organ of the accountancy office, Boro Treasurer's Dept.' It is fairly crude, in the artistic sense, with few words and lots of empty spaces. There are jokes at the expense of Fred Sellers' height: 'A shilling fund has been started to provide Mr Sellers with a collapsable [sic] ladder. Will subscribers please forward their subscriptions to Mr Wainwright, Hon Treasurer.' He did a cartoon of himself, with the headline 'A Modern Romeo (Now that Valentino is dead, he is without a rival)'. Wishful thinking, presumably. Most of it is sixth-form humour, young chaps amusing each other. Later, however, these little booklets became more sophisticated in their art work

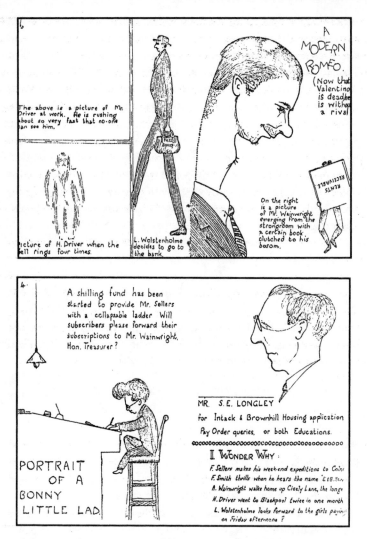

and layout, almost up to publication standards. Did he ever see himself as a cartoonist or satirist instead of an accountant? He clearly showed a talent and an interest, but he doesn't appear to have thought of it as a proper job, or ever contemplated trying to get pieces published in his local newspaper.

The office was a large one, with between fifty and sixty people all together. The Treasurer was R. G. Pye, and jokes about him appear in most of Alfred's booklets. There was a Deputy Treasurer, J. Bennett, and a Chief Accountancy Assistant, N. W. E. Hamm, both of whom in turn became Borough Treasurer. Below them were about six other qualified accountants who knew they would eventually have to move on, to get promotion. Alfred and his particular friends, all in their early twenties, were in the next ranking, trainee accountants, still plodding through the endless examinations. They sat in the open part of the wood-panelled office at their high mahogany desks, working away at their ledgers, sucking their pens, wondering what their future might be. Below them were the clerks.

Almost all of them were men. There were only two women actually in the office – although outside, on the counter where the rents were paid, there was often a couple of older women. The Treasurer's secretary was Edna Panter, in her thirties, who was also doing the examinations; this was most unusual for the period, even being allowed to try. She got through the early stages, but never qualified. Another younger woman was Betty Ditchfield who acted as the Treasurer's assistant secretary.

'A lot of the men fell for Betty,' says Lawrence, 'including several married men, but I don't think there were ever any affairs in the office. Alfred fell for Betty as well, but I'm sure it was all innocent.'

Lawrence remembers a girl in the outer office whom Alfred also liked. 'She was orginally Nellie Lynch, then became Nellie Morrison until her husband died. Then she got married again and became Nellie Myerscough. He died as well.'

One of Alfred's particular jobs in the office was to organize whip rounds for people when they left or got married. 'He had a list which he sent round, and people had to write in whether they were contributing a shilling or 1/6d. He kept this list so if *you* were leaving the office, or getting married, he'd show you what you'd contributed in the past and say well, you can't expect much, as you haven't given much . . .'

Another colleague of the same age was Bob Alker. He was born in 1909, educated at Queen Elizabeth's Grammar School, and joined the office in May 1926 as a junior clerk. He too remembers Alfred's passion for Betty Ditchfield, and later got to know her very well, as his wife, Mona, became her close friend. Betty, like his wife, was a Christian Scientist. She was also a keep-fit fanatic who didn't drink and never ate on Sundays.

'She was only small, but not curvacious the way young girls are today, but every man in the office took to her. She had a good personality. Mind you, there are men attracted to any young woman of her age, and she was the only one. She was born in 1911, so she was four years younger than Alf. When the war began, and we got younger lasses in the office, she had more competition.

'Alf took a great shine to her. He overheard her telling someone one Friday that she was planning to climb Pendle Hill on the Saturday. She got to the top and there was AW waiting for her. He was besotted by her. They had a long conversation. I don't know the details, but Betty told my wife about it later, and at the end of it, she said AW was in tears . . .'

'Later on, when I got to know her well, I discovered she felt very bitter towards men. I don't think Alf would have been happy with her, not in the physical sense. It wouldn't have worked, from what I knew of her. She was one of four children and her father had left the mother when she was young. She had been engaged to get married but her fiancé went off three weeks before the marriage. She got married late in life, marrying a widower who soon fell ill and became an invalid. She had no children. Alf never forgot her.

'We did spend a lot of time in the office discussing women, not just Betty. I can well remember Alf's pubescent sort of conversation which came across those tall desks as we sat in the accountancy office, not the sort of conversation for the ears of any gently brought up young women.'

What sort of stuff, Bob? These days, it's hard to imagine that we could be shocked by what you young shavers discussed in the 1920s.

Bob, eighty-four and a widower, was sitting in his bungalow in Garstang, looking very fit and cheerful. He has enjoyed 'hammering the superannuation fund' since he retired twenty-four years ago as Area Accountant for Norweb in Preston. 'Oh, it was just lads' talk. I remember Alf saying he'd like to give it to one particular woman. He could be a bit lurid, in both his conversation and his letters to his close friends, but he wasn't the only man to indulge in Lothario fantasies.

'He was very good at his job. I went to book-keeping classes with him when we were youngsters and had just started the exams, and the first time I saw his handwriting I was amazed. "Eeh, Alf, what lovely handwriting," I said. He was proud of it.'

In those days, of course, all schools taught handwriting as a subject, and there were fierce penalties for those who did poor work, but Alfred was exceptionally good. It ran in the family as his mother and sisters had fine handwriting. (Alice's memoir, quoted earlier, was in green ink – a colour often favoured by AW.)

'Alf used to sing in the office when we were doing up the pay packets on a Friday,' recalls Bob. 'It took a whole day, filling the little brown envelopes for all the council workers, hundreds of them. Those on duty, about six of us, had to sit in a little room and Alf would lead the singing. "One Alone" was his favourite. He wasn't really a mixer, but he was well liked.'

At home, all his spare time was still spent slogging at his examination work, apart from the cinema or watching Rovers on a Saturday afternoon. He didn't make it to Wembley for their Cup Final success of 1928, but he celebrated at a friend's house where they listened to it on the wireless.

On 20 March 1931, a telegram arrived for him at the office. It went first to the Borough Treasurer who called Bob Alker over, telling him to find Wainwright, saying it was important. 'Alf was paying out the Poor Law at the time and I said, "Here, Alf, this is for you, it's supposed to be important".'

The telegram said: 'HEARTIEST CONGRATULATIONS ON PASSING INTERMEDIATE EXAMINATION AND OBTAINING SECOND PLACE AND PRIZE.' A letter followed confirming the news, saying his prize would be two guineas and that he should come to the Annual Conference of the Institute of Municipal Treasurers and Accountants in Brighton in order to receive it.

'I went reluctantly, never having been south of Manchester before, and was glad to get back on the next train.'

A couple of years later Alfred passed the final part of the accountancy exams, and so after ten years of solid study and devotion to duty he became an Associate of his professional body, entitled to put the letters AIMTA (Hons) after his name. Which he did. And one of the first places was on a joke advertisement for a School of Municipal Accountancy – Principal A Wainwright – passed round the office to amuse his friends. Oddly, he changed the name of Lawrence Wolstenholme to Wolstencroft. An error, or an in-joke we do not know.

CHAPTER FIVE

First Lakeland Visit, 1930

Alfred Wainwright first visited the Lake District in 1930 – an event that changed his life. He was aged twenty-three, a late starter in some senses as rambling and fellwalking in Lakeland was a very popular activity for young people of the time, and there were colleagues and friends at work who had already been there. By now he had some money in his pocket, no commitments, except to his mother to whom he felt very grateful. Lakeland was only sixty miles away, after all, with regular and reasonably priced trains and buses. So what kept him? Nervousness, perhaps. He had never been away from home on holiday before. All his outings so far had been day trips. It seemed to him 'another world, beyond reach, unattainable'. He needed a suitable companion, not feeling brave enough to do it on his own, and so he 'recruited' a cousin, his word, which would indicate a bit of leaning on, suggesting that none of his office colleagues was keen enough or available. The cousin was Eric Beardsall, the son of his mother's sister Annie, who was working as a clerk for the local council in Penistone. And so they set off, with their shilling haversacks, stout shoes but no boots or waterproofs, a party of two, taking the bus from Blackburn to Kendal.

In junk shops and car boot sales you can still come across faded albums of little, poorly composed snaps of Lake District holidays taken by people long gone and long forgotten, parties of wholesome looking young men and women, striding off to open their lungs and eyes, thankful to leave the urban squalor of industrial Lancashire behind. This year Windermere. Pity about the rain. Next year let's try Cornwall. I say, after that, what about Scotland.

Wainwright was unusual in that his passion for Lakeland was total and all-consuming. It was love at first sight. His only intention was to return. Years later in 1987, writing in *Ex-Fellwanderer*, he still remembered his first impressions, the first walks, the first climbs, the first sensations.

Alighting from the bus, our first objective, according to my itinerary, was Orrest Head, a recommended viewpoint nearby. Our way led up a lane amongst lovely trees, passing large houses that seemed to me like castles, with gardens fragrant with flowers. I thought how wonderful it must be to live in a house with a garden. The sun was shining, the birds singing. We went on, climbing steadily under a canopy of foliage, the path becoming rougher, and then, quite suddenly, we emerged from the shadows of the trees and were on a bare headland, and, as though a curtain had dramatically been torn aside, beheld a truly magnificent view. It was a moment of magic, a revelation so unexpected that I stood transfixed, unable to believe my eyes. I saw mountain ranges, one after another, the nearer starkly etched, those beyond fading into the blue distance. Rich woodlands, emerald pastures and the shimmering waters of the lake below added to a pageant of loveliness, a glorious panorama that held me enthralled. I had seen landscapes of rural beauty pictured in

The view from Orrest Head: taken from A Fifth Lakeland Sketchbook

the local art gallery, but here was no painted canvas; this was real. This was truth. God was in his heaven that day and I a humble worshipper.

The mountains compelled my attention most. They were all nameless strangers to me, although I recognised the Langdale Pikes from photographs I had seen. They looked exciting and friendly. I fancied they were beckoning me to their midst. Cloud shadows chased across them as I watched, and momentarily they appeared gloomy and frightening, but with the return of the sun they were smiling again. Come on and join us, they seemed to say.

There were no big factories and tall chimneys and crowded tenements to disfigure a scene of supreme beauty, and there was a profound stillness and tranquillity. There was no sound other than the singing of larks overhead. No other visitors came.

My more prosaic cousin went to sleep in the warm grass. I forgot his existence. I felt I was some other person; this was not me. I wasn't accustomed or entitled to such a privilege. I was an alien here. I didn't belong. If only I could, sometime! If only I could! Those few hours on Orrest Head cast a spell that changed my life.

They spent their first night in a bed and breakfast establishment in Windermere, the first he had ever stayed at. Very homely, he thought, though he was annoyed by another guest who played the piano all evening while Alfred was trying to study his maps and plan the next day's excitements.

This took them up the Troutbeck valley, heading towards 'High Street, Roman Road', words he had been attracted to on the map – even now, still so alluring, if rather confusing for absolute beginners who might think there is going to be a properly marked out Roman route. They started to climb Froswick, 2359 feet high, the first real mountain Alfred had seen at close quarters, before crossing over on to the long and wondrous ridge path of High Street, feeling in every sense on top of the world, and making their way towards Ullswater.

They reached civilisation at Howtown where cousin Eric, 'who had travelled more, and acquired a measure of sophistication', insisted on staying at the Howtown Hotel. Alfred thought a hotel was too posh for the likes of him, especially in their dishevelled clothes, but they were allowed in and slept well in what Alfred considered to be luxurious comfort.

Next day, they took the bus to Patterdale and, like many first timers to Lakeland, they set off for Helvellyn, attracted by its glamour and fame and the allure of Striding Edge.

The weather was less promising, and before reaching the gap in the wall we were enveloped in a clammy mist and the rain started. Neither of us had waterproofs nor a change of clothing. Perhaps it would clear later: we were already under the optimistic delusion that afflicts most fellwalkers. The path was clear underfoot and we entered a grey shroud with visibility down to a few yards only. We went on, heads down against the driving rain until, quite suddenly, a window opened in the mist ahead, disclosing a black tower of rock streaming with water, an evil and threatening monster that stopped us in our tracks. Then the mist closed in again and the apparition vanished. We were scared: there were unseen terrors ahead. Yet the path was still distinct; generations of walkers must have come this way and survived, and if we turned back now we would get as wet as we would by continuing forward. We ventured further tentatively and soon found ourselves climbing the rocks of the tower to reach a platform of naked rock that vanished into the mist as a narrow ridge with appalling precipices on both sides. There was no doubt about it: we were on Striding Edge. In agonies of apprehension we edged our way along the spine of the ridge, sometimes deviating to a path just below the crest to bypass difficulties. We passed a memorial to someone who had fallen to his death from the ridge, which did nothing for our peace of mind.

After an age of anxiety we reached the abrupt end of the Edge and descended an awkward crack in the rocks to firmer ground below and beyond, feeling and looking like old men. Perhaps mercifully the mist had obscured the perils of the journey, making it a tightrope in the sky and concealing the consequences of a fall. The rain still sluiced down, making rivulets on our bellies. We sheltered for a few minutes at the base of the crack, recovering from an ordeal we had not expected. My cousin, looking like something fished from the sea, kept looking at me and saying nothing but was obviously inwardly blaming me, as author of the day's programme, for his present misery.

They did reach the summit of Helvellyn, and got down again, confused by what they thought was going to be a pony route, and found themselves at Thirlspot. They then tramped the six miles to Keswick, still in heavy rain, water squirting out of the laceholes of their shoes.

In Keswick we presented ourselves at a house in Stanger Street with a bed and breakfast sign, looking like two drowned scarecrows, dripping water from every protuberance and making pools on the doorstep. A lady opened the door and invited us inside. It was here that I had my first experience of the kindness and hospitality of the people of the district, an experience that was to be repeated in every cottage and farmhouse where I subsequently stayed. This lady in Stanger Street was wonderfully solicitous and concerned for us: she was a widow who had retained her husband's wardrobe. She made us take off our soaking clothes, gave us warm towels and then supplied us with jackets and trousers and shirts and socks, ill fitting but dry and warm, taking our own rags away to dry. Then she prepared a large supper and we recuperated in front of a blazing fire before retiring to comfortable beds. That woman was sent from heaven.

The next day was sunny, so they did some of the local walks around the Vale of Keswick, getting some odd looks for their strange clothes. The dead man had been smaller than Alfred, so his trousers ended half way up his legs. When they got back to their digs, they found their clothes not only dried but pressed.

In the days that followed I lived in an ecstasy of delight. We climbed to the ridges, scrambled amongst the rocks and reached a few summit cairns. We walked entranced along the valleys and lakesides. I was bewitched by everything. Here was harmony without a discordant note, and an indefinable aura of romantic charm, a mystical quality of beauty and tranquillity in alliance. The natives we met and in whose cottages we stayed overnight were all friendly and helpful, and their smiling faces reflected an inner peace and contentment as though their serene surroundings had permeated their philosophy of life.

And especially we marvelled at the freedom to roam the hills without restriction or hindrance. We could wander anywhere above the intake walls of the farms without reprimand: there were no policemen, no keep out notices, no warnings to trespassers as there were at home, but absolute freedom of access. It was wonderful to be able to wander and explore at will. The mountains, which later I came to know as fells, had open invitations to all. We walked amidst changing and often dramatic landscapes in a state of perpetual excitement.

They ended the week at Coniston, again staying in a hotel on Eric's insistence. Throughout the week, Alfred had been studying his maps, making notes, working out what was on the horizon, vowing to come back and climb everything, to cast his eyes again on the scenes of 'splendour far beyond my imaginings'.

Returning from paradise to Blackburn was a bit of a shock, plunging him from elation to despondency. Blackburn seemed even grimmer and uglier than he had remembered – and his home life seemed equally unattractive. Frank, a big strapping man of over six foot, as tall as Alfred, but with dark curly hair, had become a bricklayer. Alas, he was also turning to be his father's son, with a distinct fondness for the bottle.

Alice, who had got married in 1920 to John Fish, gave birth to her first child Jack in 1925. As a little boy, he saw a lot of his Grandmother and Grandad Wainwright, or 'Pop' as he was known in the family.

'When he was sober, Pop was smashing to play with. I'd jump on the horsehair sofa, which pricked my bare legs, and climb on top of him, pull his hair, jump all over him. But other times he frightened me. I'd hear him singing "Old Black Joe" in the kitchen. "I'm coming, I'm coming, for my head is bending low. I hear the gentle voices calling, Old Black Joe." It was his deep voice singing "I'm coming" which really scared me. Then he'd appear with his cap in his hand, and go round the room with it, to my mother, Grandma, anyone else. He was collecting coppers to have a drink. They'd give him a few, just to keep him quiet.'

Why did Emily still stick with him? 'Because she had taken her marriage vows. Her Christian faith kept her going. He was very big and she was very small. I never saw them out together.'

Annie got married in 1929 to Bill Duxbury who worked in the brick works opposite the Wainwright house.

There's a very good photograph of the wedding in which Alfred appears (*see* plate 6). He's in a smart suit, wearing a button hole, and his hair has been well brushed and flattened. Annie remembered exactly the trouble taken with this photograph, that it took ages to get everyone settled and there was some palaver about her new husband's trousers hanging down too far and they had to be pinned up. And she never liked how her brother Alfred had brushed his hair. 'It looked like he'd been hit on the head with a frying pan,' so she always said.

On the other side sits her friend Ruth Holden, her cloche bonnet pulled down well over her forehead. By the look of the bouquet in her hand, she was Annie's bridesmaid. Ruth was also a mill girl and a member of the same church as the Wainwrights, Furthergate Congregational. Her parents had both died and she lived with her sister Doris.

Was Alfred friendly with Ruth? Was there, dare one suggest it, anything between them? If so, perhaps he might have included her in his walking party the following year, when he revisited the Lakes at Whitsuntide. Or perhaps he was too shy to ask her. Or perhaps at this stage they were just good friends.

According to his own account, written years later in *Ex-Fellwanderer*, he didn't know any girls at this stage in his life. This cannot have been strictly true, however, judging by his office colleagues who all remember his interest in Betty Ditchfield, and interest in girls in general, if just as an abstract sexual concept. Betty had not gone out with him, and had not encouraged his advances, such as they were, so we have to believe that he had had no success with girls, even though he was certainly interested. In *Ex-Fellwanderer*, he writes:

'A young fellow in the office had a saying he repeated whenever the subject of the opposite sex was mentioned. "Women are all alike with a blanket over their heads": no need to be selective.'

Not very complimentary, and something few people would say today without risking being beaten over the head and branded as sexist. But he was fairly realistic about his own chances.

'I was not a good catch for any young female: I was shy, sensitive, skinny, ungainly. I had red hair and wore glasses: who would have me?'

The answer was Ruth Holden.

CHAPTER SIX

Ruth and Peter, 1931–40

Alfred and Ruth were married on 24 December 1931, at Further-gate Congregational Church, Blackburn, the church they had both attended since childhood. He was twenty-four and on the wedding certificate his job was given as clerk in the Borough Treasurer's Office. She was twenty-two, a cotton weaver. The witnesses were Doris, Ruth's sister, and Eric Beardsall, Alfred's cousin. No wedding photographs have survived, so the nearest to a wedding photograph, with them in their best outfits, is the one taken earlier at Annie's wedding.

Jack Fish, Alice's son, was at the wedding, aged six. He says he has never seen a wedding photograph, and presumes none was taken. 'But I do remember what Aunt Ruth wore – a lemon silk outfit.' Nothing significant in this. A white wedding, at the time, was normally associated with a proper wedding, with the full works, while a discreet off-white dress was used for quieter weddings.

Ruth had a slight cast in her right eye, hardly visible to strangers. According to one story she was born with it, but in another, she had hurt her eye as a child, fighting or scrapping with another girl. She was self-conscious about it and never cared for photographs, which could explain why her hat was pulled down in the other photograph. Alfred also never liked having his photo taken.

'The main thing I remember about the day was the taxi ride,' says Jack. 'It was the first time I'd been in a car of any sort. The reception was at the café run by Ruth's brother, Arthur, opposite the gates of Queen's Park, about a mile from Audley Range.'

Jack can't recall if Albert Wainwright was there, but thinks not. 'I don't think he went to Annie's wedding either. "I can't leave the house," he used to say. "I've got to look after the silver." That was his joke. What it meant was he couldn't be bothered.'

'Neither of us had any money,' recalled Alfred later on. 'Our honeymoon cost us two shillings, the price of two seats at the cinema on our wedding night.' The cinema, according to another member of the family, was the Star Cinema in Blackburn.

Alfred, in *Ex-Fellwanderer*, gives the impression that he got married because Ruth was his first and only girlfriend, which is not very gallant. 'Nobody ever regarded me with admiration. So when one at last showed an interest, I married her and left home, not easy in my mind and feeling that I was deserting my mother.'

His concern for his mother apart, he was very keen to leave home, if only to get away from his father's company, wanting to create a home of his own which might prove to be a happier place for him. He'd enjoyed visiting Ruth and her sister Doris in their house in Artillery Street, had liked the fun and liveliness of two sisters, running their own lives.

On his marriage, he moved into their house at first, then after a couple of months he and Ruth got a council house at 11 Hamer Avenue, not very far from his mother's house. It was on a rather sedate corporation estate, in a quiet road, a semi-detached house built a couple of years earlier in Accrington red stone. It had a bathroom, hot water and a garden, which his mother's house didn't have, while the street boasted a few trees and a hint of greenery.

Six weeks after the wedding my father died suddenly at the age of sixty-two. My mother shed tears but there was no grief amongst the rest of the family. Had I foreseen this happening I would never have left my mother and would have found a pleasanter house with a garden for both of us to enjoy. She was now alone in a house that had held six, her only income being a pension of ten shillings a week, more than half of which was needed for rent; clearly she could not subsist on this. I had been the main breadwinner over the past few years and I felt wretched for depriving her of my assistance when I married. I was now relatively affluent, earning more than £4 a week, twice the average adult wage. My brother and my sisters were in no position to help but fortunately I was able to augment her pension and provide her with a small radio. I wished I could have done much more but had committed myself to the responsibilities of wedlock.

It's not clear from that paragraph from *Ex-Fellwanderer* if Alfred is saying he would not have got married if his father had died earlier, or just that he would not have left his mother. 'Both of us' does suggest he and his mother living together on their own, but it might also refer to both families. All three of them together would probably have worked quite well. The Wainwrights, mother and sisters, were very pleased that Ruth had came along, and they all liked her very much, while she in theory had got a good catch, a young man, rather studious, rather quiet, but one clearly going places, moving up the social scale, from working class to professional middle class.

Their son Peter was born on 15 February 1933, while they were still living in Hamer Avenue. About a year later, they bought their first house, a semi-detached corner house at 90 Shadsworth Road. Two bedrooms, the same size as their council house, and on a busier road, but it was private, as befitted the home of a properly qualified municipal accountant.

Alfred was very proud of his son, and boasted that he had won a Bonny Baby competition. Peter has some early memories of going on outings with his father at the weekend, to Oswaldtwistle, Knuzden Brook, Ribchester and Darwen Tower. 'He would tell me the name of the hills, what we were passing, what was coming up.'

On Sundays, Peter went to Sunday School, taken by his mother, then on visits to his Grandma and his aunts Alice and Annie. He has no memory of his Uncle Frank. 'He wasn't talked about in the family. He didn't go to church and he liked his booze.'

He can't remember his father going to church with them and it would appear that around this time Alfred stopped going to Furthergate Congregational Church, much to his mother's disappointment. In June 1940, Alfred got a letter from his mother, saying how sad she was that he was no longer attending. It's a well-written letter, in good handwriting, perfectly grammatical, appealing to him to think again, telling him that God is everywhere and to Hold Fast to that which is good. There is an element of emotional blackmail, also an underlying suggestion that perhaps Alfred is not being guided right. Not just in not going to church but perhaps in other matters?

Blackburn
June 23/40

My Dear Alfred,

You have been in my thoughts so often lately. I feel I must write just a few lines to you; I want to tell you how very, very sorry I am now you have left us at Furthergate. I had hoped for big things for you, Alfred, I was *so* thankful for what you did undertake to do, it made my heart glad; but, neither the time, nor the place matters. God is everywhere, what a comforting thought! You will find Him in the little chapel at Belthorn, even as you found Him at Furthergate, I just leave you in His care, & ask you always to 'Hold fast; to that which is good': I shall always pray for you, Alfred, that you may be guided right, wherever you go.

I thank God too, from the very depths of my heart, for all you have been, and still are to

Your grateful & loving Mother.

Jack Fish always enjoyed visiting his Aunt Ruth's house, and playing with his small cousin Peter. 'Ruth gave a birthday party for him when he was about five. There were six or so other little boys there. I did some magic tricks, assisted by my cousin Joan [Annie's oldest child, born 1930]. They thought it was wonderful. Ruth always laid on a good tea party. I can't remember Alfred being there. I think he'd gone out, or he was at work.

'I liked going to their house because they had so many animals – the dog Peggy, a cat called Paddy, a tortoise, a budgie and a white mouse. Ruth took all the cousins, and Peter, out on picnics. I remember one picnic on Pendle Hill where she took a pan and water and some eggs, gathered some sticks, made a fire and boiled the eggs. We thought it was marvellous. She knew about trees and birds and that sort of thing'

*

When the war began, Ruth went back to work in the mill, to help the war effort. Peter's primary school was at Intack, near where she worked, and each lunch time he would walk to the mill and be given lunch by his mother. 'She worked what was called a six loom. It had this wooden shuttle which scared the daylights out of me. It seemed to take flight, and come zooming towards me. I'd sit down beside her machine and she'd give me a meat and potato pie which she'd taken with her to work especially for my lunch. I hated it. It always tasted of cotton. Every lunch time, everything I ate tasted of cotton.'

When he was about five or six, Peter was taken by his father for the first time to Ewood Park to watch Blackburn Rovers play, handed over the heads of the men, like all the other little boys, then dropped over the front wall so he could sit on the side of the pitch and watch. He was too young to appreciate the game itself, but he enjoyed the pies and coffee at half time. 'Dad soon took me to all the home games and eventually, as I got older, I stood beside him. No, he didn't shout and cheer. He just stood quiet. He didn't have a rattle. Nothing like that. He worked at the Town Hall, didn't he? Rattles were for mill workers.'

His mother was the disciplinarian if he was naughty and needed a smack, never his father. 'I was once caught by a policeman for throwing lumps of coke into a quarry. I'd been doing it with some other boys on the way home from school. When the policeman caught us, he made us go down into the quarry with a bucket to pick every piece up. I was late home from school that day, and got smacked. Then when my mother heard the reason, I got another smack.'

Peter has many happy memories of his childhood, of doing good things, having nice times, with both his mother and his father, but surprisingly, he has few memories of doing things in a threesome, all together. But then, of course, his father was very busy, working hard to get promotion.

*

After that first visit in 1930, Alfred went regularly to the Lake District on his annual two weeks' holiday. The following Whitsun, he managed to get up a party of three friends from his office, Eric Maudsley, Jim Sharples and Harry Driver, all of whom appeared in his office sketches and cartoons (*see* page 26). A. Wainwright was the leader, according to the meticulous notes and itinerary which he prepared in advance, promising them a comprehensive tour, seeing every lake, every valley, every mountain. 'It will be arduous, but the reward will be well worth the work.'

Their first day did not start off too well. Alfred had worked out a sixteen-mile hike, from Windermere to Patterdale – the route he had taken the previous year – which he planned to do the moment they got off the bus from Blackburn, was somewhat ambitious. They didn't arrive in Windermere until after midday, by which time the weather was appalling, visibility rotten, and by the time they got on to High Street they could see nothing, so they packed up and spent the first night in Troutbeck. The rest of the week went well. Some of the planned climbs did not get done, such as Blencathra, Grasmoor and Pillar, as Alfred had over-estimated how much they would manage each day, but they did a complete circle of the Lakes, covering 102 miles and climbing a total of 34,850 feet. It was remarkable that he had planned such a detailed itinerary after just one visit to Lakeland, but he'd always had a passion for planning routes, using maps and guide books, even to places he never managed to see.

Ruth was not a member of this touring party, or any of his later Lakeland jaunts, as far as is known, but then he did prefer to take arduous routes, the sort best suited to fit young men.

In 1936, he went off on his own to Scotland for the first time, to the island of Arran, taking a camera. He wrote up his experiences afterwards in a little photo album. The shots are mainly views, with just a couple showing him, a knotted handkerchief over his head, sitting by a stream.

The words, all of which he neatly typed out, are striving for literary effect, often rather purple prosy, not the straightforward sensible descriptions he later preferred.

I first saw Arran from the mainland at Ardrossan.

There was the wide Firth between, glittering in the sun; a few white-sailed fishing boats drifted leisurely on its waters. Far beyond, on the horizon, was a phantom island – a purple line springing out of the blueness of space, rising and falling, and finally leaping up into a precipitous mountain sky-line that fell again abruptly into misty nothingness.

I stood on the pierhead at Ardrossan and gazed across at the island. Of detail there was none. The sun was sinking fast; the shadows of the mountains had crept over the valleys, the headlands and bays were obscured in the haze of evening. Clouds lingered on the highest peaks; here alone the sun still caressed the island, touching it with a rosy radiance.

The days that followed will ever have a very special place in my memory.

I climbed all the hills, scrambled joyfully over the rough rocky summits, lay in the warm heather and marvelled at the magnificence of the views, came leaping down the steep slopes with smooth strides, paddled in crystal streams and watched the darting trout, trudged happily in the gloaming to the huge suppers that awaited me.

And every moment of every day the sun shone brilliantly from skies that were cloudless.

There was a quality in the scene I cannot easily define. Somehow, the island seemed unreal, a dream, almost as though the purple wedge that rose from the blue sea into the blue sky was nothing more than a vaporous mass that must soon dissolve and fade from sight. Yet this could not be: the outline was too well-defined, those rugged heights before me were not temporal; it was something that had not changed since first it was thrust upwards from the ocean floor. It was an island – an enchanted island. It was Arran.

I left Arran very, very reluctantly, like a lover torn from the arms of his bride. This had been more than a holiday; rather it had held the bliss of a honeymoon. An unromantic world called me back, but my eyes did not leave the Island of Enchantments until the ugly buildings of the mainland obscured my view.

Someday I will return and taste again those charms which enslaved me. I yearn for the day to come.

As Peter grew older, bigger and stronger, he began to be his father's walking companion, on short trips at first, then further afield.

In 1940, when he was seven, his father took him on a walking holiday, just the two of them, to the limestone country of Malham, Settle and Ingleton. Alfred took endless snaps of Peter standing studying the map with his handkerchief on his head, knotted in four corners. Alfred then stuck all these photos in a little album, typing out a label which he stuck at the front saying: 'PETER WAINWRIGHT – on his first walking tour: SUMMER 1940'. There are no shots of the doting father in this little album, or of any other people – only of Peter sitting by streams, gazing at little waterfalls, climbing paths, leaning on walls or resolutely walking into the distance in his little shorts and pullover, his socks round his ankles, his small rucksack on his back. It's a touching little album, showing Peter's clear enjoyment of the holiday, and the father's pleasure in his son following his own footsteps. (*See* plates 8 & 9.)

A year later, he took Peter walking in the Lakes for the first time, and again produced a little album of happy snaps. 'I remember a bed and breakfast place in Keswick,' says Peter, 'and getting up really early to climb Skiddaw. The best fun was the Halfway House, halfway up Skiddaw, long gone now, where you could get refreshments. We also climbed Catbells that holiday, took trips on the launches and fished in Derwentwater. I loved all these trips with my father.'

There was also another sort of trip, sometime in 1941, when he was eight, alone with his mother this time, a surprise trip, not anywhere very far or very exciting. All they did was travel a mile from their home, just the two of them, to stay in two rooms above a café in Queen's Park.

'I didn't quite understand at first what was going on. I hadn't realised she'd run away from my father. No, I don't remember any rows or anything. I just got up one day and my mother said we were off. I wasn't upset. I enjoyed it. I liked living beside a park. It was a good place to play. My uncle Arthur ran the café downstairs and so I got ice cream and soft drinks whenever I went down. We were there for about a couple of months, I think. I didn't want to leave. In fact, I cried when we came to leave. I'd just discovered in one of the rooms above the café boxes of model steam engines and I was dying to play with them.'

What had gone wrong with his marriage?

At the office, Alfred didn't talk about his marriage, but everyone presumed it was going well enough. Ruth complained to nobody, nor did Alfred. His mother and sisters knew nothing.

He did, however, reveal a great deal in a strange piece of composition which he wrote secretly in 1939, just eight years after his marriage, when Peter was about five. This began as a fictionalised attempt at his life story, calling himself Michael Wayne, but Peter is given his real name and after the first few pages, it is clear he is telling the real story of his marriage, a story he told to nobody in his lifetime.

CHAPTER SEVEN

Alfred's Story

Michael Wayne reached his home. There was a big fire awaiting him, his slippers were warming in front of it, his supper was laid ready. The woman was there with her book, drab, untidy, badly-dressed. She lifted her tired, strained eyes to his as he entered, but there was no smile of welcome. Her eyes fell to her book again, but now she did not read. Oh, the weariness of it all!

She had tried so hard to please him before her affection for him had gone. Now she knew it was hopeless: she never would please him. She kept the house nice, looked after his comfort as best she knew how, always had his meals ready, never grumbled, never asked questions. She couldn't make him happy; it was beyond her power. She had realised that long ago . . . She hoped he would notice that she had put his slippers to warm before the fire. But he wouldn't, he wouldn't; he never appreciated anything she did for him. This man, her husband! To her, not a man, but a relentless machine, crushing her, crushing her.

She had not had a kind word from him since the baby was born. To others, he could be pleasant enough: she knew he was popular and well liked at his work, she heard in roundabout ways of kindnesses he had shown to people he hardly knew. Oh, what had she done to earn his condemnation? How had she failed him? If only he would tell her, she would try to remedy the position. But he did not, he never told her. She did not understand him. Why was he always so quiet, so sullen? He never praised her, but in fairness to him, he never said an unkind thing either; he never found fault. What troubled him? What tormented his mind? She did not know. His face relaxed only when he was playing with his

47

son, he seemed happy then; but she had sometimes noticed a look in his eyes as he regarded the boy that made her wonder.

Wayne slumped into his chair and changed into his slippers. He lit a cigarette, and sat gazing into the fire. His face was set, without expression, but the old familiar emotions were surging through him again. Was he never to know peace and contentment? This night was no different from all the rest. It was always in the evenings when his mind was most active, when imagination ran wild and unchecked. Too late now to keep out the thoughts that should not be there. Once he had tried, but in vain, so utterly in vain: he could not. Nowadays he let them run on, making no effort to banish them. Let his imagination take him where it willed. If he were to be denied the experiences he yearned for, then at least let him dream about them, let him try to picture them, to deceive himself that there was substance in the shadows, that they may come true. One life! One life to live, and one mistake could mar it, make it intolerable! One life, one mistake!

How differently his life could have been planned! He seemed old now, old in experience; only one thing new could happen to him now – a meeting with the girl who meant so much to him – and that was not likely to happen. His life would drag on, drag on, a monotonous repetition of dull uninspired incidents that had no novelty, no appeal for him. Yet how ridiculous his attitude was, really! He was but thirty-two. He was young . . .

One night when he was out walking he was caught in a thunder-storm on a lonely road just outside the town. The only shelter available was the deep doorway of a public house, and he availed himself of it. He could hear someone thumping a piano inside, someone singing in a harsh voice, then a burst of drunken applause and shouting. His head ached; he should be at home studying, he could do an hour or two before the others came in. A gust of wind drove the rain into the doorway; he moved back and bumped into someone standing further in the dark shadow. He apologised; he had thought he was alone there. It was a girl. They talked, awkwardly enough; when the rain ceased they walked along to the town together. She told him of herself; he didn't speak much. She lived with her elder sister; her father and mother had died when she was very young. She had a slight physical defect, the result of a childish prank played on her when she was a little girl. She was a cotton weaver and worked in a big mill not far from Wayne's home. She won his sympathy from the start; he always felt terribly sorry for anyone who had suffered misfortune, perhaps because of his own experience. He shyly asked her to meet him again. Her ready consent pleased him, made him feel that he was not so hopeless after all. He did not study that night.

He saw her, by arrangement, many times that winter. He liked her company; it was better than walking about alone. She dressed plainly and was unobtrusive; she was not noisy, speaking in the dialect as other girls did, but she made silly grammatical errors which vaguely irritated him. She let him kiss her and fondle her; he liked to do these things; they helped him to forget.

But when the summer came he stopped seeing her; their favourite haunts were out of the question when the evenings were light. He did not tell her why he would not see her again, but made the false excuse of hard study. She cried a little when he left her for the last time; he cursed himself for being an ungenerous brute, and the memory of her tears haunted him: he knew he had hurt her and would have to return to her.

He did, the following autumn. She was not attractive – how the fellows at work would laugh at him – but she seemed fond of him, allowed him the liberties he delighted in. Yet he was never really happy with her as he felt he should be. At the back of his mind was always present the uncomfortable feeling that he was being both unfair and foolish: he knew little of the other sex, but he could conceive, imperfectly as yet, that some other girl may come along and be a source of much greater contentment to him. But she never came. Probably she never would, he used to tell himself; probably all girls were very much alike, and this one who now shared his evenings was not inferior, in the essential qualities, to the rest. So they drifted on into closer intimacy. She became part of his life; he began to feel that if she were not there when he wanted her, he would have a real sense of loss.

He often went to her house, where she lived with her sister. It was not a pleasant house, and was in a mean street, but it was better than his own. There, at least, was no misery; he liked to sit in a corner and watch the two of them bustling about the room, happy and contented together. But he was not satisfied with himself. He thought too much of that other girl who had no name; she filled him with restlessness and discontent. There were higher things in life, and he should be searching for them.

With the passing months there came a growing unrest. The Means Test was instituted; unless he got away from the house his father would lose his beer-money, his unemployment pay; there would be a scene. He was still seeing occasionally the girl he had met on that wet night. He had never had the heart to break off the association; she would have been distressed. He was not at all sure that he wanted to break it off; she helped him to forget his misery when she put her arms around him in the darkness and quietness of the room. Oh, but it was all so cheap, so shabby! He was drugging his mind with her kisses, trying to deceive himself that he was happy with her. He tried to shut out of his mind the thoughts that came creeping in. There were higher ideals, worthier ambitions; he should be striving for them. But hadn't he argued it all so often? They were not for him . . .

Poor pathetic Michael Wayne! He married the girl at Christmas, and went to live with her and her sister at their home. He felt acutely that he was deserting his mother, but he consoled himself with the reflection that he could afford to make her a weekly allowance. He changed homes; that was all that happened to him. There was no honeymoon. There was no happiness for him. The intimacies that he had looked forward to meant nothing, nothing. He found out then, when his wife should have shown her love for him most of all, that she did not love him. She worked hard in the house, keeping it spotless, making him good meals, waiting on him hand and foot. But she did not respond to his embrace . . . Already he was beginning to discover his mistake.

Two months after his marriage his father died suddenly. Two months afterwards! If this had happened earlier Wayne would not have left his mother. His re-action was one of profound shock; this was his first near bereavement, and somehow his memories of his father at this time were all of pleasing incidents; he thought of him at his best, not at his worst. His mother was deeply grieved, and Wayne realised now that she had never lost her love for her wayward and erring husband.

Within three months following their marriage Wayne and his wife moved out of the narrow street. He had grown ashamed of being seen walking along it: there seemed always to be gossiping old women at the doors, screaming children on the pavement. He had a responsible position and a good wage; he should not live in surroundings like that. His wife did not want to leave.

Their new home was better. It was situated on the outskirts of the town, and he quickly lost touch with the scenes of his boyhood. There was a nice garden, a bath, electric light: he had not had these amenities before.

The severance of his old associations began to work a change in him; his new surroundings helped him to forget the misery and the poverty that had been so familiar. He read better books. He began to acquire a distaste of anything cheap and tawdry. But the more his mind progressed the further he drew away from his wife. If they had anything in common before, it was rapidly going. She clung tenaciously to her old friends and her old habits, reviled him for leaving the old home.

Then his baby was born, and most of his cares seemed to vanish. He was happier now than he had ever been, and very proud of the little fellow. He made an idol of him, did everything he possibly could to bring a smile to the tiny face. Peter was a delicate baby: he had come into the world rather too soon, and until he was several months old had to be wrapped in cotton wool, and most carefully watched. Wayne adored him; his very own!

He seldom went near his mother's home. He was changing now, rapidly; nothing could arrest his change of mood. Gone were the old fears and doubts, the old feeling of inferiority. He was beginning now, for the first time, to consider himself an equal with the other fellows at work. He acquired new confidence. He quickly lost touch with the things that had so dominated his life previously. The stigma of poverty, the meanness, the sordid atmosphere – these had gone for ever. Gone for ever! He was stretching his limbs, reaching upwards. And the further he reached the nearer he came to his conception of that other girl; he felt he understood her better – and yet he did not know that she really existed! His former acquaintances irritated him with their slovenly ways and illiterate speech; he was shaking them off, leaving them behind.

He was passionately fond of his son, and liked nothing better than to be alone with him. He watched jealously the unfolding of the little mind, tutored him carefully, willingly and joyfully sacrificed his leisure time to play with him. Peter must make a success of his life; he must have no handicaps.

But the woman he had married was a source of despair to him, not because of any vicious habits but because of sheer indifference. As always, she was a model housewife. But she had no communion with her husband; he had grown strange, and she could not understand him. He was moody and silent except when the boy was in the room. He never confided in her; he had never done that. But now it was worse: he had obviously no desire to speak to her at all.

Wayne was beginning to experience torments that were new to him. He realised that his marriage had been a ghastly mistake; it had given him Peter, but nothing else. He had married someone who had been his equal. Now he had changed, for the better he thought; certainly his aspirations were far nobler. But his wife had not changed with him. She never would. She was incapable of change. It was too much trouble now to make herself look neat and tidy for her husband's benefit. He was securely anchored to her, so it was unnecessary. She took no pride in her personal appearance; she was drab, slatternly. Wayne would come home in the evenings and despair would enter his heart as he crossed the threshold. That woman, his wife! He noticed the untidy hair, the dull eyes, the uncared-for hands, the stained clothes. His wife! To love and to cherish for ever. For ever! He had never loved her. How well he knew that now. What miserable folly! She was slowly killing every generous impulse he felt for her. Her voice was harsh and ungrammatical. Once he had remonstrated with her, asked her to speak nicely and correctly; if she would not do it for his sake, then for Peter's. She had laughed at him; he would never ask again. She would never be a help to him; she couldn't be. She could only be a hindrance to his ambitions. He never took her out in the evenings; he was ashamed of her. Oh, he was so willing to start again if she would only try to understand and help him. He had married her; she was the mother of his son. They had made a mistake, but he was ready to attempt to make some sort of a success of it. Why didn't she improve herself, be attractive, speak nicely? Had she not intelligence enough to see that he was striving for a better life, to come with him? Could she not realise that unless she changed, he must abandon forever the ambitions that filled his heart? But no, it was hopeless. She could not understand. She was content to remain as she was. Already, Wayne was looking into the future, and he could see nothing there but a weary routine, no happiness. Her indifference chilled his very soul, he grew irritable in her presence. Sometimes when he heard her screaming at the boy he felt he could have struck her. This, for the rest of his life!

She found ready sympathisers in her cronies. There was no sacredness in her relations with her husband. His deficiencies were broadcast. In the little world in which his wife lived and had her being he gained a reputation for surliness and incivility and bad temper, and the more he withdrew into his shell against these traitorous remarks from one who should have been faithful, the more substantial appeared to be the grounds for her criticisms.

Wayne was lonely. He had no friends now; he had sent them away himself. He lavished all his affection on his son. He did not spoil him, and he did not try to influence him against his mother; no, he could never do that: she loved him, too, as much as Wayne did, and would have sacrificed all for him.

Wayne needed someone to confide in. His mother would have

listened, but he had drawn away from her of late years; besides, she would have been fearfully worried if she had suspected his unhappiness. There was the girl he dreamed of. How close he seemed to have come to her latterly. She had taken his mother's place as the guiding influence in his life. She dominated his thoughts, his actions. She had lifted him up, shown him the better way. Such was the power of his imagination. He loved to think about her: oh, there was nothing wrong in that. There couldn't be. He had long since ceased to argue with himself about it. He wasn't being unfaithful. She represented all the qualities that were kind and charitable; how then could she inspire unkindness in himself? His heart held no bitterness when he was thinking of her; he felt soothed and quietened, strangely comforted.

He bought a new house. He found a building society which would advance him the full purchase price and he borrowed every penny of it. He hoped that the new surroundings would influence his wife, but they did not. Latterly he was never angry with her; he was becoming resigned. He saw his duty, and for Peter's sake he must do it. But there was no companionship, no comradeship. They lived together and were worlds apart.

He did not take the last part of the examination next year. He never considered it. He could not have prepared for it. Any ambition he had ever had was killed, killed by his own foolishness, killed by his wife's stolid indifference, her lack of interest in his progress. She had told him now that she had not a scrap of affection for him; she knew he had none for her.

She still allowed him the privileges of a husband, whenever he willed. This was her duty as a wife; she felt that she had failed in nothing else that marriage had demanded and she would not fail in this. But she submitted sullenly; not once in all these years did she respond to him. His heart ached for some show of affection, for kindness and comfort. His demands on her grew less and less frequent. The restraint he imposed on himself caused him agonies of suffering, both physical and mental; it played havoc with his peace of mind. He often wondered if it was not this lack of real understanding on the part of his wife that had made their marriage such a mockery; why could she not realise that this natural relationship was absolutely vital to their happiness? Never from the start had she welcomed his embrace; if there was not communion between them on these occasions how could there possibly be on others? Latterly, with his growing appreciation of life and all that life could mean, be began almost to loathe himself when he took her in his arms. These were not moments of bliss, not precious opportunities to experience perfect joy, as they should have been; they were followed always by moods of bitter self-reproach. He was made to feel worse than a beast, and he reviled himself for surrendering to an instinct that had begun to appear ugly.

In other ways she changed very little. She became quieter, more mature. She worked hard, looked after Peter splendidly, always had an eye for his own wellbeing. She seemed resigned to the life that was now familiar. There was no communication of ideas between them; they never confided. They followed their own interests in silence. Sometimes Wayne wondered what her thoughts were. He did not think that she was altogether unhappy. Peter was the centre of her life, she had her friends, she was houseproud and industrious. She would have been friendlier to him, he knew, if he had been prepared to meet her halfway. But how could he? How could he pretend an affection he did not feel? How could he be insincere, and continue to be insincere? How could he live a life of pretence? How could he do these things, and remain honest? He could not; his thoughts would have been unbearable. At present, whatever his shortcomings, he was at least true to the dictates of his heart.

Often it seemed that a break must come soon. Twice his wife had told him that if he wanted a separation she would not stand in his way. He said nothing; there was nothing to say. Yet he pondered over the suggestion often. No, this was not the solution. They would have been happier apart, but there was Peter. No, affairs must continue like this to the end; there was no release.

He spent his holidays alone always, and came to look forward to these stolen opportunities of temporary escape with real expectancy and eagerness. They meant a change of environment and he welcomed them joyfully. Inactive holidays he did not consider: he lived them to the full, and planned beforehand every minute of his liberation. He was mentally tired; his release lay in exercise for the body. They were no ordinary holidays he indulged in. The essential was change, and he sought all chances of making the change complete. A body that was habitually inactive was on these occasions flogged into weariness by excessive effort; he found a curious pleasure in physical exhaustion, accompanied as it always was by a mind at last at rest. He liked to be constantly on the move, spending each night in different surroundings; it irked to have to return to a familiar abode. So with a body as restless as his thoughts had been previously, he wandered from one scene to another . . . His sole companion was a dear creature born in his imagination, and never yet come to life. She went every step of the way with him.

He still went to church, but not so often as formerly. His mother liked to see him there; she herself was, and always had been, a most devout attender. But there was no message for him now in the service; he had not the patience to listen to the preacher. Duties in connection with the church were thrust upon him; he did not refuse them; it was easier to accept. He performed them efficiently, without enthusiasm.

Some of his old habits clung. He still went to every cricket and football match, whatever the weather; he watched dispassionately, disinterestedly. He was losing interest, losing interest in life.

He had no friends. He never invited anyone to his house. He had too much to hide; he could never bear the humiliation. He was lonely, too. He wanted to meet people, but they would find his secrets; it was impossible. Was there no way out? He thought about it so much. Yes, there was one way. One way. It would cost money, and he hadn't any; it would mean a fight for the boy, and he must be careful to avoid any action that Peter might afterwards reproach him for; it would mean a scandal, but he could face that for such a cause. He pondered over it. No, no, it must not happen. But oh to be able to start again before every spark in him was stifled for ever. He and Peter together, a new start. Ah Peter, at once a blessing and a problem! If you were not here, your father would have been gone long ago. But you are here, and your father thanks God that you are. Dear Peter!

So one year dragged on into another. All the examinations were passed. His seniors urged him to leave the town for a better position; the juniors hinted that he was in the way of their progress. They didn't know; they knew nothing of him. If he left the town he would have to go alone, and he had lost the knack of making friends. His wife would not go with him; she had told him so. And he could not desert Peter, not for all the money in the world. Sometimes he felt sorry for his wife. It was his own fault. He had ruined her life, just as surely as he had ruined his own. He had not made her happy, had not tried to. Peter was his world now. Peter helped, a lot.

The fire had gone out; he did not know the time.

He was tired. His thoughts had carried him out of himself, soared away beyond the dimensions of earth, lost themselves in the boundless universe. They would not come back to him; they were no longer within the control of his exhausted body.

He felt suddenly weary. In the darkness he could see nothing, but he felt himself slipping, slipping into oblivion.

Gradually he became conscious that she was there, with him, she whom he loved. He had not heard her come in, but now she was standing by his chair, looking down at him. She did not speak.

He turned to her, rested his aching head against her sweet breast. She was with him, comforting him, soothing him: he was not perplexed and frightened any more. He had been wandering to and fro through the weary years, beaten, confused, despairing, suffering; now, at last, he had found refuge. All his life had been leading up to this moment. This was his home, this soft throbbing breast; he wanted no other. Could he but rest within this haven for ever, he would ask nothing more.

He stirred. He had been dreaming again, that dream which had by now become familiar. Yet was it a dream, nothing more? It was so real. He could feel her presence yet: she had not gone; she had become part of him.

He rose slowly to his feet. He stood awhile, then went out of the room. It was very late, very quiet. How close she was tonight!

He walked softly to his son's room, bent over the tiny figure in the bed. The boy was fast asleep, with the teddy bear that had been his constant bedmate since he was a baby in the circle of one chubby arm. Wayne looked at him long and earnestly, then he stooped and tenderly kissed the warm cheek.

He turned out the light, and went quietly to his own room.

CHAPTER EIGHT

Pennine Pleasures, 1938–41

There is no doubt that every word of Alfred's 'story' is true, true to his feelings at the time, to his thoughts about his marriage so far, and true to the facts about his life. The original is three times as long and contains a lot more autobiographical material – memories of his childhood and school days, his drunken father, his struggles to pass the exams, which I have omitted as they have already been described. It also contains a longer beginning, with him wandering round Blackburn, feeling soulful, which I have also omitted though for different reasons. It isn't very good and adds nothing.

Perhaps he intended it to be fictional, wanting to produce a moody soulful story, hence the name change, to disguise his identity, in case Ruth or anyone else ever found it. Then once started, he decided to tell the truth, as he saw it, and as honestly as he could. The possibility of publication presumably never occurred to him, though it has a shape and form, and the writing is polished and vaguely literary, trying for effect, in a style which is reminiscent of the pre-war period. Today, it would have been much more brutally done, with the sexual problems more graphically described. He admits she 'submitted sullenly', making him feel a beast. A marital situation which was typical of the times, though never admitted, never talked about. And who is to say it is not typical of our times, despite all our supposed self-knowledge and openness and talking things through. The difference today is that most people would not put up with it. His wife did suggest twice that they should be separated, so he says, but presumably they both felt caught, trapped, and there was Peter.

His anguish is well caught, and even heart-rending, but was he being fair? He does reveal his own brutishness, and not just in a sexual sense – criticising his wife's silly grammatical mistakes, her drab, untidy appearance, and even her 'slight physical defect', saying he was ashamed of her, fearing the fellows might laugh. He admits he was moody, did not confide in her, had no desire to speak to her. Off with his head, and everything else, so a modern feminist might instantly say, what a sexist pig, how could he treat her like that.

The Wainwright family all approved of Ruth. Their memories of her at the time are not quite Alfred's. They saw her as sociable, friendly, lively, a good housekeeper, a good mother. Not very pretty, in the accepted sense, but then Alfred was no Errol Flynn, despite some passing fancies. She might have been a mill girl, and spoke like one, but they deny she was drab, deny she ever ran him down, and say she was eager to learn and improve herself, given half a chance.

There are always two sides to every marriage and who can ever know the truth, who can ever portion total blame. One can only sympathise with both parties caught up in such a situation, making each other unhappy. Did she trap Alfred, letting him fondle her, seeing him as a good catch? We don't have her side of it, whether she ever truly loved him, or simply wanted a home and a family. Did they have some early years of happiness, with the new house, the new baby? In a letter to a friend in 1932, not long after his marriage, he gives his address as 'The Love Nest, Artillery Street', and says he is planning a walking tour with his wife at Whit. But a year later, to the same friend, in answering a list of the friend's queries, he has a headline saying, 'Re Married Life' – and leaves it totally blank.

By 1939, when he wrote that story, he seems to have no happy memories at all. In fact he admits he 'never loved her'. If that were so, then he must take the larger share of the blame. Which, of course, he was doing, writhing in his anguish.

The incident which Peter remembers, of his mother running away, probably came after this story, though the exact dates are hard to fix. There is no clue to what brought it about, whether it was caused by some specific event or the general situation, as revealed in his story. Could there have been someone else? Was Ruth jealous of Betty in the office? Did Ruth take refuge with someone, apart from her brother? She moved only a mile away, so neighbours must have known. (The building they fled to is still there, opposite the gates of Queen's Park, but is no longer a café, but an Asian-run shop, renting videos.)

Divorce had obviously entered his mind, but it was hard in those days, and socially not acceptable in respectable working-class families. Alfred was very mindful of his position in society, his job at the Town Hall, the need to keep up appearances, his personal dread of people gossiping about him or knowing his business. He was imbued with some of his mother's attitudes, stoically putting up with things, as she had put up with the drunken Albert. She at least did it cheerfully, always trying to look on the bright side, hoping for her reward in heaven. Alfred went sullen and depressed and into himself, feeling doomed for life, despite his half-dream, half-fantasy of meeting the Perfect Woman some day, some where.

Then there was, of course, Peter, the light of both their lives. How could they really split up when there was his well-being and his future to consider. Someone who tried to bring them back together was Alfred's mother. She had written to scold him about his loss of faith, which appears to have made little difference to his church attendance, but when she wrote to him about his marriage, in May 1941, when she was very ill, there is little doubt he was greatly affected by it. It was Ruth who told her about the possible separation, not Alfred himself, so she discloses in her letter. He kept this letter for ever.

363 Audley Range
Blackburn
May 28 1941

My Dear Alfred,

Forgive me, Alfred if I am interfering with your affairs, but when Ruth told me, you were thinking of separating, my heart seemed to die within me. I *do* hope it isn't true, & pray earnestly that you may come to some understanding, before it is too late.

I have thought such a lot of Peter, what will he do without his Daddy's love, a Daddy he has almost worshipped and does still: poor little Peter, I could weep when I think of him; Think again Alfred, & for his sake, don't separate. 'A little child shall lead them.' I have prayed night after night, that this little task may be Peter's.

God bless you all, & guide you in the right path.

With kindest love, from your anxious & troubled Mother.

The true state of Alfred's marriage is important for any study of his life. Not just in the strict biographical sense but because it had a vital bearing on his future work. The accepted belief, for those of his fans who have ever pondered on his motivation, is that he ruined the marriage through his obsession for walking the fells. No wonder his poor wife got fed up with him. This is a view he himself encouraged, in *Ex-Fellwanderer*, saying that she was 'unable to tolerate any longer obsessions of mine that left her out in the cold'.

The truth is the opposite. It wasn't fellwalking which caused the bad marriage – but the bad marriage which caused the obsessive fellwalking. In his story, he admits that he began to see it as an escape. 'Release lay in exercise for the body ... flogged into weariness by excessive effort ... a curious pleasure in physical exercise.' So he took every chance to get away, on his own if necessary, to wipe out the memory of his marital misery, to subjugate his sexual and emotional needs.

The most ambitious and arduous of his early escapes took place in September 1938, when he did a two-week walking tour of the Pennines. He went on his own, Peter being too young for such a long trek, and his office friends being perhaps not interested or available, or even not required. However, he did send a series of postcards back to Lawrence Wolstenholme, most remarkable in that they are the first known drawings of this sort.

He had a secondary aim in mind, not just the walk, but a project based on the walk. This Pennine walk produced his first proper, full-length book although it was not published till 1986.

The walk itself was fairly uneventful, from Settle up to the Roman Wall and back, staying at farm houses or inns. No accidents occur, no dramas, except one rumbling in the background – from time to time he hears on the wireless that Mr Hitler is threatening war, but then Peace breaks out at Munich. He travels very light, as he always did, carrying hardly anything with him.

My small rucksack was in fact virtually empty, and I could have managed quite well without it. I incline to the view, never before expressed, that a rucksack is not at all necessary on a walking tour. How some hikers can enjoy themselves beneath the weight of their huge, fifty-pound burdens completely passes my comprehension.

I have had expeditions in the Lake District without a pack, and gone short of nothing. I take a light raincoat or a cape, always; but never a change of clothes, nor an extra shirt, nor pyjamas. The clothes I wear when I set off must suffice: if they get wet, it is unfortunate for walking in wet raiment is unpleasant, but they have never failed to get dry afterwards. Pyjamas are, of course, a nuisance at all times and have no saving grace. A pair of slippers is a comfort, and additional socks are essential, but these will slip easily into a pocket.

On this occasion my rucksack contained four maps, the one in use being carried in my pocket. I had a toothbrush and a safety razor, a bottle of Indian ink and a pen, pencils and a rubber and a few postcards. I had also a miscellany of ointments and safe and certain cures for influenza, widely different in form and actually resembling each other only in the fact that they were one and all highly recommended by the medical profession.

All told, the entire contents of my rucksack would weigh less than two pounds, so that I was free to square my shoulders and stride out as quickly as I pleased.

He set off with flu (not surprisingly, since he never took a change of clothing with him on any of his walks) and was forced to exist in wet clothes until he could find a friendly farmer's wife to dry them for him over night. Otherwise he had to remain wet, and probably pretty pongy as well. Apart from one map, no drawings appeared in his book – but he did send some illustrated postcards to his friend Lawrence. He also took some photographs, none of them very good.

HEXHAM
NORTHUMBERLAND
7. 15 PM
19 SEP 48

Mr. L. Wolstenholme,
Borough Treasurer's Office
Town Hall
Blackburn.

The Priory of Lanercost

The postcards sent to Lawrence Wolstenholme
during the Pennine Walk

65

Ingleton, Wednesday.

In sun and shower—
from dawn to dusk—
having a GRAND time!
aw.

Mr. L. Wolstenholme,
Boro' Treasurer's Office
Town Hall
Blackburn.

There is no form of excitement quite like that of going into a shop for your prints. You have been told they will be ready at a certain hour; you have managed to curb your impatience in the meantime, but now the hour has struck and you are seething with anticipation. This is one appointment we never forget. There is a great thrill when the packet is handed over the counter, although you receive it with an air of indifference. You get outside, but cannot go further. You simply cannot wait a moment longer; you must look at them. You stand looking in the shop window, ostensibly regarding the display, but feverish fingers under cover of your coat are tearing the packet open. You have them now in your hand. In your hand! Look at them, fool! Drop your eyes, look at them; nobody is watching. See the results of your efforts. You have paid for them. They are in your hand. Look at them! You need wait in suspense no longer.

So you glance at them, one after another, quickly, and move away, conscious of disappointment and the sense that it is all over, life is empty again. My snapshots are always a blow to me.

On the walk, he mused philosophically on a range of subjects, all very entertaining and lively, reminiscent of the young R. L. Stevenson on his early walking tours, laying down the law, summing up humanity.

Anticipation is often more pleasurable than realisation; recollection is the sweetest of all and the most enduring. The mentality which urges you never to anticipate, never to count your chickens before they are hatched, is wrong all to blazes. Let your anticipation run riot, plan and dream of things far above your grasp, reach after them in your imagination even when reality is receding, think about them always. Plan new achievements, and set about achieving them. Failure and disappointment simply don't matter; go ahead with your dreaming, let your enthusiasm run away with you. You were made to rise and soar, and come down to earth with a bump, and rise and soar again. If you accomplish nothing else, you'll have kept the rot and the rust away. Let me warn you: it's the practical people who stay rooted on the earth, who make the money. But it's the dreamers who touch the stars. Which is the success you plan? Are you to 'play safe' for the rest or your life, or are you to adventure? You must make a choice, and make it early; and having made it, you must abide by it.

Having explained Anticipation for us, he moves on to the nature of Enthusiasm, although here he reveals some of his prejudices, or is he speaking from experience?

Enthusiasm grips a man's imagination, drives him on and on, and the hardships and discomforts of his way are nought. Enthusiasm feeds on itself. The enthusiast tingles with life and, while he yet lives, dwells with the gods.

Despite all that has been written to the contrary, I think that women are the practical sex. They do as their judgments dictate; they are not creatures of imagination. I have not yet witnessed genuine enthusiasm in one of them; often I have seen a pretence of it, but the divine spark was missing. Conventions deny them the liberty to indulge in the higher flights. Maybe their imaginations do soar sometimes, but are kept in leash and hidden. Yet I doubt it, for there are no secret enthusiasms. The man burns; the woman throws the cold water over him. Let's leave it at that, and kindly ascribe mixed metaphors also to enthusiasm.

He extols the joys of more humdrum activities, such as smoking cigarettes or supping HP sauce.

Nothing appeals to the palate more, at the end of a long day in the country, than sauce. It burns and scorches a throat jaded with too many cigarettes, makes it tingle pleasantly, and sends a glow of warmth to a starved stomach. I search for nothing more eagerly on a table; my desire for it amounts almost to lust. Let there be a bottle of sauce rearing up amongst the dishes, and it becomes the mainstay of the meal; all else, meat, fish, potatoes, being added merely for flavouring. I could eat a mound of scrapings from a stable if there was sauce in plenty to conceal the incongruity of the repast.

He muses on mists, clouds, maps and hills, especially hills and maps.

Give me a map to look at, and I am content. Give me a map of country I know, and I am comforted: I live my travels over again; step by step, I recall the journeys I have made; half-forgotten incidents spring vividly to mind, and again I can suffer and rejoice at experiences which are once more made very real. Old maps are old friends, understood only by the man with whom they have travelled the miles. Nobody could read my maps as I do. Lend a book to a friend and he can enjoy it and miss nothing of its story: lend him a map, and he cannot even begin to read the tale it has to tell. For maps are personal things which books are not. The appeal of an old map is to the memory; an old map spread across my knees closes my eyes. The older, the more tattered it is, the greater my affection for it. I recall our adventures together in storm and sunshine; an occasion, perhaps, when it slipped from my pocket and I searched my tracks anxiously, as for a lost companion, until it was found; an occasion, perhaps, when the mist was thick and instinct and the map urged different ways, and I followed the map and came to safe ground again. Ah yes, maps are grand companions. I have thrown books away, but never a map.

Give me a map of country I do not know, even of country I shall never know, and it has the power to thrill and excite me. No book has such an appeal to the imagination.

One of the recurring themes is women. It's his love of hills and walking on them which drives him on, but everywhere he goes, sex seems to rear its pretty head, if only in his own tousled thoughts. He recalls a recent train journey where someone started talking to him. 'At first, I resented his intrusion in my compartment for I had bought a nudist magazine on the platform and was fairly itching to be looking at it.' On the walk itself, he starts pining for a girl he has only glimpsed, and leaves a box of chocolates for her. He follows a pair of lovely legs in a village street, longs to kiss somebody passionately, makes love to a hot water bottle, gives the eye to a young woman he might have a chance with, until she reappears with her baby.

He goes to sleep one evening in a girl's bedroom where she has left behind her underwear. 'The bedrails were draped with silk stockings and there were wispy garments which, study them as I willed, I could not see their purpose. Whoever the owner was, she had put all her cards on the table. I had, of necessity, to play solitaire. As a result, I slept well that night.' Ho hum.

In one farmhouse, where he is sitting shattered after a very long day, he sees a young woman who fancies him.

She came into the room to view me more closely and, being pleased with what she saw, sat beside me. She had a curious interest in me, I could see. More than that, she was attracted to me. She was all smiles. She fawned upon me. She made no effort to conceal the fact that she was conquered and awaited my attention. At last, a dream come true. Sad that it should happen this particular evening. For I could only look dully at her. A man without a body cannot a wooing go.

He describes this scene as a fact, not his fancy, although it was just as likely she'd come to gape at a man who hadn't changed his clothes for two weeks. At other times, he does know when he is fantasising. His Dream Girl, the dear creature born in his imagination', once again comes into his thoughts.

I thought for a time about the day's events. And then, very softly, the girl of my dreams came to me, as she does every evening when all is still, to tuck me in and say goodnight, or to stay with me and talk quietly in the darkness. We have been companions on many a delightful journey, and known the quiet joy of comradeship; together we have broken the bonds that would keep us to the earth and soared in wonderful flight of ecstasy.

I gave her my heart long ago, and am her slave until I die. She is the dearest little person in the world, and she has become the most real. Her kiss is my last experience every night before I sleep, her warm tender lips the caress that closes each day.

Am I a fool, thus to dwell in dreams?

Almost all the way through the book he gives the impression that he is a single chap, on the loose, on the look-out – although that doesn't stop him giving advice on marriage.

To a young man seeking a wife, I would say that neatness is the first essential; a trim appearance, a dainty body, a precise outlook. Intelligence is the next virtue to seek, and it is a rare one; it is the comparative deficiency in intellect that makes woman's claim for equality with man pathetic. Next in importance is a sense of humour. But the girl who laughs loudly is to be avoided; look for one who smiles rather than laughs, whose heartiest guffaw is never more than a quiet chuckle. Good looks don't matter a great deal, and don't last, anyway; I have a partiality for blue eyes, to me they make a face look honest, but I am ready to be convinced that hazel or brown eyes signify an equally trustworthy nature. For the further guidance of the young man seeking a wife, let me add the following counsel; never marry a girl because you are sorry for her, for sympathy dies swiftly; never marry a girl simply because she is a good cook, for there are worse ailments than a rebellious stomach; keep away from the massive women, for they will go worse, and make you labour like a beast; never marry simply to get away from a depressing home, for the odds are you will jump from the fire into the frying-pan, and it is better to roast now than to sizzle for the rest of your life; beware the girl who is your senior in age and fawns on you, for you are her last opportunity, perhaps, and secretly she may be despising you and hating herself. But do not worry too much about your choice. If you picked blindfold, you could be pretty sure of getting a wife who would keep the home tidy, have your meals ready promptly, give you an amazing baby now and again, and be entirely devoted and faithful. Whether these qualities are sufficient to make you happy, depends on yourself.

It is only at the very end of the book that he reveals, almost as an aside, that he is in fact a married man, when he wonders if there will be any changes at home to his 'son, spouse, Peggy, Paddy, Micky'. The latter are his dogs and cat although that is not explained.

Throughout, his joy in writing the book shines through, his love of language, his pleasure in trying to recapture the emotions of the walk over the following long winter months while he wrote it. Did he hope the book would be published? There are enough references in the book itself to indicate this was in his mind at the time, addressing 'my reader', talking about going into print, but in his Introduction, written in 1986 when the book was finally published (exactly as he wrote it in 1938) he says it was done purely for his own pleasure, though 'three other people in the office read it and pronounced it good'.

THIS collection of photographs is intended to serve as an introduction to Mr. Wainwright's latest book

PENNINE CAMPAIGN

A stirring tale of fearless adventure amongst the High Pennines and along the Roman Wall.

Full details of this publication are given later in this volume.

Arrangements have been made with the Alké Studio for a supply of enlargements of this superb portrait. The demand will be enormous. Make sure of your copy by ORDERING NOW. Price 4ᵈ each, or with autograph, 6ᵈ each.

PENNINE CAMPAIGN will be published within a few months. The first edition will be strictly limited in number. Each copy will contain four full-page original black-and-white sketches by the author, together with a map of the journey and numerous small illustrations and photographs, and will be bound in blue limp cloth with gold lettering. The narrative of 90,000 words will be typewritten, and the price per copy will be graded according to the quality of the typed matter, viz.

21/- for original typed manuscript

17/6 for first typed copy

15/- for second typed copy

10/6 for third typed copy

This is your opportunity to obtain a volume which you will be proud to rank amongst your most valued possessions.

Mr. Wainwright's literary style is free and masterly, and reveals the sure touch of the true artist. With this book, he assures himself of immortality.

A FEAST FOR THE WHOLE FAMILY!
ORDER EARLY.

Nearing the end of his grim trek, Mr. Wainwright's face relaxes for a moment during an interview by enterprising representatives of the Northumbrian Press. (*Picture by courtesy of the Hexham Daily Star*)

Extracts from the 'publisher's' booklet announcing the publication of Pennine Campaign

I find it hard to believe that he did not have some hopes of it being published at the time, despite what he later said. He had clearly become a skilful writer, proud of his word power, who had produced a polished, finished book. Did he offer it somewhere and was rejected, and then later wiped the disappointment from his mind by putting the text into a drawer? There is no evidence that he ever formally sent it to a publisher, but there are enough clues to suggest he had serious hopes of publication.

When he'd finished writing it, he produced a lavishly illustrated 'publisher's' booklet announcing its imminent publication; this included photographs taken on the journey, a brief guide to Hadrian's Wall, and full details of the price and cover (see also page 71). Okay, this was a joke, AW enjoying himself, and amusing his friends, but doing it so carefully, with beautiful lettering and an almost professional layout, so that it looked like a real hand-out for a genuinely forthcoming book.

He also wrote a 'reader's' report of the book, as if written by a publisher's reader, the sort of report which a publisher of the day might well have commissioned, and used the name Frederick Hornby. (Well, I am assuming it is an AW joke, as the writing is a bit florid and purply, comparing the author to Priestley and Wordsworth.) It does indicate he knew something about the publishing business, to create such a good cod report.

Subject:—	*Pennine Campaign*
Reviewer:—	*Frederick Hornby.*
Reading Time:—	*Four Hours (approx)*
Date:—	*1st December, 1939.*

REPORT

It cannot be said that travel-books are the most interesting of all books to review. Too often, they are stereotyped chronicles of voyages, expeditions, or walks, whose appeal is limited to the esoteric few, who have a deeper interest in the object of the author than has the ordinary layman. Again, a travel-book which can boast of being well-written is something of a rarity. Evidently, these chroniclers do not number literary ability among their possibly manifold talents. And so it is all the more refreshing to come across a travel-book, whose author has combined literary ability with a flair for description, to produce a thoroughly interesting and highly enjoyable book.

Mr Wainwright's book is a record of his walking-tour from Settle to Hadrian's Wall, via the Dales of Yorkshire and over the broad back of the Pennines. This feat was accomplished within a fortnight, and as such bears a strong appeal to all true lovers of the walking art, while its interest to antiquarians is prompted by its object – to reach and explore that mighty bulwark against the marauding Picts and Scots, survivor of close on two thousand years of storm, wrack, and vandalism, a lasting testament to those Roman engineers who 'fashioned better than they knew' – the Wall of Hadrian.

I am not a walker nor am I an antiquarian. Yet I lived this journey – I tramped over fell and moor, through peat and bog, through heather, gorse, and bracken, in blazing heat, in icy hail, in clammy mist. I saw the Wall – the Vallum – the Ditch – I explored the ramparts and the milecastles. I talked with Richardson, I gazed loathingly at the drunken Rowley. Such is the potency of a good writer's pen.

Undeniably, the author is a master of the descriptive art. The artist latent within him is vividly revealed in his portrayal of the rural scenes through which he journeyed. Rarely using the same combination of epithets twice, in spite of the fact that where description is so vital in a book of this nature, he nevertheless manages to avoid any descent to verbiage, or pedanticism. Combined with this flair for natural description is the power of character delineation and a keen sense of atmosphere. Here his description of the little old lady who reminded him of his mother, and his outline of the atmosphere generated by the fair at Alston leap readily to the mind. I can pay no higher compliment by saying that at times I found myself comparing his style with that of Priestley's in a manner that was in no way derogatory.

The heights are manifestly the author's Elysium. With a simple, plain religion such as his, deriving its root force from the mountains and the love wherewith they inspire him, he might almost be called Wordsworthian in his outlook. And like Wordsworth, he points to the mountains and their philosophy as the balm and unguent of man's ills. But in the words of this poet, I must regretfully remind him that 'the world is too much with us'. Those who feel the call of the mountains and find their peace and solace there should give thanks and rejoice, for their's [sic] is a fortunate heritage which is the lot of few to acquire.

Philosophy, simple and homely, surely the fruits of the inspiration of high altitudes, colours this book with its rich discursiveness. It is very welcome inasmuch as it is an integral part of the journey and without it, there would be a sense of the absence of a vital ingredient. Idealism such as his dream girl can be of great help: certainly it can be a source of consolation and inspiration. All must have at some time felt the need of some driving-force in the attainment of an ideal: it matters not whether the inspiration is real or imaginary: it can never be other than real to the one seeking for inspiration.

This book has its defects as must all books. I propose to ignore over-sentimentality or a tendency to dictate. Such faults are minor ones, and have been committed by more illustrious writers than this one. Suffice to say, I derived considerable pleasure from this book: I can only hope it is a foretaste of more to come.

Wainwright clearly enjoyed writing this pretend review, but there is no doubt he was very interested in soliciting serious opinions of his book, showing it to far more than just 'three other people' in his office. He made several copies, passed it round his own office, and also sent a copy to a friend who had left the office, Walter Eric Maudsley, one of those who had accompanied him on the Lakeland walk at Whitsuntide in 1931. Eric had moved from the Blackburn office in 1932 to Carlisle and then to Hertford in 1939.

In February 1941, AW wrote to Eric asking him to send back his copy of *Pennine Campaign* as a blonde in the office wanted to read it. 'Every day the aforementioned blonde comes round to my desk and pushes her soft breasts into me and whispers "Have you got it back yet" I am anxious that she should have it, even though that may mean that she will no longer push her soft breasts into me, which same operation, by the way, I could endure until Judgment Day.'

A month later, he's still waiting. 'I felt flattered at your references to the success my book is having in Hertford, but tell my readers to be bloody handy, I want it back quick.'

It is returned at last, then Eric wants it back, having got someone else interested in reading it.

You want *Pennine Campaign* again. Such a fag having to find brown paper and parcel it up and send it! I intended to make minor corrections, and amend the title to *Pennine Journey*, but the months have sped by and nothing has been done. Who wants it this time? Anybody with 'fluence? Longland, for instance? I'd like to see it published, and anybody can have the copyright for fifty pounds: a rare opportunity for someone with business acumen, for royalties will roll in! I'll send it, if you really want to have it. But it's in tatters now. See that it doesn't get amongst the salvage.

Several friends of Eric wanted to read it this time, including his Deputy Treasurer, and also Eric's girlfriend, a woman called Bess. Eric eventually tells AW her opinion of the book, which wasn't very encouraging. 'Bess says that you can sketch even if your efforts in the literary world are crude and clumsy.'

That must have been a disappointment for him. By sending it around so many people, there was always a slight chance that someone who liked it might have connections in the publishing world, but that didn't happen. Anyway, wartime wasn't quite the right time for an unknown to break into publication. We have to accept therefore that it was a pure amusement for him, an escape from domestic un-bliss, and can only wonder how his life would have been different, if only he had become a serious author at the age of thirty-one.

CHAPTER NINE

Office Pleasures, 1938–40

During the time he was writing *Pennine Campaign*, a serious attempt at a proper book, there was still a juvenile spirit lurking inside. At home he might be trying to be literary but in the office he was still producing satirical stuff to amuse his chums such as Lawrence Wolstenholme, Jim Sharples, Bob Alker and Fred Sellers.

In 1937 he wrote and illustrated a twenty-eight-page magazine called 'This Office of Ours. 28 Big Pages – Two Magnificent Free Gifts Inside'. It was described as a Shad Production, after the street where he lived, Shadsworth Road. Most of the jokes and references are hard to appreciate now – although when I contacted Bob Alker and some of the others still alive, they all had a laugh at times and people now gone, and were able to explain a few of the references. There was an agony column for the lovelorn, with advice by 'Ann Simple', mocking people in the office.

Replies to Correspondents:
BD – Don't be afraid of hurting his feelings. Tell him to stop, if you want him to.
[BD was Betty Ditchfield]
WA – You do not say whether you are male or female. Until you do of course I cannot advise you. In any case, I should say you are now too old for it. But write to me more fully, won't you, dear?
[WA was William Ashton, a bachelor, remembered in the office for maintaining that 'marriage was a filthy occupation'.]

There were garden notes, pen portraits, embroidery patterns, poems, stories – all of them made up by AW and all in his handwriting. Many of the jokes were directed at the Treasurer,

R.G. Pye, or at N.W.E. Hamm, the Chief Accountant, or at people who were bald, tall or had a moustache, or thought to be lazy, always late, always talking, flash, puritanical; in fact, the sort of people in offices anywhere.

'*The Seven Ages of Man*' *from* This Office of Ours

THINGS WE SHALL NEVER SEE
Hair on the top of WA's head
JS running along a corridor
NWEH 's top lip
AH at his desk at 9 o'clock
Disorder in the Correspondence office
Any of the Collectors going up steps two a a time
Spittoons on the floor of the Loans Office.

THINGS WE TIRE OF SEEING
RGP sneezing
RGP waiting to sneeze
Income Tax computations
A Shaw's mouth opening
AW's six-year-old overcoat

THINGS WE'D LOVE TO SEE
NWEH as Romeo to WA's Juliet
JS running along a corridor
Mae West at the counter of the Loans Office
Forget-me-nots in JHW's desk
Look of dawning intelligence on Shackleton's face

RGP didn't actually sneeze, but when lost for words, or thinking hard, he would pull out his handkerchief, as if about to sneeze.

One of the longest pieces was entitled 'The Strange Young Man and the Beautiful Lady – a Story for the Very Tiny Ones'. It was about a strange young man, 'thin and ugly with very red hair', who was in love with a Beautiful Lady. He lived in a dark forest while she lived in a sunlit meadow. One day he told her his story, and his love for her, but she did not answer. 'Years passed and he became blind and could not then go to work and died. And when she was told of his death, the B. Lady wrinkled her fair brow and tried to hard to remember him. And last she did and she was sorry because she knew he had loved her.'

In 1939, he produced a booklet with photographs, so making it look even more professional. This was called 'Alpine Adventure – 1939' and was the programme for a proposed sixteen-day trip to the Bernese Oberland, with exact details and itinerary for every day, with a few jokes along the way. The party was divided in two, a Mobile Section and an Immobile Section. 'On the tenth day, the MOBILE SECTION joins the IMMOBILE SECTION which has been resident all this time at Grindelwald, whereupon the whole party becomes QUASI MOBILE.'

There were detailed maps of all the routes, up and down various mountains. 'Thank heavens I'm writing these names not saying them.' Our Leader had a whole page to himself. 'Alfred (True Blue) Wainwright, 1907–1939. Lone leader of many lost expeditions. Author of Wainwright's Guide to the Lakeland Fells.' A joke book, of course, as he had not written anything on Lakeland, but was his Alpine Adventure a joke?

'Oh no,' says Lawrence Wolstenholme, 'he meant it. He sent it round the office, hoping people would join the party, but 1939 wasn't a good time to plan a trip to Europe. It never got anywhere.'

When the war came, Alfred was not called up. It was deemed that his sort of local government work, and his particular position as a fairly senior municipal accountant, was vital for the good of Blackburn, so while many of his colleagues in the office went off to fight, Alfred stayed at home, his call-up deferred. (Peter, his son, has a memory of his father at some time having a medical examination, which he failed anyway, because of his eyesight.)

The war did have one good effect – it brought some girls into the office. As the younger, unqualified men were called up, they were replaced by young women. 'They were bright, lively, very modern girls,' remembers Bob Alker, 'the sort Alfred always had an eye for.'

Their arrival spurred him into action, so he wrote to Eric Maudsley in Hertford in February 1941.

I am being persistently urged by the girls in the office to form a rambling club, and this appeals to me hugely, for it is an idea I have secretly nursed in my skinny bosom for many years only to postpone it after a review of the meagre female company available. But now things are

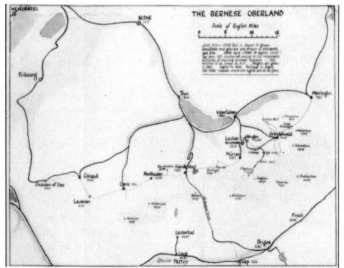

LAST STRAGGLER
FROM MOSCOW:
" Seen owt of Napoleon ?"

THE PROGRAMME
continued—

Tenth
Day
: To ** Lauterbrunnen, ** Wengen,
and *** Grindelwald.

Steep descent to the ** Lauterbrunnen Valley, famous for its cascades.
Here is the ** Staubbach Fall (980'), the highest waterfall in Europe. Climb
to ** Wengen, thence across the ** Wengern Alp (where Byron "carried
the pageant of his bleeding heart ") to the *** Little Scheidegg, where
the Jungfrau Railway starts, and where the Immobile Section should
be waiting with appropriate greetings. Bridle-path to *** Grindelwald.
Magnificent views all day. The great peaks of the Oberland hereabouts
form a stupendous mountain wall whose battlements seem to overhang
in mid air 10,000' above. Marvellous !

Eleventh
Day
: Visit to the *** Glaciers of
Grindelwald.

Ascend to the Bäregg Chalet, whence traverse to the **** Eismeer
('Sea of Ice'), a world of stupendous ice-masses amidst a grand
amphitheatre of snow-clad mountain peaks. Return to *** Grindelwald.

Twelfth
Day
: Ascent of the **** Faulhorn (8805')
A long but easy climb. This mountain is composed
of a crumbling calcareous schist (per Baedeker) and is noted both for
its rich and varied flora and its unequalled panorama of the Oberland
giants which lower up across the green pastures of *** Grindelwald.

Thirteenth
Day
: To ** Interlaken, by the *** Grosse
Scheidegg and ** Meiringen

This glorious walk passes beneath the huge basement of cliffs on which
the **** Wetterhorn is super-structed. Astounding view upwards. Easy
descent to ** Meiringen, where are the ** Reichenbach Falls, and which
ends the traverse of the Oberland. Train to ** Interlaken.

"VÖRWARTS, VOLSTENHOLME"

THE PROGRAMME
continued

Fourteenth Day	To Newchatel and *Paris. *Evening in *Paris*
Fifteenth Day	From *Paris to London. *Evening in London.*
Sixteenth Day	Back to *Blackburn

The IMMOBILE SECTION will travel direct to Grindelwald from Newchatel on the fourth day, and stay there for the duration of the holiday. No better headquarters could be chosen. Grindelwald is superbly situated at the foot of the staggering ten-thousand feet cliff on the crest of which, like monstrous watchtowers, rise the four great peaks of the Wetterhorn, the Eiger, the Mönch, and the Jungfrau. Grindelwald is an admirable centre for many delightful and varied excursions.

On the tenth day, the Immobile Section will go to the Little Scheidegg to await the arrival of the Mobile Section. If the latter do not put in an appearance by five p.m, they may return, saddened and a little sobered, and will have to get back to Blackburn as best they can. If the reunion does, however, take place, the night is to be given over to abandon and licence.

So

The MOBILE SECTION is for those restless individuals to whom adventure and sudden death have an irresistible appeal. It is for those who always like to be looking round the next corner.

The IMMOBILE SECTION is for those who can be well content to idle away the hours in Paradise, letting the loveliness of their surroundings sink deep into their souls. It is for the quiet lovers of true beauty. Recommended also for those who reckon nowt of Our Leader.

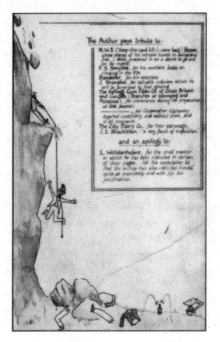

The Author pays tribute to:

N.W.E. (Keep-the-card-till-I-come-back) Raven, whose literal & his refined lunch in Switzerland was, indeed, assisted in no a desire to go and be useful.
F.S. Smythe, for his excellent books on climbing on the Alps.
Rucksack, for his associate.
J. Sharpener, for valuable criticism which he...
...
The National Gun Fund Co. of Great Britain and Canada, (branches at Winnipeg and Montreal), for conference during the preparation of this poems.
... for Corporation stationery, supplied cheerfully and without stint, and all enquiries.
The Coty Dairy Co., for their patronage.
J.E. Shackleton "a very fount of inspiration."

and an apology to:

L. Wolstenholme, for the cruel manner in which he has been ridiculed in certain of these pages. Let his contribution be that the author has also ridiculed himself quite as mercilessly and with far less justification.

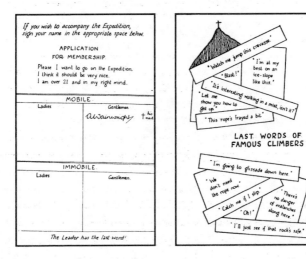

If you wish to accompany the Expedition, sign your name in the appropriate space below.

APPLICATION FOR MEMBERSHIP.

Please I want to go on the Expedition.
I think it should be very nice.
I am over 21 and in my right mind.

MOBILE.	
Ladies	Gentlemen
	A.Wainwright † his mark

IMMOBILE.	
Ladies	Gentlemen.

The Leader has the last word!

"Watch me jump this crevasse."
"I'm at my best on an ice-slope like this."
"Blast!"
"It's interesting walking in a mist, isn't it?"
"Let me show you how to get up."
"This rope's frayed a bit."

LAST WORDS OF FAMOUS CLIMBERS

"I'm going to glissade down here."
"We don't need the rope now."
"There's no danger of avalanches along here."
"Catch me if I slip."
"Oh!"
"I'll just see if that rock's safe."

different: the office is crammed with plump juicy specimens who are itching for excitement. So I am contemplating forming THE PENDLE CLUB, an association for cultured young men and women interested in walking. The blonde I told you about is as keen as mustard. Perhaps you'd better send me that Manual of Sexual Methods; I'd like to read it, in case the Pendle Club has a wet day, and I fancy the blonde would take to Method 34 like a duck to water. Send it, will you, please?

To the surprise of most people in the office, Alfred did actually organise the club, and had proper notepaper printed with himself as Vice Chairman, Lawrence Wolstenholme as Chairman and Bob Alker as Hon Treasurer. Lawrence's wife, Margery, was a member, as was Bob Alker's wife, Mona. Dorothy Coleman, the blonde in question, was Hon Sec, but there is no sign of Alfred's wife Ruth being involved, or even told.

Bob remembers only one outing, a walk up Pendle Hill, and then to the cinema. He took his camera with him and got the one and only shot of the Pendle Club, resting on top of the hill (*see* plate 10).

A picture of the Pendle Club in the cinema might have been even more interesting, judging by a letter from Alfred to Eric Maudsley, in which again he wants his book back.

You will observe with your customary shrewdness that the Pendle Club has come into being, but alas, far from being a rambling club, it is already developing into an association of Mature Men and Young Ladies

1 AW as a baby: born 1907

2 His mother,
Emily Wainwright

3 & 4 His sisters, Alice and Annie Wainwright

5 His father, Albert Wainwright

6 Annie Wainwright's wedding to Bill Duxbury, 1929. Ruth Holden and AW are seated: they married in 1931 but no wedding photo exists

7 AW and Ruth's only child, Peter, born 1933: pretty enough to enter a 'Beautiful Baby' contest

8 & 9 Young Peter Wainwright on holiday in limestone country, 1940, snapped by AW: 'I loved all those trips with my father'

10 The Pendle Club outing, 1941. Back left, Margery and Lawrence Wolstenholme;
front row, Bob and Mona Alker and AW. 'Bright, lively, modern girls – the sort
Alfred always had an eye for'

11 Ruth and Peter at High Sweden Bridge – photographed by AW on a rare family
outing

12 & 13 AW resting on the fells, 1950s. Note his formal walking clothes of collar and tie and tweed jacket . . . plus the ubiquitous pipe

1956   1961   1966

14 The Kendal Borough Treasurer's team: every five years from 1951, AW organised an office photograph. They show his suits getting tweedier, his face plumper and his spectacles becoming heavier as his eyes grew weaker. In the top photograph, 1951, Percy Duff is on AW's left

15 AW and Henry Marshall, plus an unknown woman. Marshall, Kendal's librarian, was AW's friend and the first 'publisher' of the Pictorial Guides.

16 AW on Place Fell, overlooking Ullswater, in traditional hot-weather headgear

17 Ruth at home in Kendal Green with AW's family, 1960: Alice and Annie, AW's sisters, with Ruth in the middle. Bill Duxbury (left), Jack Fish (right) plus Cindy the dog

18 AW, meanwhile, was not at home but walking alone on the fells

Who Have No Dread Of Pregnancy. The idea was originally good and completely moral, but so far the primitive urge to sit in a dark cinema and play with the opposite sex has been paramount in our thoughts, and there has been very little walking done. Hence our practice to date has been to clear off to a strange town (Clitheroe, usually), have tea, and then do a bit of groping on the back row of the local picturedrome.

Your Manual Of Sexual Methods has not yet arrived, in spite of your assurances; I am anxious to discover whether certain of my own devices have been publicly recognised; if not, I shall be able to affix an allonge for the benefit of subsequent readers.

What I am much more concerned about is the fate of my Pennine Campaign. WHERE THE HELL IS IT? There are several people here panting to read it; must I forever put them off with feeble excuses? Get it back TODAY and send it on to me TONIGHT. The Hon. Sec. of the Pendle Club has promised that I can so-and-so her when I produce it, but not before, and I should like to get this done on Thursday.

How much of this was bravado, showing off to his distant chum, letting him see what a good time he was having? There are those who maintain this was an era of sexual innocence, pre the permissive age, but on the other hand it was wartime, even if they were in safe civilian jobs. In almost all his letters to Eric there were sexual references, if just to the Sex Manual or other stimulating publications. 'I expended a penny on the current "Sun Bathing Review"', so he reveals, writing about his train trip home after a short holiday with Eric. 'This purchase being effected without a blush. A disappointing book, though – no hairs on.'

He goes on to boast about the women waiting for him, to whom he has sent postcards while he's been away.

And now I am back to the familiar life, with women fore and aft and right and left, and find myself besieged with invitations. Absence, it seems, had made their joint and several hearts grow even fonder. Dorothy is treasuring her letter, 'the loveliest I ever received' she says. Doris thought hers was 'beautiful' and has returned it for me to preserve for her out of her hubby's reach. Both wanted me to take them for a walk last night (after much indecision, I chose Doris). If ever they meet and swop confidences I shall have to flee the town: could you then find me a job? Anyway, I have made them both wonderfully happy: what does it matter that I have sacrificed honour.

There's something missing in your life, Maudsley lad, and it will still be missing when your salary runs into four figures. I told you what it was and I tell you again: go and find a little hole to put your old man in. Remember the snails, and go and do likewise.

I have just written to Wasdale Head for accommodation for Whitsun for Doris and myself and her husband and son. Later in the year Dorothy and I are going hiking in the Lakes: this might develop into an organised holiday of the Pendle Club, and if so, there will be a sincere invitation for you to come: imagine us all strewn in couples along Langstrath after the fashion of the Dovedale snails!

In a postcard written to Lawrence Wolstenholme in the summer of 1939 while Lawrence was on holiday in Keswick, he said rather enigmatically: 'I received another 12-page letter from you-know-where, and despite my disclosure of last week, yet another invitation. Surely this is a Konquest.'

There was one other club which Alfred helped to found, also in 1939, which continues to this day – Blackburn Rovers Supporters Club. It grew out of a group of his friends in the Treasurer's Office who were very keen on Rovers, talked about the team all week, and went most Saturday afternoons to Ewood Park. After all their famous achievements back in the 1880s, the club had won only one trophy since, the FA Cup in 1928, then had suffered the

ignominy of relegation from the First Division in 1936. But in the season 1938–39, they won the Second Division Championship, and so arrived back in the First Division with the newly-formed Supporters Club there to cheer them on.

A. Wainwright was the first Hon. Treasurer while James Crook, also in the Treasurer's Office, was Hon. Sec. The chairman was Fred Haslam, who also worked in the Town Hall. Another friend and co-founder was Tom Snape, a good friend of Alfred's, as was Tom's wife, Doris.

In June 1940, they organised a coach trip from Blackburn to Wembley for the War Cup Final where Rovers were to play West Ham. The FA Cup was truncated during the war, and a restricted crowd of only 43,000 turned up, and Rovers were beaten one nil.

Billy Westall who, in 1939, was working as a football reporter on the old *Blackburn Times*, remembers the Supporters Club being founded but says it was always fairly small, the Club itself was against it, and it petered out during the war not to be revived until the 1950s. All the same, it didn't stop Alfred and his chums enjoying themselves in the 1939–40 season, having whist drives and dinners in the Club's honour, singing songs and toasting each other.

The Club continued, on paper at least, for another year, with the officials rotating, Alfred becoming in turn Hon. Treasurer, Acting Sec. and Chairman. The notepaper changed as well, so they must have had some money – or access to the Town Hall's printer. It was a very happy period for Alfred, what with the young girls in the office and the football supporters' club to keep him amused and occupied, as he told Eric.

At present I seem to have more friends than ever I've had. Until a couple of years ago, I had none. I used to call Lawrence Wolst and Jim Sharples my friends, and still do, of course, but I never sought their company after office hours. I knew nothing of the pleasures of entertaining companions. That's all changed now. The most profitable evening I ever spent was the night when the Supporters' Club was formed. I was elected to office, and put my whole heart into making it a success. I've been rewarded a thousand times. The Committee meetings became a joy to my starved soul: there I found bright talk and laughter and beer, and it suited. I made friends, easy-going friends but the best in the world. Better still, with their help I rid myself of an accursed complex: it became easier to meet other people, and to be friendly with them, too. I have become a favourite with the ladies! And I like them a lot. Nowadays I never need to spend a night moping and sighing; the trouble is to resist all the invitations I get for a night out.

So that was fortunate for him. Walking clubs and football provided perfect escapes from an unhappy marriage. As for his wife, Ruth, she was being given ample excuse for running away with Peter.

CHAPTER TEN

Lakeland Dreaming, 1939–41

It would be wrong to overstate the sex'n football. As in all lives, many strands run in parallel, at the same time, often in the same place. Alfred might have had high hopes of getting some ripe young women, preferably married, to lie with him in some valley, although his fancied trip with the girls of the Pendle Club never happened, but his main passion was for the Lake District. He made regular trips there, despite wartime restrictions on travelling, and the lack of accommodation or proper food when he got there, and spent much of his spare time studying Lakeland maps and books. Baddeley appears to have been his favourite guide book.

In a letter to Eric Maudsley, he mentions a salary increase, and that he has bought not a nudist mag this time but four outdoor books. 'I have today celebrated by sending £2.14.0 to the publishers of Smythe's *Peaks and Valleys*, *A Camera in the Hills*, *My Alpine Album* and *The Mountain Scene* for a copy of each. These are magnificent books and I advise you to follow suit.'

Eric was still living in Hertford, a boring landscape, so AW maintains. At least when he was based in Carlisle, he had been handy for the Lakes.

What on earth persuaded you to leave this fairest spot of England for life on a miserable plain? Money, was it? The Royal Mint itself wouldn't induce me away! Now, more than ever before, flat country gives me the pip. A flat landscape is a picture only half-finished; it contains nothing to arrest the attention; there is no satisfactory horizon; the gaze wanders aimlessly over the scene and trails away to nothing; there is no background, no climax. It's like a story without a plot.

During 1939 and 1940, amidst the fun and games, he had frequently been trying to organise proper walking holidays with his friends, the sort they had had in the early 1930s when he first discovered Lakeland. In April 1939, he wrote to Lawrence Wolstenholme, hoping that he and Jim Sharples would agree to one more Lakeland jaunt, before they all grew old together.

Mr Wolstenholme:
This is you as seen by me.
Not such a stunner for good looks, are you?
One thing I admire about you, however, is that you are always willing to help anyone in financial straits..

— Yours very sincerely,

A. Wainwright.

P.S. By the way, can you lend me a shilling for to-night.
Thanking you in anticipation,
I am, believe me,
Yours truly A.W.

90 Shadsworth Road,
Blackburn,
15th April 1939.

Dear Lawrence,

That week we spent under canvas at Stonethwaite is still so fresh and poignant a memory that it came as a shock to me to realise, one evening last week, that six years have fled since then. Six years is a long long time, when we are looking forward; an incredibly short interval when we pause and look back. When we were at Stonethwaite, Jim had but recently attained his thirtieth birthday, yet the rest of us, so much younger, regarded him as a veteran campaigner; you were a carefree bachelor of twenty-four, with no immediate prospects of marriage; Peter, now a big rough lad, was only a few months old and I was still lost in the wonder of him.

You haven't changed much during these six years, nor has Jim. Indeed, it would be extremely difficult to find even the slightest evidence of change in either of you. You've both sort of grown on me, almost as though you were additional limbs; I should feel lost if you were no longer in your place, and I cannot possibly imagine you other than just as you are. I haven't changed, either; not in the essentials. I think we know each other pretty well.

We are getting to that stage now where the gap between ourselves and the youngsters who are newly-appointed to the staff is widening to an alarming degree. We are mature. The newcomers treat us with deference and respect; we are, to them, middle-aged, halfway to retirement. This seems ridiculous: we are young men yet. But it is a fact that has caused me much sober reflection of late. We are getting on, no doubt about that. If we were footballers, we should be veterans now. We are above conscription age. Too old! The thought appals.

We three, you and Jim and me, are the last links with the quiet, peaceful years before the War. Those who are coming after us are different. They can't be depended on, they can't settle down. They can't pick out the things that really matter; they change friends too easily. They don't like climbing hills; they think it must be utter boredom to sit idly by a stream tumbling down a mountain side. They wouldn't dream of buying a map and studying it. The sort of holiday we like best has no meaning for them. Heather, to them, is a weed.

I've thought a lot lately of the good times we used to have together in the Lake District. We introduced other members from time to time; they proved fickle, and one by one they have dropped off. Nowadays there are no expeditions, no squabbles over leaders and vice-leaders or equipment, no wild suggestions for sleeping in trees and caves ... There are the three of us still with a passionate regard for Borrowdale, for the sunny track from Watendlath to Rosthwaite, for Helvellyn and Gable and the rest of them, but we are alone in our devotion.

That week at Stonethwaite was our last holiday together.

Six years ago!

I've taken to solitary wandering since then, and revel in it, but I can't help feeling how grand it would be to have another week in Lakeland with Jim and yourself, as we used to. Remember those impossible programmes we prepared? They all somehow started with Ill Bell, didn't they, and then went on to Patterdale, Keswick, Rosthwaite, Buttermere, Wasdale and Langdale; always the same way round. There was always the thrill of securing lodgings, the furtive explorations along low dark passages in search of the lavatory, the huge suppers, and then to crown the day, the glass of beer in the local inn.

We are not too far gone to do it all again, and enjoy it. Our programme would have to be more reasonable. One summit a day must suffice; we would have to stick to the passes more, and be content to look up at the tops. But the meals would be no less enjoyable, the beer no less good.

What do you say? For auld lang syne I think we should go again, the three of us. Perhaps not this year, for other plans may already have been made. But next year? Whitsun 1940, perhaps?

Think about it. Let your wife see this letter.

I have sent a similar message to Jim.

Most of the qualified accountants of Alfred's age in the office, such as Lawrence and Bob Alker, were permanently on the look out for possible situations elsewhere, knowing there was a hard core of three or four above them who wouldn't leave now, and a group of youngsters below who were waiting for them to move on. Each week they searched the job ads in the *Local Government Chronicle*. Alfred fancied one in South Africa and, not to be left out, drafted an application letter for his amusement.

'Tiger Kloof'
Shadsworth Road,
Blackburn.

Messrs. Davis and Soper, Ltd.
Agents of the City Council of Port Elizabeth,
54, St. Mary Axe,
London, E.C.3.

Gentlemen,

I respectfully beg to apply for the position of Assistant City Treasurer to the Town Council of Port Elizabeth, and offer the following particulars in support of my application.

Since my infancy I have wanted to be an Empire Builder and have a matted beard. I have trained and disciplined myself with these two ends in view. I have deliberately infused into my home the atmosphere of a Last Outpost of Civilisation. For years I have walked the streets in dusty shoes and unkempt clothing. I claim not to have had a proper wash since Mafeking night, and I stopped shaving as soon as I saw your advertisement. Gentlemen, are these sacrifices to be in vain? Davis and Soper, I plead with you both. You especially, Soper. You want your frontiers pushing back, don't you? You want discipline in the Bush, don't you? You want the native women clothed, don't you? I suggest respectably that I am just the type for the job.

I am a Britisher, thank God, of extraordinary appearance and strong religious beliefs. I enjoy good health, am six feet tall, and have a top set of perfect teeth. I can shoot from the hip after a short delay. I am very lean and hungry, and look rather sweet in a turban. I have red hair and a russet beard which is kept severely pruned in deference to the wishes of my present employers. After years of arduous and exhausting practice in the secrecy of my chamber I have cultivated and perfected a proud, defiant 'Shoot-then-and-be-damned-to-you-I'll-die-with-my-honour-untarnished' look which cannot fail to impress the Colonels' daughters.

I have long wanted to visit South Africa. I had, in fact, intended to lead a Gold Rush to Johannesburg in June, 1939, by way of the Atlas Mountains and Mount Kenya, using for the first time covered wagons with pneumatic tyres and sliding roofs. Ah, gentlemen, the lure of it all! How it grips the heart! Those magic evenings standing on the verandah of the clubhouse with a bottle of whisky in one hand and a gill of quinine in the other, 'twixt the noise and bustle of a tiny community and the eternal silences of the boundless veldt, 'twixt bores and boers. A whispering breeze sweeps down from the kopje, eddies around the kraal; your old school tie stirs tremulously; then it is gone. Suddenly from the dark forest comes the distant roll of tom-toms, the kangaroos in the compound start hopping about all over the shop, your quinine slips from your nerveless fingers and shatters in a thousand fragments. You laugh, harshly, unmusically . . . You must go. Your feet turn habitually to the little whitewashed building in the corner of the kraal. You cannot wait any longer. You remember, dully, that you haven't been since after breakfast yesterday morning . . . That's Africa, lad!

I enclose a testimonial from James Pitts, V.C. who relieved Ladysmith whilst in his cups, and 50 coupons cut from 'Africander' Tobaccos.

I am fully qualified for the position, having seen 'Trader Horn' twelve times, and if I am honoured with the appointment it will be my constant endeavour at all times to strive to maintain the dignity of the office.

Your obedient servant,

A. Wainwright

One of the bright young men in the office was Clifford Singleton, born in 1922, who joined the office in 1939. In the list of staff salaries for February 1941, written immaculately in AW's hand, young Clifford was right at the bottom. AW by this time was the eighth most senior person, on £26–5–0 a month. Clifford eventually qualified, moved on, but returned to Blackburn in 1968, becoming Borough Treasurer and Chief Executive: he retired in 1985.

'When I joined the office at seventeen. AW was thirty-four and seemed a very senior figure. I was the junior in his department, working to him, on on my first day, he called me to his desk and said: "Now, Singleton, I've got some good advice for you. Be in this office every morning at nine o'clock." Then he paused. "Now you may find it lonely at first . . ."'

COUNTY BOROUGH OF BLACKBURN.

FINANCE AND GENERAL PURPOSES COMMITTEES.

SALARIES OF STAFF *for the month ending* 28th February 1941

Pay Order Ref.	Name	Unemployment Book No.	Employer's Contributions			Gross Salary			Employee's Contributions			Nett Salary			Remarks
			Sup'n	H. & P. Ins'ce	Unemp. Ins'ce	£	s.	d.	Sup'n	H. & P. Ins'ce	Unemp. Ins'ce	£	s.	d.	Income Tax
	Finance Committee (continued)														
	BOROUGH TREASURER'S DEP'T														
6580	R. G. Rye	One month's salary	5·13·6	·	·	112	10	·	5·13·6	·	·	77	·	2	29.17.6
6581	J. Bennett	do	3·2·6	·	·	62	10	·	3·2·6	·	·	48	3	9	11.3.9
6582	N.W.E. Hamm	do	2·1·8	·	·	41	13	4	2·1·8	·	·	37	19	7	1.12.1
6583	A. Shaw	do	1·10·0	·	E	30	·	·	1·10·0	·	E	26	13	6	3.16.6
6584	J.H. Wallbank	do	1·9·2	·	E	29	3	4	1·9·2	·	E	23	12	10	4.1.4
6585	J.W. Richardson	do	·	·	E	29	3	4	·	·	E	26	4	9	2.18.7
6586	W. Ashton	do	1·7·11	·	E	27	18	4	1·7·11	·	E	22	18	10	3.11.7
6587	A. Wainwright	do	1·6·3	·	E	26	5	·	1·6·3	·	E	24	18	9	·
6588	J. Sharples	do	18·5	·	E	26	5	·	18·5	·	E	25	6	7	·
6589	F. Sellers	do	1·3·0	·	E	22	19	4	1·3·0	·	E	21	11	7	4.9
6590	L. Wolstenholme	do	1·3·0	·	E	22	19	4	1·3·0	·	E	21	6	4	10.0
6591	N. Porter	do	1·3·0	·	E	22	19	4	1·3·0	·	E	21	4	·	12.6
6592	R. Alker	do	1·3·0	·	E	22	19	4	1·3·0	·	E	21	11	2	5.2
6593	J. Charnley, per Mrs M. Charnley	One month's salary (less 1envy/day)	1·0·6	·	·	7	1	8	1·0·6	·	·	6	1	4	£17.6.8 less 28 days @ 3/2s
–	F. Holgate	–	1·0·6	·	·	1	·	4	1·0·6	·	·	·	·	·	·
6594	H. Tallow, per Mrs B. Tallow	One month's salary (less 1envy/day)	1·0·6	·	·	8	2	8	1·0·6	·	·	7	2	4	£17.6.8 less 28 days @ 2/6 ·
6595	L. Jacobs, per Mrs S. Jacobs	do	17·0	·	·	6	15	3	17·0	·	·	5	18	3	£17·0·1 less 28 days @ 6/6.10
6596	A. Westhead, per Mrs E. Westhead	do	17·0	·	·	7	16	1	17·0	·	·	6	19	1	£17·0·1 less 28 days @ 2/6·
–	J.L. Crook	–	12·10	·	·	·	12	10	Annual 12·10	·	·	·	·	·	·
–	T. Wright	–	15·5	·	·	·	15	5	15·5	·	·	·	·	·	·
–	R. Barker	–	12·10	·	·	·	12	10	12·10	·	·	·	·	·	·
6597	R. Woods	One month's salary	14·2 0·3·8 0·3·6	·	·	14	2	8	14·2	0·3·8	0·3·6	13	1	6	·
–	J. Wilding	–	8·10	·	·	·	8	10	8·10	·	·	·	·	·	·
6598	H. Hirst	One month's salary	8·10 0·3·8 0·3·0	·	·	8	16	8	8·10	0·3·8	0·3·0	8	1	2	·
–	N.W. Tennant	–	10·7	·	·	·	10	7	10·7	·	·	·	·	·	·
–	J. Rothwell	–	8·6	·	·	·	8	6	8·6	·	·	·	·	·	·
6599	J. Reid	One month's salary	8·6 0·3·8 0·3·0	·	·	7	1	4	8·6	0·3·8	0·3·0	6	6	2	·
6600	C.H. Singleton	do	6·11 0·3·8 0·3·0	·	·	5	14	10	6·11	0·3·8	0·3·0	5	1	3	·
			31·2·10 0·14·8 0·12·6			547	6	2	6·8·4 27·13·6 0·14·8 0·12·6			455	2	11	58·11·5
–	Superannuation Fund	Employees' Superannuation Deductions										27	13	6	·
–	do	do	paid by Corporation									3	16	6	·
–	do	do	and recoverable									·	12	10	·
–	do	Department's Equivalent Contribution										32	2	10	·

Staff ledger, in AW's immaculate hand

Young Clifford had no inkling of AW's office passion for Betty Ditchfield, but he has a vivid memory of AW's skill and affrontery as a forger. 'There was one day when a load of cheques were returned from the bank, because we'd forgotten to get the Treasurer's signature. It was a sacking offence for the person who'd made the mistake. When AW heard what had happened, he asked for the cheques and then signed each one in the Treasurer's name. They were re-presented to the bank and no one was any the wiser.

'But I was more amazed when he did the same thing with a mortgage. These were very serious affairs, for big sums like £200. They had to be signed by the Mayor, the Treasurer and the Town Clerk. They had been signed all right, but the person working on them knocked over a bottle of ink and ruined one completely. He was in a terrible state. Then someone suggested he went to see Mr Wainwright. AW got a blank, and filled in the three names, signed it on behalf of the three individuals, and off it went. No one ever found out.'

Clifford Singleton is in the only staff photograph which exists from this period in the Treasurer's office, taken on 7 October 1939 as a record of the younger staff about to join H. M. Forces. It was taken by Bob Alker who was very proud of his photographic prowess. He sent a note round the office, saying where and when it would be taken, asking people to sign if they were going to turn up. A. Wainwright was one of those who signed – but he was practically the only one who failed to turn up on the day. 'That was typical of him,' says Bob. Bob himself is in the photograph, on the far left, as he was using a delayed exposure. The two office women can be seen – with Betty Ditchfield to the right, at the front, hair parted in the middle.

It was Bob Alker who, in September 1941, spotted the advertisement for a job in Kendal and pointed it out to Alfred. 'He'd been on leave and missed it. It was the last day for applications but I said, "Go on Alf, this is the thing for you." I knew he'd tried for a job at Ambleside, and not got it. I had a vested interest in him getting this position. I wanted his job.'

Alfred wrote off, even though it wasn't such a well-paid

position, offering only £275 a year, rising to £315, as an account-ancy assistant. It would mean a drop in salary if he got the job, as he'd had a rise in the autumn of 1941 and was now earning £350. He took with him to the interview a glowing reference from Mr Pye, the Blackburn Borough Treasurer, which mentioned the prize he had won, ten years previously.

Three others had applied for the job, but Alfred was sure he would get it. 'None of the others had my qualifications or experi-ence.' One of the people on the interviewing committee was Jimmy Richardson, then a Kendal Councillor and magistrate, one of two Quakers conducting the interviews. He rememembers asking Wainwright why he wanted to move to Kendal from a much bigger authority. 'He said Kendal was the nicest spot he'd ever visited and it would be a joy to live in this area.'

CHAPTER ELEVEN

Life in Kendal, 1941–47

Alfred took up his new job in Kendal at the end of November 1941, moving into digs in Burneside Road. While he looked for proper accommodation, his wife Ruth, who was not at all keen on the move, and eight-year-old son Peter were left behind in Blackburn, moving into the house of his sister, Alice Fish, at 363 Audley Range, along with their cat Paddy, the dog Peggy, Andrew the tortoise, plus a mouse and a budgie, names not known.

It had taken him a long time to achieve his heart's desire. Over eleven years had elapsed since that first Lakeland holiday which had so inspired him. He was now coming up to his thirty-fifth birthday, his working life was almost half over, having spent twenty-one years at Blackburn Town Hall where he had begun to feel part of the furniture, part of the surroundings.

In some ways, it was like retirement. He was coming to a small, sleepy office in a small, sleepy rural town. The Blackburn office had been about five times the size, always busy, with lots of overtime, especially now during the war when so many of the qualified staff had been called up and inexperienced girls had to be taught the systems, and anything else they could be taught. According to Bob Alker, Alfred left the office with everyone's good wishes, presented with some money and a camera, but a bit annoyed with the hierarchy. He'd put in a number of extra hours on some emergency electricity generating work and was upset to get only £35 in bonus money when the seniors got so much more.

His new job in Kendal as accountancy assistant sounds reasonably humble on paper, but in practice he was third in the hierarchy – with only the Borough Treasurer, Mr W. E. Carter, and the senior accountancy assistant ahead of him. These were the three qualified municipal accountants. Below them were trainee account- ants and clerks, about fifteen in all in the office. He was better qualified and more experienced than his position normally de- manded – in fact, he was better qualified than the Treasurer himself.

'At Kendal it was dead easy, a doddle: I could have done it standing on my head. It was a complete change. For years after- wards I never lost the feeling that I was really on holiday. I walked to the office through green fields and amongst trees beside a river, and there were hills in the distance. Life was good.'

There had, of course, been some hills not far from Blackburn, but his immediate life had been totally industrial, in a large city of some 120,000 surrounded by mills and factories, back-to-back houses – although it did, of course, have a First Division football team, something the whole of Cumberland and Westmorland had never had. Kendal was still in Westmorland in those days, the largest town with a population of some 20,000, but not the county capital for that was Appleby. It did at one time have a textile industry, though not on the scale of Blackburn. In the fourteenth and fifteenth centuries, Kendal was a noted wool centre and was famous for a type of cloth known as 'Kendal Green' which Shakespeare mentions in *Henry IV*.

Kendal today is still basically a market town, handsome rather than pretty with its grey stone buildings, but with several thriving local industries – K Shoes, Provincial Insurance and Kendal Mint Cake. It is the southern entrance to Lakeland, with a very confusing one-way system, but does not depend on tourism the way that Windermere, Keswick and Ambleside do, managing to have an all- the-year life of its own, with a great many cultural and artistic attractions. It has a ruined castle which was built by William Rufus, and which once belonged to Thomas Parr whose daughter, Katherine, was born in the castle. Kendal's other famous resident was the painter George Romney who died in the town in 1802. Kendal was neither in nor out of the Lake District National Park in 1941 when Wainwright arrived since the concept was not created until 1951; then it cleverly kept itself a mile outside, despite the fact that the Planning Board's headquarters is in the town.

Alfred adored his new life from the moment he arrived, and was instantly typing ecstatic letters to his friend Lawrence Wolston-holme, back in Blackburn.

'Stanegarth'
Burneside Road,
Kendal.

Thursday evening,
December 4 1941.

Dear Lawrence,

Fancy sitting down to write to you, old friend, and not knowing what to say!

What would you like me to talk about? What do you want to hear?

Shall I tell you how, when I set out for the office this morning, there was a white mist shrouding the valley, softening the lines of the old grey buildings I am learning to know well, making mysterious a scene that is fast becoming familiar? And how, up on the nearby hillsides, the tops of the trees showed faintly through the haze as though they were afloat, suspended, belonging neither to earth nor sky? Shall I tell you how, as I sit at my desk, I can hear the seagulls screaming on the river? Or try to describe the cleanness and freshness of the morning air as I walk along to the town, the strange stillness of the atmosphere, the quietness: those indefinable charms which no visitor to the Lake District ever forgets?

But need I speak of these delights?

You know them so well.

Already I am under the spell.

This is different, vastly different.

It matters not a scrap that nobody here cares tuppence about me, or wonders who I am and whence I came. I am a lover come back to his first and best love, and come to stay. I have cast away, without regrets, the black boots of my profession, and put on joyfully, with relief, the comfy slippers of semi-retirement. Now I am content. Now for half a lifetime of doing what I want to do! Now watch me go rustier and rustier and enjoy the process of disintegration. When my mind itself is corroded and worn out, I shall die. Then I will go to heaven, and not know the difference.

Yes, Lawrence, the prospect pleases.

Nobody here knows me, yet I am surrounded with friends: the tall trees by the river, the enchanting path over by the castle, the birds and the squirrels in the wood; and all around me, most faithful and constant of all, the unchanging hills. Soon I shall have other acquaintances: people will come to know me, smile at me, whistle after me as I walk along. Time will bring them. If I could only hope for a small part of the affection which people in Blackburn have shown me I should be quite happy.

This morning as I turned the corner of the road, a street-sweeper called out a cheerful 'Good morning' and bestowed on me a most engaging smile. In less than a week I have gained a brand-new acquaintance!

I shall look out for him tomorrow.

There, you see, Lawrence, is the way life must start again for your old pal.

Alf

A few days later, this time in handwriting, he says that he is a changed man, he has become 'benign'.

The role I am assiduously fostering now, with some success, is that of 'Patriarch of the Fells'. A fine upstanding figure of a man, no longer young, with white locks flowing behind him as he faces the wind in the high places, a tireless and appreciative walker on the hills, with a kindly (yet a little sad) smile and a warm greeting and helpful advice for those he meets on his wanderings. On the hills I am as a king in his kingdom, with a friendly blessing for all my admiring subjects. I have even been known to pat the heads of youthful fellow-travellers. That's AW, now.

I only want to be remembered to Miss D, nobody else.

AW
Best writer in Kendal

That final sentence is interesting, still thinking about Betty Ditch-field. The 'Best writer' refers to his artistic handwriting, not any creative writing, as he explains in his next letter to Lawrence, on 12 December 1941.

Unquestionably I am the best writer in Kendal. Having lots of time to spare and no interruptions and no questions asked I go about leaving a trail of artistic efforts in the various books, which evoke excited comment from the staff, much to my gratification.

Kendal is delightful. So is life in Kendal. So is work in Kendal. After the clatter and clamour of the Borough Treasurer's Office at Blackburn, I am, by comparison, encompassed by a deathly calm. Everything here is on so tiny a scale that I feel like a giant playing with a child's toys. Cashbooks are written up once a month, in five minutes, and reconciled every six months. Some of the ledgers are posted twice a year; the others (including Education) not until the end of the year, so that there is some resemblance to the old bookkeeping questions we used to get in the R.S.A. Examinations: given a trial balance, prepare the ledger accounts and Balance Sheet (40 marks). And certainly I am not harassed by dam-silly Reports on Progress, etc. 'Have reminders been sent re unpresented cheques?'. I pause to smile.

Your letter was very welcome. (So will Jim's be when he is finally moved to reply.) More dreamy and soulful than ever, am I? Perhaps you're right. Maybe I am drifting into a state of coma again. I want to, because I work better when I am torpid. The mood will burst with a loud bang, however, when its purpose is served, and then, out of its agony, will be delivered Wainwright's First Lakeland Classic.

With regard to your other principal point, I refuse to be inveigled into a discussion of the female sex in this correspondence. That can wait until we are face to face once more.

Before I forget! Tomorrow I move into my first Lakeland home, so please note the address: 19 CASTLE GROVE, KENDAL.

19 Castle Grove was a council house which came through his job. It was something of a come-down from his self-owned semi-detached in Blackburn, but it was attractively built in grey stone with a view of the ruined Kendal Castle through the front window. Once it was his, Ruth and Peter were commanded to join him.

Peter remembers travelling to Kendal in the furniture van with his mother and the animals. 'She fell out at Garstang. I always used to tease her about that. There were no street lights, because of the war, and when the van slowed down for something, she thought it had stopped. She opened the door, and the dog jumped ahead of her, and it pulled her out.'

Peter started at the local primary school where he was mocked for his strong Blackburn accent. 'Someone shot me with an air rifle – just because I'd said bunfire for bonfire.'

In the early days at Kendal, Peter has a clear memory of all three of them going on local walks, which is also mentioned in Alfred's letters to Lawrence. Was Alfred perhaps making a fresh stab at being a family man, including his wife for once in his activities, which he had never done in Blackburn, turning over a new leaf now that he was feeling a new, benign and happy man?

19 Castle Grove,
Kendal.

Sunday evening,
January 11 1942.

Dear Lawrence,

Today it has snowed all day. But in Kendal one does not crouch over the fire. Today I and my family have been up the valley to Kentmere, which looked more Alpine than ever through the falling snow, then over Garburn Pass and by the fell-road back to Windermere. We have seen robins, rabbits, a heron, grouse; and for an hour watched a shepherd with four dogs rounding up his flock on Garburn before driving them down to a lower pasture, for soon the snow will be deep.

Well, sonny, how are you? How's everybody in the old concentration camp? I can hardly imagine the horror of it now; the change has been so complete. Details are fading a little: first door on the left round the corner, wasn't it? What was that name we gave to it – 'draghouse' or something of the sort, wasn't it? Yes, I remember now: 'the house of a thousand drags'. Ah yes, that comes back clearly on reflection. Let me see if I can recall the number of your telephone (how posh you are, having a telephone!) . . . 26, wasn't it? And wasn't there a girl in the office called – sorry, I forget the name. Yet I seem to remember her. Or was that all a dream?

Blackburn is gone, so soon. Kendal is real. The world has turned over. The crumbling ruins on the hill, the dark pines on the fellside, the racing river: these are real, more real, seemingly, than Salford and Victoria Street ever were. The grey old town in its circle of purple and golden fells: this is real. The gaunt grey mountains, shrouded in new snow, harsh and bitterly cruel in midwinter, yet curiously compelling: these are real. All else is imaginary; nothing else has meaning.

Come away, Lawrence! While you have youth and red blood in your veins, come away! Come to this land of perpetual wonder, and forget the dingy past. Come where the air intoxicates as champagne, where the birds sing merrily all day long, where a well-satisfied populace wear fat smiles of deep contentment, where life is easy or earnest as you care to make it, and only money is unimportant. Leave behind the lustreless prose, and come to the sublime poetry of life!

First give my love to those I have loved.
And to those I still love.

Then come home to the hills!
Alf

In his reply, Lawrence must have cast some doubt about the change in his friend, and presumably asked about his love life.

Tuesday evening,   19 Castle Grove,
February 10 1942.   Kendal.

Dear Lawrence,

For some reason which is not clear, you persist in harping about ladies in your communications. From time to time you make references, sometimes vague but more often pointed, concerning my past interest in the other sex which are entirely unwarranted.

You remember best, it would appear, the sham A.W., the poseur; the man of furtive downward glance and lascivious habit, the willing prey to morbid phobias, the evil creature of sinister nocturnal missions. Apparently you never knew the real A.W.

All those unhealthy tendencies I have shed as easily as a garment. They were quite superficial. Believe me, your remarks about 'hillocks' and 'valleys', doubtless intended to tantalise me, arouse no feeling whatever. Blue-veined milky bosoms interest me not at all. If I admire a supple curve it is with the eyes of an artist.

Lawrence, I once sat on a boulder at the foot of Sty Head Pass and gazed up at the Napes Ridges for two hours without blinking. Fifty yards away, at Burnthwaite, there was a huge feed awaiting me: I was both tired and hungry after a hard day. Yet I could not take my gaze away from the rocky pinnacles above me, and not until the setting sun drew his concealing shadow across the scene did the fascination depart ... Now I submit seriously that no woman, however shameless her antics, could compel my attention to such a pitch of absorption. Let her reveal herself to the uttermost whisker, and let sweet seductiveness do its darnedest – and still I would greatly prefer to sit on a stone with an empty belly and aching limbs and look at a naked mountain.

No, Lozenge, you have got my heart's desire all wrong. I left Blackburn not merely satiated with women, but gorged. There were no lofty peaks there for me to regard, and willy-nilly I found certain passing interests in the depths. When the chance came for me to cast these petty charmers aside in favour of holier joys I was off like a shot, with heart triumphant. Was it not so?

On Saturday afternoon I climbed the Helm, a strange isolated hill two miles out of the town, which sticks up above the countryside like a stranded ship with keel upturned. Snow-covered and detached, it looked as if terrific winds had piled up a mammoth drift, for the gorse and bracken on its steep sides were deeply covered beneath the glittering whiteness.

I made my way slowly to the top, ploughing through snow that was pure and virgin (dam the word!). The panorama was indescribably beautiful. Morecambe Bay, Arnside, Grange, the great wall of the Lake mountains, Shap Fells, the Sedbergh Hills, the Pennines: these were the boundaries of my vision, and within the circle were five hundred miles of country wondrous fair to look upon. I was uplifted and enriched by the scene. These are the conquests I seek, the objects of my endeavour, the virgins I prefer to grind beneath me.

Yes, I was in Blackburn on the 31st ultimo, but why the croak of triumph? I came, not to bury Ceaser [sic], but to complete the B.R.S.C. accounts for 1941.

I shall be there again on the 21st instant, for another dib in the fleshpots.

How is sweet Nell of Old Witton? Why doesn't she write?

I duly cashed your Money Order at the Post Office, a la Billy Bunter, and forthwith made my way to the tuckshop, where I bought a lovely book called 'Mountains in Flower', a collection of photographs of alpine plants in their natural surroundings. Note that I could have bought a dozen french-lettres with the money. Sorry to confound your theories still further!

I have found a kindred soul here in the person of an adorable young lady who answers to Marjorie. She is a typist at the Health Office next door. We talk wistfully of Wharfedale and Malham and Dent, and of Teesdale and Muker and the Lakes, and together we sigh and yearn for the sunny weekends to come. She's a sweet child. And a healthy one: I have checked her particulars from her medical report for superannuation. She's 26, weighs 100 pounds, stands 5'2", is sound in wind and limb, and the condition of her urine is satisfactory.

So roll on, ye sunny weekends!

Alf

This is a nasty letter.
Don't mention 'em again.

A month later, Alfred is in a more sombre mood, beginning to feel nostalgic for his old friends and old places in Blackburn.

Wednesday evening,   19 Castle Grove,
March 4 1942.   Kendal.

Dear Lawrence,

When I closed my books at midday last Saturday and came out into the street I had completed a quarter of a year's service with Kendal

Borough Council. A quarter of a year! It's been a long time, and in many ways a lonely time; yet the incidents of my last few days in Blackburn are so vividly engraved in my memory that I find myself still able to live them over again in detail – and often do, for my idle thoughts are all of Blackburn folk: there is, as yet, nobody here to occupy my attention out of office hours.

I recall my last visit to Ewood: how carefully I deliberated which way I should go to the ground on this final occasion, for there were many familiar and oft-tramped alternatives, all dear to me, before deciding at length to follow the route of my earliest pilgrimages twenty years before, by way of Old Bank Lane and Longshaw. I proceeded very sedately and soberly, like a man going to a funeral. And you may be sure I lingered long after the players had left the field, surveying this scene of past glories from a favourite position by the scoreboard ere I turned sadly away ... I can recall every detail of the B.R.S.C. [Blackburn Rovers Supporters Club] Party on the Friday night before I departed, and of my last hours at the Snapes' house, when I sat and watched the clock.

Most of all, perhaps, my thoughts revert to that Saturday morning which brought to an end my long and revered association with you all. I had worked hard for some weeks in an attempt to get everything straight and about eleven o'clock I suddenly realised that all was completed; there was nothing else for me to do. From that moment I was no longer part of the office. I had but to wait until twelve o'clock, and then put on my hat and walk out for ever. One by one old friends came to say a hearty goodbye, or to whisper farewell, and gradually the room emptied. You were there, head down over your books, as ever; Miss D was talking to me by the safe; nobody else remained. How unreal the scene; how well I remember! Then Miss D slipped away, I was ready to go, and you came across to wish me godspeed. You did not see how earnestly I gazed across the room before I closed the door, at the old desk and the rickety chair which would know me no more.

I have walked once more the long mile of Audley Range, along the old familiar pavement where every crack in the flags is remembered well. I have seen again, from a distance, 90 Shadsworth Road. I have gazed at the barrage balloons with a new interest.

I was minded to call on you during this last brief visit, to inspect at close quarters the collapsible knee and more particularly the flat bottom mentioned in your letter. (I always had a partiality for bottoms). However, I learned that you had then been back at work for a week, and so let the opportunity pass.

About half of my presentation money has been spent in the purchase of pictures. One especially, my main purchase, I am pleased to have acquired, because I have long coveted it; every time I have been in Keswick in recent years I have gone round to Abrahams' to look at it. Now old Abrahams has sold it to me, and it is mine. I lift my eyes, and can see it now. 'Buttermere and High Crag' – a well-loved scene.

The other half of my present has been expended in tobacco and razor-blades and liquorice-all-sorts and other sundries. When next I go to Keswick I shall, however, atone by spending the monetary equivalent in the purchase of further photographic gems of Lakeland.

Last Sunday I went to Skelwith Force and Elterwater, returning by Red Bank and Loughrigg Terrace and Rydal. The days of prodigious effort are gone; now I can stroll as slowly as I please, and sit on a wall for a smoke. Time doesn't matter any more. I have no programmes to rush through, and no burdens to carry. There is no longer any need for desperate hurry. The Brathay Valley, awakening to springtime beneath the snowy domes of Wetherlam and the Pikes, was really beautiful, while the view across Grasmere from the Terrace was never more entrancing ... Then home for a smashing tea, and an idle evening spent sleepily gazing into the fire and thinking of absent friends. It's a nice way to spend a day, Lawrence!

Alf

Please remember me (in a gentle undertone) to Miss Ditchfield and to the infant Teresa.

Teresa is not another girl in the Blackburn office but the new-born daughter of Lawrence and his wife, Margery. In Alfred's next letter to him, he finishes with what appears to be some good news about his own family.

Wednesday evening,   19 Castle Grove,
April 8 1942.   Kendal.

Dear Lawrence,

Many thanks for a very welcome and 'newsy' letter.

Your little pen-picture of the infant Teresa was delightfully expressed, and I am pleased to learn that you have succeeded in winning the affections of this winsome maid – such a faith cannot do other than keep your heart and mind clean, and inspire you to the gallantry of a Galahad.

And Nellie starts afresh at Whitsun! This was good news, and here's my 3/6 for the subscription list. This marriage will be a success, and blessed with much issue (for she is remarkably fertile). We do not correspond, bad cess to her; so would you please remind her that she owes me two shirts?

As for Dorothy's chances of happiness anew, I ha' ma doots, and I suppose you have, too.

Now I must take you to task. I cannot understand your vehement objection to my 'hugging the past' as you wrongly term it. I don't hug it at all, and certainly nothing would ever induce me to return to the old scenes. But remember that Blackburn has thirty-five years of memories for me; and pleasant reminiscences are as much a delight, and as wholesome a joy, as a good meal or a classical concert or a tramp over the hills. What do you do when you listen to Mozart and Offenbach and all the other ancients but hug the past and find a present delight in doing so? There's absolutely no difference. And would you have me forget Jim and yourself – and my mother? My roots in Blackburn went pretty deep, son!

But, if you are in any doubt, let me assure you that the transplanting has been a complete, overwhelming success. I am a thousand-a-year man in everything but cash. I am an outrageous success at work, and am happier than ever I was. I can step out of the office on to a passing bus and in a few minutes be on Orrest Head, or in an hour on Loughrigg Terrace – and how fearfully shabby Revidge and Ramsgreave and Shadsworth are by comparison! I can stroll through the fields behind the house after tea, and in five minutes reach a stile whereon I habitually recline, for before me in splendid array I see the Crinkles and Bowfell, the gap of Mickledore, Gable in magnificent isolation, the Pikes, Fairfield – and not yet has the scene failed to send a quiver through me. No, if you mistake reminiscence for regret you are hopelessly wrong. My only regret is that you and a few others are not here to share the good things with me.

Plans for the future, which you assume to be non-existent, are going on apace. The new bungalow is planned down to the last detail: 'twill be built of the familiar grey-green stone and slate familiar to these parts, and be dry-walled so that the wistaria and clemati can grip; it will stand high on a hillside, by a wood, with the open fell behind. It will merge harmoniously into the landscape. The view from the big windows at the front will comprise many miles of the loveliest country God ever made, a park where I may wander at will, and from my seat by the ingle I shall see this view as a picture, ever-changing, set in the frame of the window. I might, even then, think occasionally of Audley Range and Shad, but do you imagine that I shall be 'hugging the past' and wanting to return? Not on your bloody life, you silly old bugger. Only the name of this desirable residence remains to be chosen, and at present I am licking my lips over LINGMOOR, GARTH and WANSFELL. Names like these would be inane in Lammack Road, but up here, where they belong, they sound grand and same and in tune with the surroundings.

The Wainwrights made their first major ascent last Sunday week, having a great time on Red Screes, in snow still waist-deep. This, by the way, is the first recorded ascent of this peak in 1942.

Kindest regards to Marjorie and yourself. I hope to be able to answer definitely your other cheeky query in my next letter. From the few potent signs around me I should hazard a guess at mid-September!

Alf

In his next letter, Alfred does not mention Ruth's pregnancy, if of course that was what he meant by 'potent signs', but reveals the story behind some other news – that he could be about to be called up.

Tuesday evening,   19 Castle Grove,
June 2 1942.   Kendal.

Dear Lawrence,

My terse communique to the effect that I was joining H. M. Forces, you say, left everyone impatient for more detail. Nobody turned a hair, I'll bet. That's five weeks ago; any of you could have settled his 'impatience' at the cost of a 2½d. stamp. I used to think when I worked there that the staff of the B.T., myself excluded, were the most bovine unemotional selfish crew I ever struck, and I see no reason to change my opinion. Only yesterday Tennant wrote to me, and mentioned that, my letters apart, he has not had even a word from any member of the office since he joined the Forces. It's bloody rotten, you know!

Anyway, what happened in my case was this. The day before I wrote Jim from Patterdale (where, by the way, I had a perfect cameo of a holiday all in a weekend) the Kendal Council were informed that my deferment expired on the 30th inst. and thereafter I would be liable for military service. I lost no sleep as a result of this harsh decision, but it proved so repugnant to the Treasurer that he called a meeting of the Finance Committee forthwith and two members were deputed to go to London to make a spirited protest. They went a fortnight ago, innocents abroad, had a most cordial interview and returned with the news that it had been agreed that I should be deferred indefinitely (the terms, I suppose, being similar to yours). No written confirmation has yet arrived.

I was in the company of Fred Percy Haslam during Whitsuntide. On the Saturday I was sorely tempted to ask him if Nellie was being married that day, as I suspected she was from an earlier letter of yours. But no, I could not venture the question; I dare not retire to a lonely bed with the knowledge that she was at that moment being well and truly blocked while my own much-more-deserving organ lay adroop for want of company. I had the news next day. Strangely I saw a girl that day, at Giggleswick, who reminded me very much of her; and another at Grasmere on the Tuesday who was her spit an' image, even to the kiss-curls on her cheek. But these were mirages. Then, at work on Friday afternoon, I happened to be walking through the General Office and glanced casually through the open door. And there, gesturing wildly to attract my attention, was Nellie Myerscough, alias Morrison, alias Lynch. No doubt about it, 'twas she, and looking lovelier than any human being has a right to look. My brain did a little somersault; it seemed so *odd* that she should be there, in the Borough Treasurer's Office at Kendal. I was introduced to her new husband, a pleasant but unimpressive youth almost lost to me in the glow of his wife's radiant personality. I thought their gesture in calling at Kendal to see me was extremely nice; we camped for half an hour and I did no more work that day. Funny how things work out, isn't it? To my dying day I shall be convinced that N would rather have it from me than from Frank or anybody else.

Later, in the same letter, Alfred gives an insight into his domestic situation, and also does some boasting.

When we have stayed at boarding-houses in the past we have often espied a mild insignificant man pottering about the kitchen while all our contacts have been with the lady of the house. That meek quiet creature is the husband, and gradually I am assuming a similar position. We have already had a great many visitors at Castle Grove, but until Whitsuntide they have come only for a few days, and never more than two at a time. But now the relatives are upon us with a vengeance. We had three all Whitweek, there is one next week, and then we are continuously booked up for bed and full board until August with never a respite. Sleeping three or four in a bed could be quite jolly if there was a preponderance of young and healthy females but I don't relish the idea of being sandwiched between an uncle and a brother-in-law. There is ample room in the house to sleep a dozen; it's beds we're short of; we've only two, and they both rattle like hell. We mustn't have any honeymoon couples here!

Can I visualise the time when I walk into the B.T's Office Blackburn and the majority of the staff whisper 'Who's that?' I can visualise the time when I enter that same office and everybody falls flat at my feet in reverent awe, for already I am well on the way to being as great a CELEBRITY as Wordsworth was. As yet, I cannot give details, but ere long it's going to be your greatest claim to notoriety that you knew Alf Wainwright. So when I am a great man I will patronise your office with my presence, and to show that I have lost nothing of my humility I will bring my photographer to take my picture sitting at the old desk.

Besides, if I called now I might be offered a cheque for the £35 owing to me for work done on the Generating Extensions, and it would hurt me to have to accept it after all these months.

Best wishes for a really happy holiday.

Alf

The big news, about which he could not reveal details, but which would make him a CELEBRITY, was nothing to do with his writing career, despite vague if fanciful references over the last few years that one day he would write a wonderful Lakeland book. It was a modest but fairly important local position he had been given by Kendal Borough Council to organise their 'Holidays at Home' programme. This was a Government-inspired scheme to stop people travelling away for their holidays, as there was a war on, by laying on attractions in their home town. Alfred, as Secretary to the Holidays Committees, was given a free hand in forming committees and making arrangement for concerts, dances, sporting events and assorted competitions to amuse the local populace during Kendal Holiday Week, 3–8 August 1942. AW himself did the illustration at the front of the programme.

He obviously enjoyed organising the Holiday Week – and it did him a lot of good, socially and work-wise. In his letters to Lawrence there had been no mention of making any new friends yet, of either sex, and all that harking back to the good old days in Blackburn would indicate a bit of homesickness, for his old friends if not the old environment.

It is always difficult in a rural as opposed to an industrial area to make new friends and contacts. Blackburn was used to strangers, ever since the eighteenth century, absorbing Irish and Scots and assorted newcomers looking for work. The Wainwrights were Yorkshire folk, after all, but were quickly accepted. Cumbrians are notably suspicious of 'offcomers' and it can take years if not decades to be properly integrated. 'They summer you, they winter you, they summer you again, then they might say hello.' So goes the old saying. Alfred was not naturally an outgoing, sociable sort of person, but being forced to organise these committees and bring people together made him well known in the town. And admired for his good work, so he himself boasted.

Wednesday evening
August 12 1942.

19 Castle Grove,
Kendal.

Dear Lawrence,

Kendal's holiday Week is over.

It's been an outrageous success, of course. It couldn't have been otherwise, with me bossing the show. Talk about superb efficiency! Everything went like clockwork, and the sun appeared whenever he was wanted. The arrangements, planned to the last detail, worked so smoothly that I was left with nothing to do during the week but watch the events and eat ice-cream. Aldermen and Councillors were my errand-boys. The Mayor came at a whistle . . . A Wainwright Production!

It's all been very enjoyable, and there's no doubt the experience has been a profitable one for me. You will have realised that I have at last decided to pull my light from under the bushel, the result being that I have been acclaimed on all sides as an artist of outstanding ability. I have had commissions to draw landscapes, which for the moment I have declined; I have other plans, big plans. My next job is to design a new cover for the Kendal Parish Church monthly magazine, at the request of the Vicar; then I shall start on the biggest and loveliest job I ever undertook, that of putting Kendal right on the map. It's a grand grand place, Lawrence. I intend to do a series of sketches of the town and neighbourhood, accompany them with a narrative, and offer the lot to the Council as the Official Handbook for the years of peace when the holiday crowds return. This isn't something you'll get by enclosing a stamp; it will have to be paid for, but, believe me, what a success it will be! Out of the immaturity of countless expedition handbooks will come the Super Guide-book, and I shall love preparing it, for Kendal was just built to be drawn and written about. It will be my book, all of it; written, illustrated and designed by Wainwright – and I have found just the printer who will make a really high-class job of it.

So I'm a big noise here now. I'm in a town where ability is appreciated, and civic pride counts a lot.

There'll be a statue to me before I'm through.

There is no record of any Wainwright Handbook to Kendal, alas, for the idea sounds good, and it would have been his first venture into public print. One of his earliest known drawings is of Abbot Hall, dated 1942, so that might have been intended for his Handbook.

Alfred was also writing long letters to his old friend Eric Maudsley, now in the army. He boasted to him about his proposed Kendal guide book, and other literary ventures which he was contemplating.

Future generations, when they think of Wordsworth and Southey and Coleridge and de Quincey; will think of Wainwright also. All my energies are now devoted to this aim. I am engaged on a work which will bring me fame, and enthusiasm for it is running white-hot; life is deliriously exciting. I haven't left myself time to tell you of my plan in detail, but believe me, this is Wainwright attaining a new best. And backing me up are friends with the stuff that counts in an enterprise of this sort. Today my researches took me on a first visit to Shap, where, by the side of the infant Lowther, in a sleepy hollow of the fells, I spent an enjoyable hour amongst the primroses gazing at the ruins of the old

Abbey. I wore flannels, not khaki. I listened to the myriad voices of nature, perfectly attuned, not to the raucous call of the sergeant-major . . .

The thing most worth seeking in life, Eric, is beauty. Make no mistake about that. I couldn't be persuaded to swop this existence for any other. I have reached the foot of the rainbow, and here, sure enough, is the pot of gold I have been seeking – beauty so exquisite that it makes the heart leap with exultation, loveliness so enchanting that it brings tears to the eyes. This is wealth, real wealth; it is free of tax, and it is mine forever . . .

So leave me here with my dreams and my plans, in the Lakeland I love so passionately.

Write to me whenever you wish.

And fight my battles for me, that's a good chap.

Tell me when the war's over!

Your old pal,

Alf

Eric, in his reply, complimented him on his letters which led AW to further promises – not only of books to come but also the admission that writing and drawing had been his real purpose in coming to Lakeland.

I agree with your remarks re Wainwright letters. They are good, unquestionably. Actually, you know, I came here to write and draw. Wordsworth and Wainwright, these two! Here are some of the prospective titles chosen for my books:

MEN AND MOUNTAINS, by Alf Wainwright.

ONCE I CLIMBED A HILL, by Alf Wainwright.

HERITAGE OF THE HEATHER, by Alf Wainwright.

MOUNTAIN MEMORIES, by Alf Wainwright.

Demy 8vo, profusely illustrated, 10/6 each.

The real classic, however will not be published until about 1960. My life's blood will be in it: it will be my memorial. This, of course, will be WAINWRIGHT'S GUIDE TO THE LAKELAND HILLS.

Look out for these publications on the bookstalls, in vivid yellow jackets. And please buy a copy, for auld lang syne!

None of these books appears to have been attempted, although it is fascinating to see what he was planning at this early stage: had he, one can only wonder, begun mapping out the seven Pictorial Guides to the Lakeland Fells in his mind? He was, however, working hard on his drawings of local scenes and buildings, sending examples to his old friends, such as Lawrence.

Friday evening,   19 Castle Grove,
October 2 1942.   Kendal.

Dear Lollipop,
I've had *one* letter from you in the past *four months*.
    Shame on you!

Blea Tarn: taken from A Fourth Lakeland Sketchbook

Bob will have given you, or will be giving you, a print of my 'Blea Tarn, Langdale'. This isn't my latest drawing, and it isn't my best; it's my first, and because it is the first, the prelude to many, I have had thirty copies made, regardless of cost, for my new friends and for those whose encouragement in the past I have not forgotten. I could have sold these thirty copies in five minutes, and wallowed in wealth for a few days, but that would spoil the idea.

I hope you like the picture. I claim that it is eminently suitable for tacking up in the lavatory and surveying moodily during the throes of excretion, or in intervals of noisy urination.

There was then a slight gap in their letters, much to Alfred's fury. Lawrence has apparently not been replying, despite Alfred's long and newsy letters until, in the end, he becomes quite vitriolic about the behaviour of someone he had presumed was one of his oldest, closest friends.

Friday evening,   19 Castle Grove,
November 20 1942.   Kendal.

Dear Lawrence,
It was a very great surprise to me to receive your letter the other day.

The trees were in new leaf and the birds were mating when last you wrote. It was springtime.

Now the trees are bare of leaves and the birds have gone to warmer lands. Spring has passed, and summer, and autumn. It is winter again.

In the meantime I have written to you occasionally, sent things I thought you would like to see. They brought no response until this week.

It grieved me deeply, angered me almost, to be ignored thus. It is discourteous, to say the least, not to reply to letters received. Good manners demanded that I should have an acknowledgment that my communications had safely arrived. Nothing came, however, and it is now some time since I deleted your name from my list of correspondents and erased you from my mind. One does not write to a man who is dead nor think of him. Your word, inertia, is not half strong enough. Even with this latest belated effort you make the admission, as though it were a joke, that it would not yet have been written but for your wife's entreaties. You should be grateful to Margery for propping you up thus and reminding you of ordinary moral decencies which should be observed, but this time she was too late. Thoughtlessness has cost you a friend.

I will reply to your letter, but I tell you frankly that there are other things I would much rather be doing tonight than writing to you.

In a few days time I shall have been at Kendal a year, and it has been a year of sublime contentment, of progress, of rapid advancement towards the attainment of an ambition that was born early and somehow survived the ghastly, soul-destroying environment of the Blackburn Town Hall. I look back on those years with horror.

Coming here was like escaping from a foul pit.

There are no days of desolation and gloom, as there were then. There are no days when things go wrong at work, no days of desperate endeavour, no weary nights of overtime, no rush jobs, no office squabbles, no R.G. wanting to see me, no interferences, no questions asked, no kow-towing to little Ceasers [sic] who ought to be shot.

In twelve months I have earned for myself a classical reputation. My ledgers, illustrated and illuminated, are things of great beauty. There is nothing here to cramp my style, no jealous criticisms and senseless comments, and I have flourished exceedingly. There is positive joy in working in these happy conditions. I am *very* highly thought of, and the Council's special pet. My flair for the artistic has been quickly recognised, and applauded. Unlike the dullards who govern Blackburn, here are men of breeding and intellect and imagination; men, moreover, to whom civic pride is a religion, not a sham. And with justification, for is this not a lovely old town and are there not centuries of proud history in its mellow grey stones?

So I prosper. Kendal folk have a reputation for clannishness, but I have blasted my way right through the outer shell and find now that every man has a smile and a kind word for me. I was one of the gentlemen of Kendal who took the Mayor to Church last Sunday, and am to be found in my place at all civic functions. A wealth of tradition still clings to Kendal, and I find its varied ceremonies of absorbing interest.

I keep the Education, Gas, Water, Electricity, Rating, Housing and Superannuation Accounts of the Council as they have never been kept before, and yet have lots of time to free-lance. Much of my time in future will be spent at the Museum, for the Council have asked me to take it under my control and look after it. Now Kendal Museum is a very remarkable place; I'd as soon drop in there to look round as go to the pictures. It is widely acknowledged as the finest in the North of England; it is not a place of death, as yours is, but a live, exciting place which attracts hordes of visitors. Now it is mine, to display the exhibits, to publicise, to curate and to catalogue. Could there be a more delightful hobby? I have long wanted a collection of birds eggs: now I have ten thousand at one fell swoop, gratis. A public-minded citizen has provided the funds to build an extension: I shall enjoy spending the money.

My work, then, is a joy to me. But it is the hours of leisure which make life in Kendal a delirious delight. At 5.30 I promptly forget about the office (my aggregate hours of overtime since I started here are precisely nil) and continue from the night before my plans, fantastic, exhilarating, wildly exciting, for a future which has bounded much nearer and is now within my grasp. These dreams are no longer transient and far away, but *real*.

Lawrence did reply to this letter pretty quickly, but it did not calm Alfred down. He was still upset that his friend was proving such a poor correspondent.

Wednesday evening,   19 Castle Grove,
November 25 1942.   Kendal.

My dear Lawrence,

Sorry to butt in on wages, but I must insist that the 'privilege (sic) of having the last word' be mine. So get 'em balanced, in a fashion, and stuck up, and then lend me a cavernous ear.

First let me thank you very sincerely for your condolences and those of the unnamed others in the office.

Then let me say that your letter afforded me acute delight. Listen. When I first knew you, back in the days of silent films, you were a romantic: you had a flashing eye, a fiery tongue, a ready temper. Sadly I have watched the years change the baleful glare into a bovine stare; calm the tempestuous flow of your invective, damp almost to extinction the flame that once burned so brightly within you. You are not as you were, by a long chalk. The Wolst of recent years has been characterised by meekness, timidity, submission – and I exhort you to save these qualities, such as they are, for your old age. When you were a youth you had dreams; now these are gone, too. You are growing old too fast, Lawrence, much too fast. I don't like to see you straddled with cobwebs. I preferred you as a man of passion, of action.

And now, at last, I have roused you from your torpor. Every word of my harangue was designed with this end in view. Far from being a 'hysterical outburst' it was written, as you should have guessed, with a placid smirk on my venerable visage. It worked. For the first time you are inspired to send me a letter which is not a doleful diatribe of distress, and not only that but you reply within 48 hours. Furthermore, your reply is couched in the violent language I hoped for. I rejoice. The red blood is flowing again.

Now actually it doesn't matter whether you write me letters or not. A letter received is a letter to be answered (it is with me, anyhow!), and when I tell you that in the past twelve months I have received over 200 (TWO HUNDRED) personal letters from folk who still think a lot of me, you will appreciate that this drain on my leisure time is hindering the fruition of my Major Plans. So you can please your damn self.

The only passage in your letter to which I bow my head and agree is that all have not my ability to wield a facile pen. How I wish they had! Oh, how I wish they had!

I had better mention that I shall be sending you a card at Christmas. I would not like to place you at a further disadvantage.

Your old pal,
Alf W.

The condolences at the beginning of this letter were to do with Alfred's mother, Emily. She died in Blackburn on 13 November 1942, aged sixty-nine. Her personal possessions amounted in value to £182.16.2, which included her bedstead, bedroom suite, sewing machine and two easy chairs which were sold for £17.15.0. There was also a settled estate worth £572 which appears to have been in the form of a property, left by her father, R. D. Woodcock the ironmonger, which, on her death, was distributed amongst her four children, Alice, Frank, Annie and Alfred. It is not clear if during her lifetime she had any income from this property, in the way of rent, which would have helped during the years her husband was out of work, or drunk.

From his mother's settled estate, Alfred eventually received a total of £174.5.0, enough for a good deposit for a bungalow, on the lines outlined to Lawrence, but this was not done. He remained in the council house.

The possible pregnancy, also mentioned to Lawrence, came to nothing. Ruth never had a second child, nor was it explained what happened.

These regular and lengthy and very well-written letters to Lawrence lasted during the first two years of his residence in Kendal, then petered out. Alfred treated them as compositions,

The Parish Church of Windermere: taken from the parish magazine dated January 1949

writing them carefully, in good decent English, trying for effect in his landscape descriptions, and trying to amuse and entertain in his gossip and news.

Lawrence, looking back today, cannot remember why he stopped replying to them. He and Alfred didn't fall out. It was part laziness, not having his friend's facility with a pen, and part business, having a young family and a demanding career. Lawrence went on to become Borough Treasurer of Blackburn in 1953, a job he held until he retired in 1971.

Alfred's boasts about his success with Kendal Holiday Week were true. He continued running them throughout the war years, and they doubtless played a big part in his promotion to Borough Treasurer. This happened on 1 August 1948, following the death of the then Treasurer.

Alfred had now got to the top of his profession – at a relatively young age, just forty-one, for a Borough Treasurer. He was in the middle of landscape which he loved, handy for exploring almost every point in Lakeland. His artistic talents were finding some expression in drawing churches and local buildings. His writing skills were hardly being used at all, except in letters to his old Blackburn friends, most of whom he was slowly losing contact with. Domestically, things do appear to have been a bit better in the first year or so in Kendal, with all three of them going on occasional family outings, but this didn't last long. A state of undeclared war returned between him and Ruth. But he did have one ready-made companion when it came to walking.

CHAPTER TWELVE

Lakeland Walking, 1948–52

In 1948, as befitted a Borough Treasurer now on a salary of £900 a year, Alfred and his family decided to move out of their council house into something more select. He bought a plot of land at Kendal Green, on the edge of the town, looking over the valley of the River Kent towards the Lakeland mountains. He had the house purpose-built, incorporating his own ideas, and set to work on the garden which was on a steep slope. It was formerly a hen run and needed a lot of work and imagination. He set himself a five-year plan, doing drawings of paths to be created, trees to be planted, cairns to be erected, boulders to be found and assembled into little crags. In his mind, he wanted to have a miniature Lake District right in his own back garden.

Peter, now aged fourteen, was at Kendal Grammar School. He'd failed the Eleven Plus, having missed a lot of schooling when, at the age of ten, his appendix burst, but his father had paid for him to go to the Grammar School, which you could in those days until it became free after the 1944 Education Act. In the summers, Peter went walking with his father. In the winters, he had to sit quietly while his father drew.

'Dad would come home in the evening, set up a folding chair by the inglenook, not say a word to anyone, and start work at his drawings. He seemed to be doing drawings in all his spare time. He did about six Christmas cards of Kendal views for Titus Wilson, which they printed and sold, so I suppose he got paid for them, and also drawings for various churches and organisations.

'While he worked, we were not allowed to talk. We didn't have a TV, as that would disrupt him. We had no heating in the house, just the one fireplace, so that's why we all stayed in the living-room, to keep warm. I suppose he was selfish, making us keep quiet, but that was his nature. My mother knitted or read and I did my homework. My mother was only allowed her friends in when he was out.'

It would appear that he did have hopes of having his drawings properly published – not just as single Christmas cards – judging by a letter to him from Titus Wilson Ltd. on 27 January 1949. At the time, this was one of Kendal's two leading printing firms, the other being the Westmorland Gazette. The firm later changed hands, and the files are missing, so it has not been possible to contact anyone who might remember what precisely Wainwright had in mind when he sent them two books of pen sketches. These books had apparently gone missing, according to the letter, but had now turned up. In returning them, the director of the firm mentioned that Wainwright's work was so good he could get himself a job as an engraver any time he wanted.

These sketchbooks presumably contained drawings only, but in his mind we know from a letter he wrote to Lawrence Wolsten-holme in July 1949 that he was still thinking of writing something on Lakeland one day.

Tarn Hows

The crazy season is in full swing – that of spending nights alone on the mountains. The weather has aided and abetted wonderfully this summer, and the exciting memories I have hoarded up for old age (which seems as far off as ever!) are pearls beyond price. Best of all, perhaps, was a glorious red sunrise seen from Harrison Stickle in a purple sky, while Langdale below was choked with cotton-wool clouds and seemed like a huge curving glacier, from the sheepfold below Rossett to Loughrigg, where it was joined by another glacier coming down from Grasmere. Out of this sea of white cloud rose all the familiar peaks of Lakeland, curiously detached, but warm and rosy and friendly in the early sunlight. Another lovely dawn was witnessed from Scafell Pike: at 3 a.m. I could see quite clearly the outline of the Isle of Man, and its winking light-houses, and the Scottish hills were so distinct that they seemed on the fringe of the Lake District. The sun came up like a ball of fire, immediately touching the stones of the summit with a warm, ruddy glow where before they had been ashen-grey: and it was unearthly to watch Gable and Bowfell and Pillar and the rest of them all light up, one after another. Below, the valleys were filled with white mist . . . Another time, last month, I was most luxuriantly sunbathing on Bowfell at 5 a.m. and watching shadowy Langdale slowly coming to life. Experiences like this have a heavenly beauty about them that sort of gets me in a soft spot. I hunger for more. I really must get my Lakeland book written. I shall have to do it finally in self-defence! There's an article in tonight's Lancashire Daily Post (North Edition) about another borough treasurer, and a recital of the weird habits of Kendal's b.t., who spends his Saturday nights sleeping (sic) on hill-tops. This will take some living-down: as ever, I have many critics of my conduct, but a perfectly serene and untroubled mind sends me about my daily affairs with a happy smile for everyone. Water off a duck's back, that's me!

The summers were for walking, not drawing, and as Peter grew bigger and stronger he became his father's companion on his long-distance walks. 'Dad being Dad, his walks got longer and longer, and my mother soon dropped out. I went with him all over Lakeland and to Scotland. I remember staying at Crianlarich when we walked five miles extra to Tyndrum, just to find a chip shop. Dad liked his after-dinner walk, which meant we often walked another ten miles on top of a hard day. The longest we ever walked in one day was thirty-eight miles.'

Peter remembers no rows or disagreements on these walks.

They were done mainly in silence. 'I did as I was told, but I loved being there. He didn't like staying at youth hostels, as there were too many other people there, especially big groups which he hated. We'd often take a tent and sleep out all night. We pitched our tent one night on Piers Gill, on Scafell, at 9.30 in the evening. It was freezing cold and hard to sleep, but Dad woke me at two in the morning to climb to the top of Scafell Pike and wait for the sunrise. Then we went back to our tent and fell asleep.'

Wainwright always made a feature of being a solitary walker, but now and again he did meet up with others heading in the same direction, and gave them the benefit of his company – and studied silence. One of the people he sometimes walked with was Weaver Owen who was manager of Lloyds Bank in Kendal from 1949 to 1955 and lived in Windermere Road, not far from Kendal Green.

'Some time in 1949 we found ourselves standing at the same bus stop one Sunday morning on the Windermere Road,' remembers Weaver Owen, now aged eighty-four and living in Banbury. 'I'd always been a keen walker and before the war spent all my holidays youth hostelling. I kept on meeting AW, on the same bus, and now and again we found we were planning to go on the same walk. The first walk we did together was up Nab Scar which he found heavy going.

'I always found him courteous and helpful, quietly spoken with usually a gentle smile on his face. On the other hand, I never heard him break into unrestrained laughter. He was the Hon Treasurer of the Kendal Mid-day Concert Club, but he never went to any of their concerts. I never heard him discuss books he had read. His passion was maps.'

They even spent one night together out on the fells, setting off from Kendal on a Saturday afternoon, after the banks had closed and Weaver Owen had finished work. 'We took the bus to Staveley and walked up the Kentmere valley to Mardale. We travelled light, with iron rations, not even taking a razor with us. We came across a sheep on the tops, lying on its back, imprisoned by the weight of its fleece. AW didn't know you should push it over so it could get back on its feet. We slept out in the open, or tried to. I didn't sleep a wink because of the midges. His pipe kept them off him. On the Sunday morning, we meandered down to Patterdale, had a cup of tea and caught the bus back to Kendal. We hadn't met a soul the entire weekend.'

A few years later, after Weaver Owen had left Kendal, he wrote to AW, reminding him of their walks together, signing himself by his christian name. Well, they had slept out together.

AW was not caught so easily by this rush of familiarity – and, using his office address, replied: 'Dear Mr Owen (or Weaver, if you prefer it, although personally I don't)'. He thanked him for his letter and memories, agreed to have a walk with him on his next Lakeland visit, but chided him for leaving Kendal for the southern flesh pots. 'Life here goes on as smoothly as ever. I miss your cheerful smile, but, to be quite honest, so inflexibly have I set my course that your departure was no more than a ripple on a placid sea.'

In all these early walking years, regardless of the length or difficulty of the route he'd planned, Alfred set off in ordinary clothes.

'We had no special walking clothes at all,' says Peter. 'Dad always walked in shoes and his suit. I was in short trousers, till I was fifteen or sixteen. There were no jeans in those days. He had four suits, all tweed. His best one was for council meetings. His second best was for work. Third best for walking. Fourth best was for gardening.

'We had no anoraks either. We tried an oilskin cape once, but you got blown away in that if there was any wind. Then we tried those cheap plastic macs, but they immediately got torn to shreds. We spent a lot of the time frozen stiff, so cold we couldn't move our hands. We were always coming back on the bus absolutely soaked. I know he boasted later that he was never ill on the fells, but I remember him having terrible colds.

'He never minded the rain, never moaned. If it got really bad, he'd turn his pipe upside down to keep the rain out. He only ever got upset with the weather if it was too bad to light his pipe. I used to say our tracks could be followed by the trail of match sticks he left behind. His pipe was in his mouth all the time, but mostly he was sucking it, not smoking it.

'He never rushed anything. He always walked slowly but, with his long stride, he covered a lot of ground and we usually completed an ascent quite a lot faster than has been given in the guide books. It was when he was making field notes that the pace really slowed. He stopped every few yards to take photographs or scribble on OS maps, or light his pipe. In those days, I liked to get the climbing over before stopping.

We did once race down Place Fell to Howtown and on to Patterdale because he was desperate for a cup of tea before we got the bus home. He sent back for hot water three times and we had ten cups each. We were in Langdale once and he misread the bus time table, getting Dungeon Ghyll confused with Chapel Stile. That was another panic. But mostly we walked slowly. Typical of Civil Servants, doing everything slowly.'

Peter smiled at the recollection of his father, the great expert, making these occasional mistakes. Forty years later, he could remember the exact places, the exact details of things that went wrong, and it obviously gave him much pleasure, then and now, to realise his meticulous, pernickity father could be human after all.

'He was always pretty clumsy. He'd never climb a wall unless he had to. He lacked co-ordination between feet and hands, so we'd walk hundred of yards to find a gate or a style or even a sheep hole to crawl through. I had to push him up Jack's Rake on Pavey Ark once, but he never liked me mentioning it. He was good on hills but not on rocks. He avoided ever having to use his hands for climbing or scrambling. He could walk anywhere, but not climb or crawl. When we got up to the first crag on Mickledore, he just stared at it, then we turned aside and ascended Scafell via Lord's Rake. His favourite descent was on his backside.

'He had a strange way of weeding his garden. He'd lie down, full length, within reach of the weeds, and weed away, then when he'd finished, he'd roll over to reach the next lot. He was quite comical.

'I only once remember him losing his temper. We came across a huge group of Boy Scouts on Lord's Rake. They were walking far apart from each other which he thought was dangerous. He thought if the first one knocked a boulder down, it could knock them all over like nine pins, so he shouted at the Scout Master, telling him that walking like that wasn't allowed.

'I beat him once, pointing out a path from Ennerdale to Pillar which he'd missed, one which had been in existence before the plantations. I'd gone on my own and found it, but he wouldn't believe me. He said it didn't exist.'

Peter's regular long-distance walks with his father lasted throughout his teenage years, until around 1953 when he was aged twenty. That year he took up cycling instead of walking.

'Nothing to do with my father. I always enjoyed my walks with him. It was just that I got in with a gang and joined a cycling club.'

Peter's holidays with his mother continued for many years. Sometimes they were also joined by her sister Doris or other friends and relations, but never by his father. 'I have no memory of them ever having a holiday together. They always went their separate ways. One of the earliest holidays I had with my mother was to Blackpool, with Aunt Doris. I got lost and the police had to come and find me. I got smacked for that.'

Very often on these holidays, Peter's cousin Jack Fish would come along, as company for Peter, even though he was a few years older. He had passed the scholarship exam for Queen Elizabeth's Grammar School in Blackburn, the first in the Wainwright family to go there. By 1950, they had moved on from Blackpool to having holidays abroad. In that year, Jack went with his Aunt Ruth and cousin Peter by coach to Italy, price £26 all in, the first time they'd been abroad together.

'After that, I went with them abroad most summers – to Switzerland, Austria, Norway, Italy, ' says Jack. 'No, Uncle Alfred never came with us. Never.'

Peter left school at sixteen. He'd done quite well in the end, getting 8 'O' levels, but his father had fixed him up with a job, so he left before the Sixth form. 'Dad knew Mr Crowdy, manager at the Gas Works, who had a vacancy, so I started there as a trainee gas engineer.'

In 1953, he was offered a better job, at the Gas Works in Windermere. It involved shift work so it was necessary for him to move to Windermere. 'My mother was very upset when I said I was leaving home. She said that if I did, she'd leave too – and get a divorce from Dad. She'd said that before, when I was young. But I wanted the new job – so I left home and she did nothing.'

Peter moved into a house in Windermere with four other young men – and for the first time in his life did all the normal-young-men-things he had never done before, such as going on pub crawls. At Kendal Green, he'd never had friends home. 'It wasn't just my dad. I was pretty shy when I was young and didn't have many friends anyway.'

Alfred lost his young walking companion for ever when Peter left home, and no one took his place, not on a regular basis. In Blackburn, he had had quite a group of office colleagues he'd gone walking with, but in Kendal, as Borough Treasurer, he did not mix as much, keeping himself and his private life separate.

But he did make two new male friends who remained close to him from then on. One of them was A. H. Griffin, usually known as Harry, the noted Lakeland author, journalist and rock climber. He's still producing books at the age of eighty-four, and fell walking, though he finally gave up rock climbing aged seventy-eight.

Harry was born in 1911, brought up in Barrow and joined the local paper aged seventeen. Four years later, he was fired, for demanding more money, and got a job in Preston with the *Lancashire Evening Post*, before moving to the *Daily Mail* in Manchester. During the war, he began as an army private and ended a Lt. Colonel with the 14th Army in Burma.

After the war, he didn't want to return to city life, as rock climbing in Lakeland had always been his first love, so he settled in Kendal, becoming Northern Editor of the *Lancashire Evening Post* in 1946, working with a small staff of two reporters and a photographer. He also wrote a weekly column in the paper called

'Leaves from a Lakeland Notebook' which he did for forty-six years. In 1951, he began his fortnightly 'Country Diary' on Lakeland in the *Manchester Guardian*, as it then was, which he still writes.

He prided himself on knowing everyone in Kendal, as a good local reporter should, but can't remember the first time he met AW, but probably around 1948. 'I have an image of going to his office one day, to talk about the rates. I think I disturbed him at work on some drawing which he quickly shoved in a drawer.

'I knew Alf did a lot of walking and he sometimes asked me things about places he hadn't yet visited. I often offered him a lift home in his lunch hour as I lived in Windermere Road, but he usually refused. I did see Ruth when I went to his house once, but I wasn't introduced formally. She was there, but scurried away. I gathered they didn't speak. It all seemed a bit mysterious. On my brief glimpses, she seemed an unsmiling person, living under great strain, but Alf must have been a difficult person to live with.

'I went walking with him several times – and he was one of the clumsiest walkers I've ever been with, with very large feet. We went up the Troutbeck Fells once and on the way down, I ran, as I usually did, climbing over a wall on the way. At the bottom, there was no sign of him. After twenty minutes, he appeared and in response to my enquiry, simply said, "I don't climb walls".

'Another time he asked me to take him to Doves Nest Caves on Rosthwaite Fell, in Borrowdale. You have to climb a little to get in, just a scramble up some rock steps, very easy, a child could do it, but Alf took one look at it and said, "I'm not going up there". I'd brought a rope in my rucksack, so I suggested I should tie him on, then he'd be all right. "I'm not going on that rope," he said. So he never did get inside the cave.'

The other friend Wainright made, from his early years in Kendal, was Percy Duff. His hobby was motorbikes, not walking, so their connection for many years was restricted to the office.

Percy Duff was born in Kendal in 1922. From the Grammar School, he joined the Treasurer's Department as a junior clerk in 1938. When Wainwright arrived in 1941, as accountancy assistant,

Percy became his pupil, but he doesn't remember much about him at this time, as a few months later he was called up and served in the Royal Artillery for the next five years. He returned in 1946, by which time AW had become number two in the office. 'He was very meticulous. Everything had to be exactly right. If you got things right, there were no problems and he was very helpful.'

Percy eventually became Wainwright's Deputy Treasurer and his closest friend in the office, despite the fifteen years age difference. 'He wasn't a worldly man. I remember him asking me one day how one rode a motor bike. How could one stay on going round corners. It had him baffled.'

On one occasion when there was a bus strike, Percy drove him to the head of the Langdale valley for a day's walk and home again in the evening, but was not invited in. He was never introduced to Ruth, but she came to the office once so he got to know her by sight. 'Alf never talked about her or his marriage in any way. He was very careful of his Public Position. No details were ever revealed about his private life. Outside the office, he wouldn't acknowledge folk and could appear very aloof. But inside the office, everyone liked him. No question about that. He generated great loyalty.'

Was he a good Treasurer? 'I'd say he was a better accountant than a Treasurer. His books were immaculate. But he wasn't as good at the public side of being Treasurer. He didn't circulate a lot, and didn't like it when he had to. When I succeeded him, however, his last advice was, 'Always support the Mayor.' By this he meant accompany the Mayor, whoever he or she was, on things like the Mayor's Sunday parade through the streets. He hated doing that, but he did it.

'He didn't care for modern machinery. When adding machines and calculators started coming in, he wouldn't have them. He wanted all columns of figures written out – and in ink. Not in pencil. If you brought a sheet of figures to him in pencil, he would say, "Have you no faith in your ability to add?" All our ledgers were in ink.'

AW arrived every morning at ten minutes to nine, carrying the keys to the strong room which he usually opened up. Percy carried the other set of keys and usually locked up at the end of the day. It was a very happy office, says Percy, with no office politics or intrigues. 'We all knew our own place. He was very fair. He allowed office parties, when it was someone's leaving or Christmas, and we would have cakes and sandwiches. He wouldn't come, oh no. He would sit in his own room while we had our party in the next room, but we'd send him in a sandwich or two and a piece of cake. I don't think he was meaning to appear aloof. He was just shy. He wasn't interested in office gossip, but he had a wry sense of humour which the juniors didn't quite realise.

'It was his idea to begin the office photographs. We had what was called a quinquennial, which was an outside valuation by actuaries of our superannuation fund. He decreed that henceforth, on the quinquennial, we would also have an office photograph taken. It was his little quirk. We started them in 1951, his first quinquennial as Treasurer, then every five years. I've still got copies of every one.'

Over the next fifteen years, the photographs in essence hardly changed (*see* plate 14), with the same number of staff, around fifteen, sitting in the same football team pose, three rows, with the front row on chairs, with AW as boss in the middle, managing what has to be called, for him, a definite grin. Even the demeanour and dress look much the same, making it hard to tell which year it is. In 1951, the front row men have their arms folded. In 1956, 1961 and 1966, the hands are lower, on laps, but still together. On close inspection, AW can be seen to age and grow plumper. In the 1951 photograph, he is wearing a rather fashionable-looking pin-striped suit. After that, he moves into tweeds. His specs are wire framed at first, then grow heavier as his eyes get weaker.

He not only did his work conscientiously but took on several outside appointments, such Hon. Clerk to Kendal Museum and Hon. Sec. and Treasurer of Kendal Borough Band.

A Happy Office then, with people contented with their lot, no rows or aggravations. Unlike his Home Life where he and Ruth continued to go their own way, not contented with their lot, but

Continuing our wonderful series:
"A.W. in Strange Postures"

No. 218:
A.W. on Striding Edge,
15th May 1952

apparently making the best of it, doomed into a loveless, silent marriage from which there seemed no escape for either of them. Ruth had her annual holiday to foreign parts, her dogs, some local friends, but was always careful to keep them away from Alfred. He had his endless walks, which took him away most weekends in the summer, staying out as late as possible, and his garden. Twice a year, he went through to Blackburn, on his own, to see Rovers play, and also visit Doris Snape, widow of his old football-following friend, Tom Snape which, according to Peter, made Ruth rather jealous.

But there was a feeling of unfulfilment. In a letter to Lawrence Wolstenholme in November 1950, he is still thinking of Betty Ditchfield. In the same letter, he says he has dug out some of his satirical bits about the old days in the Blackburn office which he is sending to Lawrence. There is also a mention of *Pennine Campaign*, the book he completed in 1938, although Lawrence appears to have forgotten its existence. Was he contemplating getting it published, or simply thinking longingly of things that might have been, of books he might have written?

In 1952, he came to the end of his self-appointed gardening duties, doing in a couple of years what he'd planned to take five. He had grown heavy and overweight, up to 15 stone, thanks to Ruth's cakes and home cooking, compared with $9\frac{1}{2}$ stone when he'd first arrived in Kendal during the early years of rationing. What was he going to do for the rest of his life? He still needed an escape, something he could throw himself into, an obsession even, to take his mind off his marital woes and the mistake he had always regretted making. He needed something which would occupy his winters and his summers, use his artistic, organising and writing talents and tire him out physically and mentally.

CHAPTER THIRTEEN

Writing Book One, 1952–54

Perhaps the most remarkable thing, amongst the many remarkable things about Wainwright's Pictorial Guides to the Lakeland Fells, was that he set himself thirteen years to finish his self-imposed task. At the age of forty-five he sat down and formulated what had been simmering in his head – carefully planning the rest of his active life, giving himself a job which would take up every moment of his time, until he was due for retirement. The possibility of illness, personal tragedy, work problems, domestic upsets, new people in his life, loss of interest, loss of energy, never came into his mind. Once the idea had hit him, he was a man possessed.

It wasn't quite an original idea. Guides to Lakeland had been appearing since 1770, the year of Wordsworth's birth, so the poet at least had a good reason to moan, as he later did, that tourists were now ruining the place, not like it was when he was a lad. This cry has continued for the last 225 years with people looking back, if only to last year, and bewailing the changes. Wordsworth did a Lakeland guide book himself, in 1820, which sold better at the time than his lovely poetry, so much so that a clergyman once asked if he had written anything else, apart from his guide book. Wordsworth, like almost every Lakeland guider, gave us the benefit of his views on what was exquisite or ugly. He complained about humanity ruining the landscape, such as people painting their cottages white or planting uniform rows of larches. So, opinionated guides weren't new, either.

Eighteenth-century guides, such as Gilpin's in 1772, were very hot on guiding you to exact spots, by exact routes, where you were meant to stand at specific 'stations' and admire the 'Picturesque'. This notion was later criticised for bringing the hordes all to the same place and taking the adventure out of walking, a criticism later thrown at Wainwright.

Detailed maps and routes up and down the main mountains were not new either and had appeared for at least a hundred years.

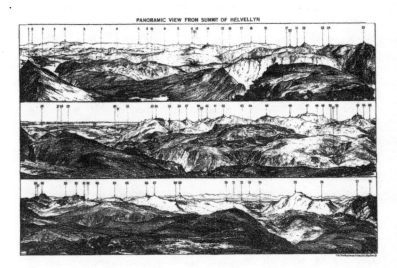

Otley's panorama to the south-west from Helvellyn (1833) and Baddeley's view from the twentieth edition of Guide to the English Lakes

I have in front of me Jonathan Otley's 1833 *Guide to the Lakes* which has a panorama, admittedly very simply drawn, from the top of Helvellyn. Baddeley's *Guide to the English Lakes*, which first appeared in the 1880s and was endlessly updated for the next eighty years, was the one which AW admired best and was excellent on maps. The twentieth edition, which appeared in 1953, had twelve full-colour maps, the sort you pulled out from the pages, plus three very good Bartholomew panoramas drawn in pen and ink, with blue for the sky and lakes. All the above mentioned guides tried to be comprehensive, covering towns and transport as well as walks and weather, with bits of botany and geology thrown in.

Wainwright's aim was much more specific. He was only interested in the fells. Baddeley was good on Helvellyn, giving five different routes up, but his guide covered only the twenty best-known Lakeland fells. Wainwright's self-imposed aim was to climb and record every fell in Lakeland, some 214 of them, giving the ways up, the ways down, what was to be seen on top and the connecting ridges. He divided Lakeland into seven sections, his own divisions, not copying any writers who had gone before, and made a plan of attack, working out how long each section would take him to complete. He couldn't drive and had no car, so everything would have to be done by public transport.

Why? Well, as he himself always said, it was a love letter. 'One man's way of expressing his devotion to Lakeland's friendly hills . . . conceived, and born, after many years of inarticulate worshipping at their shrines.'

As we have seen, some form of Lakeland book had been in his mind for many years. He had boasted about it to friends, fantasised about doing it, promising himself he would manage it one day. He had completed one book, now nearly fifteen years ago, without drawings or illustrations, full of his personal observations and experiences and carefully crafted prose, but in 1952 that still lay in his drawer, unseen by the public. This time he was embarking on an instructional rather than a literary exercise, recording what he had seen and done, using his graphic skills and his accountancy brain to organise all the elements. For whom? We have to believe the initial purpose was solely to amuse himself, for that was what he always said.

'I was working for my own pleasure . . . gathering together all my notes and drawings and a host of recollections, and putting them in a book so that when I became an old man I could look at them at leisure, recall all my memories, and go on fell walking in spirit long after my legs had given up.'

How did he come to divide Lakeland into seven compartments? 'The Lake District', however one defines it or draws its boundaries, is basically circular. Wordsworth, in his 1820 *Guide*, likened its shape to a wheel, which was neat, with the lakes and dales radiating from the centre like the spokes of the wheel. Most writers, in covering the Lakes, usually start in the middle, somewhere near Windermere, then wander round, vaguely in a circle, before coming back to the centre. Another way is to divide Lakeland into north and south, with the boundary being Dunmail Raise. This is a useful division as, traditionally, the natives on either side stuck to their own region. I still feel, as I move south over Dunmail Raise, that I am entering a different land, with different accents, suspecting that I am almost in Lancashire. Coming north, southern Lakelanders feel that once over Dunmail Raise they are virtually in Scotland.

Wainwright was, of course, looking for geographical divisions, ways of neatly carving up the landscape into manageable mouthfuls. One has to assume at some stage he got out a large map of Cumberland and Westmorland, as it then was, and started pencilling in dividing lines. Maps were his main reading, always had been, rather than books, and he could study them for hours, imagining routes, negotiating obstacles, working out how much he might do in a day, a week, a year. He had by now visited most lakes, most valleys, most mountains, and knew the terrain pretty well.

His first job was to decide the ultimate boundary. The National Park had recently been unveiled as a concept and delineated as a territory in 1951, but he largely ignored it, restricting himself to the high ground. (The National Park boundary goes further west than Wainwright's, taking in parts of the coast.)

What he did, first of all, was draw a straight line connecting all the extremities of the outlying Lakes. This worked perfectly on the west and the south sides, and fairly well on the east, including in its artificial boundary all the high-ish ground, usually coloured brown on old maps, but it didn't work nearly so well on the north side. A straight line, for example, from the far end of Bassenthwaite to the top end of Ullswater would roughly slice through the flanks of Skiddaw and therefore miss out ten reasonably sized fells to the north, such as High Pike and Carrock Fell. Anyone knowing the region would want them in as they are the natural guardians of the Skiddaw range, separating the high land from the plains. Then there was the problem of little Binsey, stuck out on its own, but well worth having inside his family of fells. So instead of a lake, he took Caldbeck village as his notional northern point, drawing his line from Bassenthwaite Lake up to Caldbeck then down to Ullswater. Thus, with a bit of fiddling, he had everything he wanted inside his own boundary.

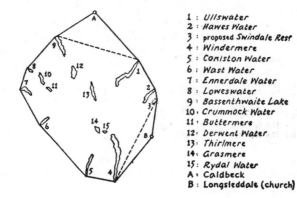

1 : *Ullswater*
2 : *Hawes Water*
3 : proposed *Swindale Rest*
4 : *Windermere*
5 : *Coniston Water*
6 : *Wast Water*
7 : *Ennerdale Water*
8 : *Loweswater*
9 : *Bassenthwaite Lake*
10 · *Crummock Water*
11 · *Buttermere*
12 · *Derwent Water*
13 · *Thirlmere*
14 · *Grasmere*
15 : *Rydal Water*
A · **Caldbeck**
B : **Longsleddale (church)**

The external boundaries of Lakeland as depicted by Wainwright in the prelims of each of the Pictorial Guides

Creating his internal divisions was a matter of making use of the natural or existing boundaries – lakes, valleys, passes and roads. He aimed for sections which contained well-defined groups of fells, but were separated sufficiently by a lake or valley from the next section. It is noticeable that none of his seven sections is connected to any adjoining section by a ridge, thus a reader only needs to concentrate on one book at a time, which was good thinking.

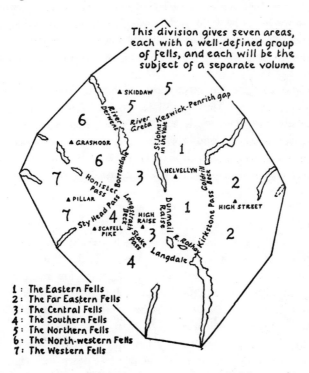

Wainwright's division of Lakeland into seven areas which he turned into the seven volumes of the Pictorial Guides

He used all the obvious and most notable dividing lines in Lakeland. Books One and Two for example are separated basically by the Kirkstone Pass and Ullswater. Crummock water, Buttermere and the Honister Pass separate Books Six and Seven. Langdale separates Books Three and Four. He also had to bear in mind his means of communication, how he would be able to tackle each section by public transport. Note how the dreaded A591, from Ambleside to Keswick, separates Books One and Three, except at the top where he decided to use St John's-in-the-Vale as his right-hand boundary, rather than the A591. He had an option there – and could have put High Rigg in either Book One or Three. There must also have been a lot of deliberation about the final line between Books Four and Seven: his main boundary line is clear enough, from Wasdale to Borrowdale, but around Sty Head he had to make certain choices. Perhaps the watershed played a part.

He did not give the exact reasons for each decision about his boundary lines, and we can only guess at what was in his mind, but finally he had to work out the length of each book – how many fells to include, and how many pages to devote to each fell, whilst trying to keep each book about the same length.

His definition of a Lakeland fell was, first, height, and secondly, individuality – was it enough of a hill in its own right or merely a slope of another. In Book One, his cut-off point appears to be around the 1400-feet mark, and he included none below that. But by Book Four, he has included a couple nearer the 1000-feet mark. In Book Six, he dips right down to include Castle Crag in Borrowdale at 985 feet, the only time he goes below the 1000-feet mark. (And he does have the grace to call Castle Crag a 'protuber-ance', rather than a fell, saying he has included it because it is so 'magnificently independent'.)

Before he began the first page, it is clear he had his overall plan of attack worked out, his time schedule laid down for tackling a total of 214 fells – an arbitrary number, inside his arbitrary bound-ary, but all gloriously clear cut in his own mind.

Looking now at the shape of his chosen area, you can see that it is circular, and if you consider Book 1 and Book 3 as being his two central sections, then Books 4, 7, 6, 5 and 2 rotate round the edges – just like the spokes of Wordsworth's wheel.

*

He started the first page of Book One, the Eastern Fells, on 9 November 1952. This was not the nearest section to his house in Kendal, nor the easiest for public transport. For that, he would have been better beginning with Book Two, covering what he called the Far Eastern Fells, but the Eastern Fells were handy enough, using the main bus route to Windermere, Ambleside and Keswick. It was also a very popular area, containing Lakeland's most glamorous, most visited mountain – Helvellyn. Was this a factor in his choice, even though he was doing it for his own amusement, so he declared, not thinking at this stage of any possible readers?

The first page he completed that November evening, using a mapping pen and a bottle of Indian ink, depicted the ascent of Dove Crag from Ambleside – reliving in his mind exploration work already done, notes already made, memories stored away and photographs propped up in front of him. He never did drawings in situ, whilst standing there. On his walks, he had always taken photographs and they were the basis of all his drawings.

His own photographs, taken with a cheap camera, were pretty poor. Around 1950, he started taking them to a local photographer in Kendal, Ken Shepherd, who worked from his home in Windermere Road, specialising in weddings and portraits, and had his own dark room. Previously he had been a photographer with the *Westmorland Gazette* and the *Carlisle Journal*. 'He came to me because he was disappointed by what the chemist had produced, so I made new prints from his negatives. I did all his photographs for the next forty years. He'd get the negatives back from the chemist, then bring them to me. He was a genius at doing his books, but hopeless at anything mechanical. He once offered me some tea, when I took his photographs round to him, but he didn't know how to make it. "Do you pour the hot water on the tea?" he asked me.'

Wainwright worked from the best of his photographs, not exactly copying them, although when placed side by side you can see where they have come from, but making artistic interpretations, showing more detail, highlighting crevices and shadows, picking out individual boulders, isolated trees and even tufts of grass. The

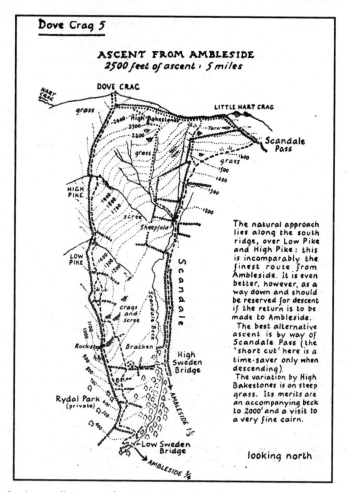

Dove Crag 5

ASCENT FROM AMBLESIDE
2500 feet of ascent · 5 miles

DOVE CRAG

HART CRAG

grass

LITTLE HART CRAG

2400 High Bakes

2300

2200

Tarn

Scandale
Pass

grass

1600

grass

1500

1400

1300

1200

HIGH
PIKE

1900
1800
1700

scree

Sheepfold

The natural approach
lies along the south
ridge, over Low Pike
and High Pike: this
is incomparably the
finest route from
Ambleside. It is even
better, however, as a
way down and should
be reserved for descent
if the return is to be
made to Ambleside.
The best alternative
ascent is by way of
Scandale Pass (the
'short cut' here is a
time-saver only when
descending).
The variation by High
Bakestones is on steep
grass. Its merits are
an accompanying beck
to 2000' and a visit to
a very fine cairn.

LOW
PIKE

1400
1300
1200

S
c
a
n
d
a
l
e

crags
and
scree

Scandale Beck

1100
1000

Rockets

Bracken

High
Sweden
Bridge

900

AMBLESIDE 1½

Rydal Park
(private)

800
700
600

500

400

Low Sweden
Bridge

looking north

AMBLESIDE ¾

---

sky is usually ignored, which is hard to do in pen and ink anyway,
but the foreground is always very detailed. Some drawings are
literally thumb-nail size, filling up gaps, while others are full-page
illustrations. Given space, he usually added a few decorative features, such as strategically placed sheep and sometimes the odd
figure, walking in the distance or sitting on a boulder. He has
himself on Clough Head, sitting with his pipe, looking towards
Blencathra (*see* page 174).

Ullswater
from the
north-east ridge

In Book One there is also a very interesting and unusual full-page illustration, St Sunday Crag 8, which is a view of Ullswater from the north-east ridge. Look at it carefully and you'll see a woman sitting admiring the view, seen from the back, and wearing what appears to be a 1930's-style bobbed hair and frock. He never revealed who this was, or even agreed it was a real person but three of his old Blackburn colleagues, including Bob Alker, are convinced they know who it is – Betty Ditchfield.

His maps were his own creation, devised by himself, with his own symbols, giving a three-dimensional effect, showing tarns lying flat, rounded hills, steep slopes and walls which turn corners, yet all making sense – and all totally accurate. He claims in the book that it is 'free from inaccuracies', which is always a hostage to fortune, encouraging the pedantic to nit pick.

The words were also in his own hand. After all, he set out to write the book for himself, so it was a sort of superior, polished version of a personal notebook, not prepared for a typesetter to print out. He used a careful hand-printed style, aping printer's type, to make it as legible as the real thing, but much more artistic. As we know, his handwriting since his early office days was always immaculate, even when sending letters to friends; he never scribbled them. He wrote most things twice all his life, even humble letters, so that the finished, sent version is always completely without corrections, mistakes or rubbings out. (The original letters to Lawrence contain no splodges, no crossings out.)

He devised two forms of hand-printing, one up and down and one more sloping, like italics, to give variety to every page. He varied the size, big and small, which is easy enough, but he also managed a form of what is called 'bold' by pressing harder and broader with his pen and making certain letters or words stand out, moving into double stroke capital letters for headlines. At first glance, his handwriting does appear uniform, but if you look carefully at almost any page of his Guides you'll see four or five different styles, blending together, but giving texture and variety and 'colour' to every page. In his accountancy ledgers, he prided himself on his letters and his figures being as neat and tidy as each other. On a larger, more complicated scale, he was making everything on every page of his Guides as artistic as possible.

As part of his attempt to give a printer's feel to his handwriting, he made sure that the left-hand side of every line was exactly aligned, the way metal type would do it. At first he didn't bother to justify on both sides – leaving the right-hand side to end wherever, as one does in a letter. The following July, after *eight months* of work, he decided he didn't like the look of this and so

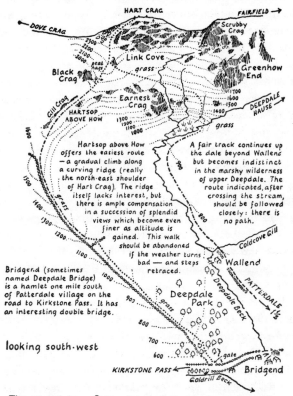

ASCENT FROM PATTERDALE
2,300 feet of ascent : 4½ miles from Patterdale village

HART CRAG

FAIRFIELD →

← DOVE CRAG

Scrubby Crag

2300
2200
2100
2000

peat hags

Link Cove

grass

Greenhow End

Black Crag

Gill Crag

Earnest Crag

1700
1600
1500
1400

DEEPDALE HAUSE →

HARTSOP ABOVE HOW

1300
1200
1100
1000

grass

1600

Hartsop above How offers the easiest route — a gradual climb along a curving ridge (really the north-east shoulder of Hart Crag). The ridge itself lacks interest, but there is ample compensation in a succession of splendid views which become even finer as altitude is gained. This walk should be abandoned if the weather turns bad — and steps retraced.

A fair track continues up the dale beyond Wallend but becomes indistinct in the marshy wilderness of upper Deepdale. The route indicated, after crossing the stream, should be followed closely: there is no path.

1500

grass

1400

1300

1200

1100

900

800

Coldcove Gill

Wallend

PATTERDALE

Bridgend (sometimes named Deepdale Bridge) is a hamlet one mile south of Patterdale village on the road to Kirkstone Pass. It has an interesting double bridge.

1000

900

grass

Deepdale Park

Deepdale Beck

PATTERDALE 1½

800

looking south-west

700

600

gate

KIRKSTONE PASS ←

Goldrill Beck

Bridgend

The ascent from Patterdale is far superior to that from the south. The Link Cove route especially is an interesting climb through the inner sanctuary of Hart Crag, the scene being impressive, *but it is quite unsuitable in bad weather.*

Sample page from Book 1 showing the roman and italic forms of hand-printing

scrapped the *hundred or so pages* he had written so far, doing the work all over again, this time the lines justified on both sides. He went even further and set himself the task, which no printed page ever achieves, of never splitting a word and using a hyphen. Madness, in a way, as who would ever notice such an unnecessary perfection, but it was part of his obsession, his self-imposed desire to get things exactly as he wanted it.

His handwriting looks perfect, almost inhuman, certainly not the human handwriting we see coming out of schools today, but if you study it clearly you can see imperfections, letters varying, unequal gaps appearing between words as he strives not to use hyphens. In 1994, the computer department of a well-known northern university created a 'Wainwright typeface', which they offered to Michael Joseph, his present-day publisher, as a commercial proposition. They turned it down as being too good. The spaces were computer correct, the letters identical, but the overall effect of every page was total blandness.

His chosen layout of the book was rather strange, and when I first read it, I admit I found it a bit confusing. There are no page numbers, for example, which makes it hard to look things up, and no index at the back but, of course, once you study his system, which took him a long time to perfect, it is all very logical and in fact gives more information than the normal guide book. The fells appear in alphabetical order, not according to height or geography, and each fell has its own page numbers, with occasional cross references. Once again, it was his own creation.

Now for the words themselves. Reading the Introduction today, and being perhaps a mite too critical for what was after all his first attempt at a guide book as opposed to a literary exercise, he did let a few clichés creep in. 'Dappled in sunlight ... magical atmosphere'. And in explaining what he meant by the Eastern Fells, there is a certain clumsiness, perhaps due to his own self-imposed constraints of fitting words to gaps and not using hyphens. 'The western boundary is formed by the deep trough of Dunmail Raise and Thirlmere, a great rift of which the principal road across the district takes advantage.' Hmm. That sentence should have been re-done, or redrawn. Now and again there were faint echoes of Baddeley. On Helvellyn, Wainwright said it had an 'aura of romance' while Baddeley said it had a 'halo of romance' which is neater.

Once the book was underway, he quickly gave up his attempts

at purple prose and settled down to plain, decent English, giving simple descriptions, instructions, explanations and advice. From time to time, his own personality seeps out, the first clue we have to the man behind the words, which is what we always want – well, I always want – when I read any sort of guide book, measuring the writer with his opinions.

He makes it clear he loves summits as they appeal to 'walkers with red blood in their veins', a favourite expression of his; he moans about people on the top of Helvellyn leaving litter from their packed lunches, and feels sorry for Little Mell Fell. 'It seems an oversight of nature that the sheep here are not born with webbed feet,' so he remarks about a marshy bit on Great Dodd. 'Here man tried to tame nature', he writes about White Side, 'and in due course nature has its full revenge.'

An important element in his decision to walk every fell was the appearance of new Ordnance Survey maps on a scale of $2\frac{1}{2}$ inches to the mile. They fascinated him, as maps always did, but also gave him much more advance information for planning his routes, more things to look for and record. Until then, he'd been walking with one-inch maps, which don't show things like walls or fences. He dedicated Book One to The Men of the Ordnance Survey 'whose maps of Lakeland have given me much pleasure both on the fells and by my fireside'.

The walking and recording for Book One, drawing and writing and laying out, took up all his spare time over the next three years. He lost time re-doing those hundred pages and he was also, of course, preparing a system and method which would last him over thirteen years and seven books, hence Book One took longer than the others.

Weekends were his main walking time, summer and winter, but mostly summers. On a good Lakeland summer day, you can almost get two days, as the light goes on until well after ten at night. He got into a routine of catching the 8.30 bus to Keswick, and the 6.30 bus back, usually managing an evening meal in Keswick before catching his bus, as he was never in any hurry to get home. He always ate fish and chips, what else, at the same time in the same Keswick caff so that Winnie the waitress knew what to order the moment he appeared in the doorway.

His garden became a jungle and, so he revealed in *Ex-Fellwanderer*, published in 1987, his 'domestic relationships withered and died'. This was not strictly correct, as we know his marriage had long since withered and died, but he was nearer admitting the truth when he added that the books were a form of escape.

'Some people escape in dreams but I was fortunate enough to live in a perfect dreamland that actually existed. I was always happier pulling on my boots in the morning than putting on my shoes. On a day when I didn't have to wear a collar and tie I was a boy again. If I was heading for the hills, and not the office, I could set forth singing, not audibly, heaven forbid; just in my heart. I was off to where the sheep were real, not human.'

When he had completed the fells for Book One, at Christmas time 1954, he added some Personal Notes in conclusion. He revealed he was from Blackburn, and that this book had been twenty years in the making, ever since he first came from his smoky mill town and set eyes on Orrest Head, but without giving away the nature of his employment or where exactly he now lived in Lakeland. He said that his wanderings had been solitary but had given him many memories, such as one which insistently returned to his mind – about a newt. A newt? So he said. One he had spied swimming around in Hard Tarn. Was this a joke, which no one has ever explained, or a touch of the purple prose again?

He said the book had not been written 'for material gain' nor for posterity, but for his own pleasure. He finished by revealing that as he was writing the last sentence, his thoughts would now be on Book Two.

He knew by then he would have readers. He had already made the big decision to publish, go public, and give everyone a chance to share his pleasures, but of course he did not know how many readers he might have, or whether posterity would have the slightest interest in anything he had done.

CHAPTER FOURTEEN

Publication of Book One, 1955

Anyone fortunate enough to have a copy of the first edition of Book One of Wainwright's Pictorial Guides to the Lakeland Fells has not only got a miniature work of art but a collector's item. It won't ever be as valuable as the 1901 first edition of Beatrix Potter's *Peter Rabbit*, which recently sold for £55,000, but there are connections. They have Lakeland in common. Both authors did their own words, illustrations and layout. Their books were a similar small size. They were both self-publishers.

Wainwright, like Miss Potter, decided to go it alone when offering his first book to the world. The normal reader, whether picking up the first or the hundredth edition of these respective books, will hardly notice any difference, for the contents always were, and always will be, exactly the same. Only certain clues inside the front pages will give the game away.

The signs to look for with Wainwright are 'Published in 1955 by Henry Marshall, Low Bridge, Kentmere, Westmorland'. This little book cost only 12/6d when it first appeared in May 1955. Two thousand copies were produced, compared with only 250 of the first *Peter Rabbit*, but today you will be lucky to find a reasonable copy for under £150.

In *Fellwanderer*, Wainright gave his own brief explanation of what happened.

By the time Book One was finished, I had begun to feel that other walkers also suffering from, or rejoicing in, Lakeland fell fever, might find some use for it. Perhaps I could be an accountant and an author too. I had become quite fond of my little infant, but it was a poor frail thing and I daren't risk exposing it to the mercies of a publisher. I couldn't face the probability of rejection. That would have hurt, and anyway publishers aren't fellwalkers and wouldn't understand. What did they know of Sharp Edge who sat at a London desk? What did they know of mountain silence who lived in a world of tumult? So I took it to Sandy Hewitson, a local printer. Sandy wasn't a fellwalker either, in fact with only one leg he couldn't be, but he was a better man than most with two: and he was a craftsman who saw in the job a challenge to his ability. I asked him how much it would cost to make copies. He said, how many copies? I thought I could reasonably expect to sell 500 – you can always find 500 people ready to try anything once. Costs were worked out – 500 was clearly uneconomical. It had to be 2000 to bring the unit cost down sufficiently to permit a reasonable selling price. I asked how much 2000 would cost – £950. I said I had only £35. He said never mind, pay me when you sell them. Sandy is dead now. He was kind to me. Kind men leave a gap when they pass on. The other sort are never missed.

I was helped at first by Henry Marshall, the Kendal Librarian, who attended to the distribution and despatch of the books. He advised me that it would never do for my name to appear both as author and publisher – a sure indication that no recognised publisher could be persuaded to undertake the responsibility – and so I borrowed his name, which, in any case, had more dignity than mine. I especially liked the Henry. I never disclosed what the Christian A of mine stood for. It suited me to hide the truth of this affliction. But it isn't Aloysius, if that's what you're thinking.

Wainwright wrote these words in 1966 so his memory was pretty fresh, but did he tell the full story and did he give due credit to all the people concerned? That reference to his own name, for example, is interesting because he always insisted it must only be given as A. Wainwright, which is how it appeared on all his books from then on. It became a running joke, not revealing his true Christian name, part of his endeavour to keep out of the limelight, even to the extent of denying who he was. The other joke was to tell people he was called A. Walker.

Yet before Book One appeared, he printed 2000 leaflets, for which Bateman and Hewitson Ltd. charged him £3.15.9 (plus £1.1.0 for the zinc block). One side of the leaflet was an order form. The other side was an advance announcement of the book – in which his name is given as Alfred Wainwright. It was only

PRINTED
by
BATEMAN AND HEWITSON L^TD
KENDAL

from engravings by
THE NORTHERN
PHOTO·ENGRAVING C^O L^TD
MANCHESTER

PUBLISHED IN 1955
by
HENRY MARSHALL
LOW BRIDGE · KENTMERE · WESTMORLAND

just before publication, therefore, that he had second thoughts.

Henry Marshall is dead, so it is hard to establish exactly how he and Wainwright came together, and what their relationship was, but from his daughter, Gillian Murphy, and from Donald James, who was his assistant at Kendal Library, and later Librarian himself, a picture emerges of someone who took his job as 'publisher' very seriously. (Incidentally, Gillian, who was seventeen in 1954, a pupil at Kendal High School, still refers to Wainwright as 'Alec', which was what she thought he was called.)

This is to announce the publication of a book
that is quite out of the ordinary

• Primarily it is a book for fellwalkers, for those who know
the fells intimately and for those who know them but little •
It is a book for all lovers of Lakeland
It is a book for collectors of unusual books

It is the first volume of a series under the title of
A PICTORIAL GUIDE TO THE LAKELAND FELLS

This first volume is
BOOK ONE : THE EASTERN FELLS
describing the Helvellyn and Fairfield groups

Hand-printed throughout, with 500 illustrations
(drawings, maps and diagrams) in its 300 pages,
it represents an original idea in the making of books
• The author is *Alfred Wainwright* of Kendal

Its price is twelve shillings and sixpence
Copies are obtainable from bookshops in Lakeland,
or by post (for sixpence more) from HENRY MARSHALL,
LOW BRIDGE, KENTMERE, WESTMORLAND

Marshall was born in the Mile End Road, in the East End of London, on 18 July 1906 so he was just six months older than Wainwright. He trained at Bethnal Green Library, a well-known breeding ground for librarians before the war. He never liked

THE EASTERN FELLS

ORDER FORM

The book will be addressed
exactly in accordance
with the particulars
you state alongside
BLOCK LETTERS, PLEASE

Name ....

Address ....

....

....

This form should be sent
with a remittance for 13s
to
HENRY MARSHALL
LOW BRIDGE
KENTMERE
WESTMORLAND

Cheques may be made payable to H. MARSHALL

London and so, as Wainwright did, schemed to get away, arriving in Kendal as Borough Librarian in 1938. In the 1950s he and his wife and three young children moved into a very attractive house not far from Kendal – Low Bridge House, Kentmere – which had the River Kent lapping round its large garden. A drawing of it appeared on the top of his notepaper.

Marshall was an active Rotarian, a church warden, and a keen walker and climber, learning rock climbing from Harry Griffin. 'He'd never done a single hill, not even Orrest Head. He was a bit of disaster on our first rock climb, up Middle Fell Buttress in the Langdales. He said his balance was poor, blaming it on the fact that he had one brown eye and one blue. But we became close friends. He was a delightful fellow. It was from Henry Marshall I first learned that Alf was doing a guide book. He was rather surprised when I asked him how it was getting on.'

It's not clear how Marshall and Wainwright first met, although they did go walking together and Gillian has a photograph of her father and AW, with a woman, resting on a cairn. It seems more likely they met through being Borough officials. Marshall, as the Librarian, often came to the Treasurer's office, so Percy Duff remembers, as they did the Library accounts. By visiting the office, Marshall would have heard about Wainwright's book, perhaps seen the contents, known he was thinking of having it published, and so suggested they should produce it together – Wainwright as author, Marshall as publisher. Gillian has a memory of her father saying that Wainwright at one stage did try to place the book with a proper publisher, but can't remember any names, which is why her father suggested going it alone. Wainwright himself always gave the opposite impression – that he never tried. He was against any London publisher fiddling with his creation. No one has ever come forward to say they turned down Wainwright, but then every London publisher turns down hundreds of ideas every week.

They were never close friends, Wainwright and Marshall, before or during their partnership, being totally different characters; they simply came together though a joint project, each spurred on by an idea. Marshall was a sociable animal, clubbable, extrovert, eager to please, practical, energetic, ingenious.

'He continually found original ways to eke out the Library's limited resources,' remembers Donald James. 'While I was working with him, he decided to re-partition and re-shelve the Library. There was no question of bringing in an architect or a library supplier – he wanted to do it himself. He did a few sketches on the back of an envelope, brought in a joiner from round the corner, then he was up a ladder himself, pulling down plasterboard. One joiner left in a huff because Marshall was using his tools.

'He always preferred to buy books through small retailers, rather than large library suppliers. He thought he could get cheaper book servicing that way. He liked the company of booksellers and got to know many of them personally.'

Deep down, Marshall had an entrepreneurial instinct, although he wasn't in it for the money, and it was this, combined with his contacts in the local book trade, which persuaded Wainwright to agree to his offer to act as publisher. Marshall ordered impressive-looking headed notepaper and set aside a room at his home to serve as his office.

The printer they chose, Sandy Hewitson, specialised in printing leaflets for the Town Hall. So both Wainwright and Marshall knew him from their respective departments. It would appear that

Marshall did most of the initial production arrangements as Wainwright at this stage knew nothing about printing, assuming art work had to be the same size as the intended page, not understanding about the processes of reduction and enlargement.

Wainwright's reference to Sandy Hewitson, quoted earlier, and his public thanking of him, hides the fact that Bateman and Hewitson Ltd were not technically the printers of the first book, even though their name was on it. They were a small jobbing printers, good at headed notepaper and leaflets, but unable to take on anything as large or complicated as a properly bound book, not having the appropriate machinery. At this stage, however, they had already been taken over by the much bigger and better equipped Kendal firm, the Westmorland Gazette.

The *Westmorland Gazette* had begun life simply as a newspaper in 1818, during a general election. It was backed by local Tory money, and its first editor was young Thomas de Quincey, recommended for the job by his friend, William Wordsworth. He lasted fourteen months before being sacked for missing the London news, not contacting the printers and not coming to the office, all things a proper editor should really try to do. There was a loss of £42 on the first year, but after de Quincey's departure, things improved and they became a printing firm as well as a newspaper. In 1955, apart from their own paper, they were printing two well established monthly magazines, *Cumbria* and *Dalesman*, plus occasional books.

The Printing Manager of the Westmorland Gazette in 1955 was Harry Firth who had joined the firm four years earlier, aged thirty-four. He was born in Bradford in 1917 and became an apprentice printer with the Westminster Press group in 1933, the company which had taken over ownership of the Westmorland Gazette.

'One day I got a call from Sandy Hewitson, just along the street. He'd been approached by a Mr Wainwright to print a guide book and wanted me to take a look at it, as it looked too big a job for them. I went round and was amazed. I couldn't believe one man had hand-drawn every page. He wanted it reproduced exactly as he'd done it and set it out. I don't think anybody since the days of the monks had ever produced a completely hand-written book. I told Hewitson that we could cope, but we were all taking a chance, printing an unknown author, who couldn't actually pay for the costs at the time.

'From the very beginning, Westmorland Gazette were the printers but Sandy was the front man who dealt with the client, which is why his firm's name went on the early books as being the printer.'

Not everything could be done in Kendal: the engraving of each page had to be done elsewhere as, at this stage, the Gazette did not have the equipment. Sandy gave the job to the Northern Photo-Engraving Co Ltd, in Manchester. Their bill, for what was described as 297 'fine line Zincos', came to £296.13.3 and was submitted to A. Wainwright, at the Municipal Offices, Kendal, on 8 March 1955, plus a bill for leaflets and envelopes. Under their agreement, this did not have to be paid until the books started selling. The Gazette's bill for the actual printing, which they kindly kept back until 28 September that year, came to £526.15. The grand total, therefore was going to be around the £900 which had originally been estimated.

In preparation, Wainwright had transferred the total capital he had available for the venture, the sum of £35, from his personal account at Martins Bank to a new account, set up to run the publishing company. All that was needed now was to get some orders, send copies out, and collect the money. If any. It no doubt helped his cause that he was Kendal's Borough Treasurer, someone in theory who should know about money, someone a local printer considered worth trusting, but he was trusting himself as much as they were trusting him. It was a large financial undertaking, taking on a debt of £900 with only £35 in the bank; if it failed it might well ruin his career as well as his bank balance.

Harry Firth went out with Wainwright and Harry Marshall as soon as the first edition was ready, visiting the local bookshops, hoping for orders. Marshall knew the bookshop managers anyway, but wanted Wainwright to show his face as well, even though he was never at ease when it came to social chat or selling himself.

'We filled the back of the car and went to Windermere, Bowness, Ambleside and Keswick,' says Harry Firth. 'Marshall went in and did most of the talking. I made a note of the orders, writing down the number each shop wanted.'

It is normal in self-publishing, as I know from my own experiences, for the author and 'publisher' to go round in the flesh and solicit orders, but I've never heard of the *printer* going round as well. I asked Harry Firth about this. 'You have to realise we were not a big firm. We had no salesmen at all, so it seemed a useful thing for me to do. After all, we wanted our money back as well.'

The retail price of Book One was 12/6, quite expensive for a little guide book when you consider that the cost of a new hardback novel was then around 7/6, but it had been an expensive book to produce, with so many engravings. At £900 for 2,000 copies the unit cost was therefore around 9/- so selling at 12/6 was not going to leave much margin for profit. 'AW just wanted to get them printed, and wasn't thinking of profits.'

The first 2,000 had no dust jackets – so be careful of any dealer who offers you a first edition, with cover. 'I didn't think of it, nor did AW,' says Harry Firth. 'He hadn't designed anything. The books were meant to be carried in the pocket on the fells, so a cover seemed unnecessary.' Both the pages and the Rexine cover were rounded; in modern editions, the corners are square. Further, the early editions were bound in a different colour (to match the colour band on the jackets when they arrived), and only changed to green when the books transferred to Westmorland Press.

Wainwright and Marshall's next job was to get some publicity for their book. Even a tyro author and first-time publisher know that it is one thing to get your books into the shops, but they won't leave the shops unless people know they are there. They'd sent out 1,400 of their 2,000 leaflets, and waited for orders to come in. As soon as they had bound books, they sent out copies to the local papers for review, and also to the *Manchester Guardian*, still in Manchester in those days. Wainwright also sent out free copies to likely people who might help the book along, such as the Director General of the Ordnance Survey and the Archbishop of York. The

Archbishop's secretary replied to Miss Thompson, Wainwright's Town Hall secretary (which suggests AW was sometimes using her for his own private use, tut tut), saying that the Archbishop did have a great love of the Lakes, but that at present he was recovering from an operation. Wainwright sent copies to his old friends in Blackburn. Bob Alker still has his first edition – and remembers that with it came an invoice, for the full price. Well, books have to be sold somehow.

Marshall sent off a copy to the British Museum knowing, as a professional in the field, that they have by law to be given a copy of every new book. He and Wainwright also contacted their colleagues in local government elsewhere in Cumberland and Westmorland, asking them to try to get their local bookshop to stock copies. The Town Clerk of Penrith bought three copies – and sent back a cheque with a nice letter saying it was 'the best book in this line I have ever seen', and promised to chase W. H. Smith.

The next stage was to arrange some advertising, despite the fact that they were working on a capital sum of only £35, with the books still to be paid for. Wainwright wrote to *Cumbria*, the magazine printed by the Westmorland Gazette, but produced in Clapham, north Lancashire, asking for their advertising rates. They were not as high as he expected and so he booked a whole page, price £10, for the June 1955 edition, also enclosing a note asking for some editorial coverage opposite his advertisement. A bit cheeky, but why not.

The first published review appeared on 27 May 1955 in the *Lancashire Evening Post*, written, surprise surprise, by AW's friend, Harry Griffin, although he did admit he knew AW. 'I have already told the author he runs the risk of taking all the adventure, the joy of discovery, out of the fells by the very completeness of his work.' Apart from that small criticism (which he still believes to this day) it was an extensive, informed and well-written review. 'I sincerely believe,' he wrote, 'it to be the most remarkable book of its kind about the Lake District ever printed.'

The *Westmorland Gazette*'s review appeared the next day, 28

May, and praised the format. 'A unique production ... hand printed facsimile form which is as readable as mechanically set type. Apart from the artistry of it the volume is a guide which no fellwalker or peak-bagger can really afford to do without.' It noted that Mr A. Wainwright was Borough Treasurer of Kendal, the printers were Bateman and Hewitson, and that the gold-embossed cover was 'a durable and wealthy one'.

The *Keswick Reminder* said it was 'excellent' and the *Carlisle Journal* described it as a 'must' – both these reviews being written anonymously by the same person, George Bott of Keswick. On 10 June 1955 a review appeared in the *Manchester Guardian*, which was a bit of luck and had nothing to do with Harry Griffin, nor did Wainwright have any other friends or contacts there. It reproduced what it called one of the author's 'vertical sketch maps' and said the book was available at 12/6 from Henry Marshall, Low Bridge, Kentmere, Westmorland, which is just the sort of plug any first-time author and publisher dreams about.

Perhaps not quite as influential, but jolly pleasing all the same, was a mention in *The Sanitarian*, the journal of Municipal Sanitary Inspectors, which said that Mr W. B. G. Rigg, Chief Sanitary Inspector, Kendal Borough, will be pleased to post copies to colleagues, price 13 shillings including postage.

In acknowledging his cheque for £10 for the full-page advertisement, the publisher of *Cumbria*, Harry Scott, wrote back to Wainwright saying that he had seen some of the original pages for the book – courtesy of Harry Firth – and congratulated him on a 'remarkable piece of work'. This was Wainwright's first unsolicited bit of praise, and he wrote back to say that he couldn't remember ever receiving a kinder or more generous letter.

'I welcome your opinion particularly because it was always in my mind when I was compiling the book that I would take it over to Clapham when it was finished to see if you would publish it! Then when the job was done, I hesitated. It seemed to me then to be unfair to ask anyone to risk money on something so different. I decided to stand the risk myself. That's how it comes about that I now find myself suffering the anxieties (and enjoying the excitements) of putting a new book before the public. At the moment, I feel like a man going to the gallows!'

The letter is interesting in that it shows publication *was* in his mind from an early stage, despite what he later said, but it shows fairly conclusively that he never submitted it to any proper publisher.

Bill Mitchell, editor of *Cumbria*, was dispatched to Kendal to interview Wainwright, in order to write a little editorial about the book. He too had marvelled at the original pages, having been shown them by Harry Firth, who had arranged the interview. It took place at Wainwright's office, in an upper room at the Town Hall. Alas, Wainwright proved unsatisfactory as a interviewee. He wanted the free publicity, knew how important it was for an unknown author, but couldn't bear to do all the things first-time authors are expected to do. 'After twenty minutes,' remembers Bill Mitchell, 'it was clear that he wanted to retain his privacy. Instead, he quizzed me about the number of words and type of illustration of the proposed feature.'

Bill Mitchell then sent Wainwright a list of questions, asking him to type out his answers, which he did. The replies are rather stilted, giving nothing away about himself. The question asking for 'any interesting experiences' was obviously meant to illicit an amusing and easy-to-use anecdote, but AW wasn't going to play that game. Bill Mitchell has no memory of the replies to the questions ever arriving at *Cumbria*, so perhaps having typed them out, Wainwright never posted them. The surviving copy, found after he died, appears to be a top copy, corrected by hand.

Q. What impelled you to write this book?
Oddly, perhaps this is a question I have never asked myself and I am not sure that I can answer it satisfactorily. Certainly it cannot be answered in a single sentence. Ideas grow, like habits, until they become a way of life. What planted this particular seed in my mind is difficult to say. Perhaps I was born with it. Looking back, I seem always to have had a passion for hill-walking, even when a small boy; other enthusiasms have come and gone, but my love of the fells has been constant. As far back as I can remember, mountain country has attracted me and mountain literature

and maps have been my favourite reading. The growing supply of mountaineering books, with their inspiring photographs and diagrams, must have influenced me considerably. It was always an ambition of mine to climb Everest (it used to be my fondest wish to die on the summit, but I've grown up since then!) The Everest books fascinated me and I studied them intently: in imagination, how often have I toiled upwards towards its summit! Well, I could never go to Everest, but there was Scafell, and Helvellyn, and all the other fells I knew so well. They too had lofty ridges and hidden recesses, and, in winter, snow and ice; away from the paths there were wide areas of lonely territory to explore, places where few walkers go. Gradually the fells have taken the place of Everest in my life; they have provided the outlet for the climbing and exploring urge fostered by the many books of mountain travel. Some years ago I started to put a notebook and a pencil in my rucksack, and to be methodical in my wanderings. Later I started to be methodical in my notes, too. Every fell had to yield the answers to the same questions: the details of its structure, the best routes of ascent, the secrets of its untrodden places, the views from the top. I regarded them all as Himalayan giants, and myself as a lone explorer. The game took a hold on me as nothing else has ever done; it became a completely absorbing pastime, but more a passion than a pastime. For every day I could spend on the fells I had six in which I could do no climbing; these I started to spend in carefully putting my notes into more attractive form and planning future expeditions. The map of Lakeland had now become a vast territory for exploration, and I planned my walks as though conducting a military campaign. You remember the war maps, the black arrows of advancing troops, the pincer movements, the mopping-up operations? That's the way I worked, but my thoughts were not of war, but utterly at peace. A tremendous impetus was given to my investigations by the re-publication of the $2\frac{1}{2}''$ Ordnance Survey maps, which, though not up-to-date, contained a wealth of interesting detail and provided a fuller appreciation of the meticulous accuracy of the cartographer's art. With these fine maps as examples, my rough notes would never do for me now: the job I was tackling must be done properly. I must make my own up-to-date maps, my own diagrams, my own drawings, all carefully designed and presented as attractively as I could. Writing is a form of drawing, and it was natural that I should try to describe the fells in words, but only where necessary to supplement the illustrations. I started to put pen to paper in earnest, hesitatingly at first. That was in November 1952 and by Christmas 1954 I had completed the first part of my plan.

Q. Why does the book appear in this particular and unusual fashion, that is, entirely from hand-written manuscript?

Because the book was intended originally only as a personal chronicle of my observations, so that everything in it, the notes as well as the illustrations, was prepared by hand. The thought of publication came much later, when it began to appear to me that my observations would be of interest to others who shared my regard for the fells. So it is that the book that has emerged is nothing more than my own personal notebook, reproduced exactly as I penned it, and embellished with an introduction and a conclusion which serve the purpose of explaining the plan to which I have worked in compiling the information.

Q. Have you had any training in art or book-illustration?

No, I have had no training in drawing, but, because the fells were never out of my mind, I have for years occupied much leisure time in translating into pictures the vivid impressions I had of them. At first, I started to do this idly, but it quickly became an absorbing occupation and to me a very satisfying one because I found that by building up a favourite mountain from a blank sheet of paper I could experience the subtle joy of feeling that I was actually engaged upon the ascent physically as the familiar shape came in to being under the pen. To me, this was a discovery of some importance. I could now sit in my chair on a winter's evening and bring Scafell or Gable into the room with me. When I could not go to the hills I could make them come to me.

Q. You must have a remarkable amount of patience?

I don't think patience is the right word. Patience lies in doing a task unwillingly. When a task is done because it is enjoyed, it is enthusiasm.

Q. Have you had any interesting experiences during the making of the book?

If you mean during my walks, yes. Every walk is an interesting experience in itself, doubly interesting because it is walked with a definite purpose. I could not begin to detail my experiences now, although someday I hope to – when the Guide is finished. In general, I would say that the most intense experiences have occurred during nights spent on the fells. Occasionally (not often, and only in Summer) I have bivouacked alone in high places; these occasions remain vivid in memory! Nobody who has not done it can imagine the splendours of sunset and sunrise from the summits, the eerie stillness of the hours of darkness, the joy of being on the tops at dawn when the larks are rising. I recommend this to everyone who loves the fells, but I recommend company to all but guide-book writers.

Q. Do you always go alone?
Invariably. I prefer to go alone, and must be alone if I am to get any work done. One cannot concentrate and comprehend another's conversation at the same time. Besides, I should be a poor companion, for my walks must often seem to be erratic, leading into unfrequented corners, zig-zagging where there is no need to zig-zag, sometimes returning to the same summit two or three times during the course of a day. In fact, I have often reason to be thankful that my antics are not being observed!

Q. When do you expect to finish Book Two?
All being well, in the Autumn of 1956.

In a draft for an accompanying letter, apparently never sent either, Wainwright said he was enclosing a copy of the *Lancashire Evening Post* article, which has some biographical information, but he would prefer any piece about him to be in narrative form rather than an interview. In this letter, he also revealed things were not going well with the book. 'In fact, I'm ready to agree to anything to get a bit more publicity.' One problem had been a rail strike which had disrupted postal deliveries. 'At least I'm making that the excuse for the negligible response so far.

'Only 70 odd replies have been received to the 1400 leaflets sent out. Griffin's excellent article has produced only three enquiries and the June *Cumbria* only two! All this is a tremendous disappointment. Fortunately, the shops are doing better, but I don't know whether more than 150 copies have been sold as yet. On the brighter side, the reviews of the book have been excellent and I have had an offer (not accepted) from another publisher to publish the six volumes that are still to come. Still optimistic, I believe everything will be OK in due course. We'll see.'

He does not give any details of this publisher's offer, and it might only have been a vague suggestion, from perhaps the

Westmorland Gazette itself, but he was very worried about the slow sales – even more so when *Cumbria* decided not to use Bill Mitchell's interview. Harry Scott wrote to apologise, saying that some of the material had already been in the *Lancashire Evening Post*, and it was their policy not to duplicate stories, but in a future issue he would try to do something.

Publication of the book had been aimed for the Whit Bank Holiday in May 1955, traditionally the beginning of the tourist season in Lakeland, as opposed to Easter which can often be pretty cold. It wasn't until July, with the rail strike over, that the book began to sell in any numbers, and then it was basically due to word of mouth. Lakeland lovers slowly discovered it for themselves.

The first fan letters from readers arrived as early as June – sent to Henry Marshall's home, as that was the only address which was given in the book. Marshall himself answered all the trade queries, and some of the fan letters, but passed anything on addressed to Wainwright personally, as the author. Wainwright answered them all, either on Marshall's notepaper or from his office, not giving away his home address. He was particularly thrilled to receive a fan letter from the Lakeland author, W. A. Poucher, and in his reply said how much he admired and had used Poucher's books.

In July, the first foreign fan letter arrived – from a Stanley G. Harris of Chicago, who had somehow got a copy of the book, although he had never been to England. He hoped to visit Lakeland, with the Eastern Fells in his pocket, and asked for advice on the best months to come. He also put in an order to Marshall for the next six books, wanting them sent to him the minute they were published.

'He did come to Lakeland not long afterwards,' says Marshall's daughter, Gillian. 'We were most impressed because he had his own bank – Harris Bank. He and his wife stayed at the Langdale Chase Hotel, very posh, and my parents invited them to have Sunday lunch with us. What he really wanted was to meet Wainwright.'

Percy Duff, Wainwright's Deputy Treasurer, recalls Harris coming to the office to meet Wainwright, with everyone getting in a flap because they feared that Mr Harris, being an American, would ask for a cup of coffee and they only had tea. They usually took their sugar straight from the bag but for this important visitor they cleaned an ashtray and used it as a sugar bowl.

Gillian's memory of the summer of 1955 was of packing up books, every evening after she had come home from school, along with her younger brother. Every order came to Marshall's house, and was dispatched by hand, unless it was a relatively large one, which would be sent direct from the printer. 'If we got any orders ourselves, my father promised us half a crown on every copy sold.'

On 28 June 1955, Wainwright had received sufficient orders, and banked enough money, to make the printer a first payment of £100. The following month, he paid over another £100. By September he had paid a total of £400, almost half way. In February, 1956, oh joy, he paid off the last £100 owing. His debt to Bateman and Hewitson was now nil.

One of his fan letters was from Weaver Owen, the local bank manager with whom he'd once spent a night on the fells. AW wrote back to him on 7 February 1956, honouring him with some big news, and also telling him some old news which Weaver had not been aware of at the time.

Book One goes into a second impression at Easter (this time with an attractive 'jacket'). Book Two will be finished on September 30th, but publication will be held over until the following Easter. Thank you for your very generous remarks about my efforts. It pleases me to recall that you were the first person I told about my plans. (Grasmere bus stop after a hurried descent from High Raise). Remember?
AW.

The second impression, of 1000 copies, came out at Easter 1956 – complete with the attractive dust jacket. Harry Firth, the printer, ran off extra copies of the jacket, and put out a notice to the effect that those who had bought a jacket-less copy, could pick up one for free at the printer's, or by sending a stamped addressed envelope. 'We got more requests for that cover than we'd actually sold books. But it meant we started to acquire a huge mailing list.'

The cult of Wainwright had begun.

CHAPTER FIFTEEN

Pictorial Success, 1955–63

The success of Book One meant little in AW's office. Percy Duff, his closest colleague, remembers him being very apprehensive when it came out, worried that he would lose money, and then his quiet pleasure when it took off and they decided to reprint, but no one else in the office was really interested. It was the Treasurer's hobby, fellwalking, they always knew that, and it was nothing to do with them. It was many years before they realised how popular his books had become. Meanwhile, he got on with his job, always first in, often staying late for council meetings, attending to all the voluntary duties he had taken on as treasurer or secretary to various local organisations, most of which, such as those in the arts and music, held little interest for him.

As Borough Treasurer, he could appear very much a nit-picker, writing rather alarming and official letters on relatively humble misdemeanours, or suspected misdemeanours.

Dear Sir,
  I have today received your letter accepting the tenancy of a house on the Hall Garth Estate.
  There was a pound note in the envelope containing your letter. I do not understand why this was sent and should be obliged if you would let me know the reason. I will keep it until I have your explanation.

Mr Tate, the gentleman in question, went along to the Treasurer's office, very puzzled. 'Now then, young man,' so Wainwright said to him, 'what's the explanation?' Mr Tate could only suggest that his wife had put the pound out for the coal man, but by mistake it had gone in the wrong envelope. 'Mr Wainwright accepted my explanation, and produced the pound forthwith. Looking back, I can't image that even forty years ago, a pound would have been thought of as much of a bribe.'

In the town, when his first book started to sell well, most people did not associate the name A. Wainwright with their Treasurer, assuming it could not be the same person. Readers of Book One, and the subsequent Pictorial Guides, had no personal details to go on, as his day job wasn't given, or where he lived, nor his christian name. No photograph ever appeared. He had tried, in those early months, to do his bit towards publicising the first book, but once it had taken off, there was no real need. He was invited to appear on local radio, but refused. Instead, Henry Marshall agreed to be interviewed. 'Marshall was much more worldly than AW,' says Percy Duff. 'He knew what people wanted.'

As each book came out, Bill Mitchell wrote a bit about it in *Cumbria*, usually reproducing several drawings provided by Harry Firth, but held back from using a photograph of the author. He had managed to get one snap, from behind, of AW smoking his pipe, his shock of hair now going white, but kept it in his drawer, knowing AW was ultra private and that it would only annoy him. Many of those who bought his little books, but read only the sections on the climbs they were going to take, gave no thought to who the author was, or whether he was in fact still alive.

They were quite proud of him back in Blackburn, at least amongst his old colleagues who realised that all his bits of gifts had come together, that he had done what he always said he would do. Remote members of his own family wrote to congratulate him. One cousin from Penistone told him that his talent for drawing had come from Grandfather Wainwright – his father's father – who had apparently done a number of pen and ink sketches. One of them, of a railway viaduct near Penistone, had been sold after his death, and the family always wished they'd kept it.

Walter Laycock, from the Borough Treasurer's office in Black-burn, wrote with a long technical query about an old Rate Contributions book, but managed a word of praise in his last paragraph, if a bit begrudging. 'I have perused your book and take off my hat to you for a piece of magnificent workmanship, but the only time my interest quickened was on reading your reference to a newt.'

Wainwright's reply was much more to point.

I do wish you wouldn't bother me with such silly things as specific rate contributions when there are mountains and rivers and lakes and so much else far worthier of discussion.

All I remember about the Blackburn office is that there was a Bank Transfer Book with a column headed 'Tick'.

Thank you for your richly merited words of appreciation about 'The Eastern Falls'.

Now let me get back to my maps, and stop bothering.

Betty Ditchfield was sent a personal copy of Book One and, by the look of her grateful reply, not charged for it, but Wainwright must also have added some notes and memories in an accompanying letter to her, perhaps on the lines that she was still his fantasy woman. In her reply, she told him very sharply to snap out of it. 'The human sense is reluctant to be aroused from sleep, the realm of its foolish and mistaken dreams cannot deny that the figure you have outlined as mine in your prolonged mental aberration is just a person of your own fancy and wishful thinking. I haven't really changed – just changed mentally . . .'

She then advised him to read some spiritually uplifting books, which she listed, plus page references, and the letter ends in a welter of confused but very sincere religious utterings. Perhaps it was just as well he had never progressed very far with Miss D. Anyway, the fells were now his new passion, taking up his time and his dreamings.

In Harry Firth, the Westmorland Gazette printer, he had acquired a new friend who occasionally gave him a lift when he was going on his walks. They climbed Great Gable together, twice, and Red Pike, and Wainwright, taking a break from his Lakeland books, invited Mr Firth, as he always referred to him, on a holiday with him to Scotland.

Wainwright never discussed his marriage with Harry, or made any reference to Ruth, but now and again he would talk to Harry about Peter. 'When we were coming back from that holiday in Scotland, we stopped in Carlisle for a cup of tea in a café. AW looked at his watch and said he didn't want to get home before such and such a time. That struck me as odd. I was longing to get back to my wife and family. I suppose that was when I realised that all wasn't well, but I didn't speak to him about it.'

As each book was published, a little leaflet was inserted advising readers when the next would appear, encouraging them to place an order. 'Every book was eagerly awaited,' says Harry, 'and each time we sold about 500 copies in advance, getting the money in cash, cutting out the bookshops.'

Wainwright would never go to the Gazette's offices or print works. Harry had either to go to the Town Hall and meet him in his office, or visit him at home. Nor would he deal with other people, except Harry. 'The managing director of the whole Westminster Press group, Bill Morrell, became a great AW fan and he made my life hell,' said Harry, 'wanting me to arrange a meeting with AW. In the end I pleaded with him to do it, just as a favour to me. So AW agreed to come to the office for fifteen minutes and meet Morrell. He was completely ill at ease – and never agreed again to that sort of thing.'

Book Two, The Far Eastern Fells, came out at Easter 1957, and was dedicated to the memory of 'The men who built the stone walls'. It was still priced at 12/6, and printed by Bateman and Hewitson, but this time the engravings were done by the Westmorland Gazette. Henry Marshall was still the publisher. Harry Firth has no idea what their financial arrangement was but he thinks that Marshall got either twopence or threepence per book sold. In Wainwright's bank statements for 1955–57, he was paying regular payments to Marshall of £5 a month in the first year, which then went up to £10, but this may have been for postage only.

In Book Two he griped about Manchester Corporation, and how they had ruined Mardale, attacked grouse shooting and admitted he did not like encounters with cows and young bulls. He began making sweeping but harmless generalisations, calling a bog on Loadpot Hill 'the worst bog in Lakeland' and said that a boulder on Yoke 'may well be the biggest boulder in Lakeland'. As a change from sheep, he drew a young deer on The Nab, but not very well. Once again, he included one drawing of himself – on Harter Fell – sitting in his jacket with his back to a cairn, pipe in mouth, rucksack at his feet (*see* page 175).

For the first time, he was openly cavalier about rights of way (something which has subsequently caused certain problems and complaints). His explorations of the Deer Forest on The Nab were conducted without permission; he was not detected but comments that 'this may have been due to his marked resemblance to an old stag'.

In his Personal Notes at the end of Book Two he thanked everyone who had written kind and encouraging letters after Book One. 'There have also been offers of hospitality, of transport (I have no car nor any wish for one), of company and of collaboration and of financial help – all of which I have declined as gracefully as I could whilst feeling deeply appreciative, for I am stubbornly resolved that this must be a single-handed effort. I have set myself this task, and I am pigheaded enough to want to do it without help. So far, everything is all right. Sufficient copies of Book One were sold to pay the printer's bill, and here again I must thank all readers who recommended the book to others, for it is perfectly clear that, lacking full facilities for publicity and distribution, it could hardly have succeeded otherwise.'

Not a word of thanks to Henry Marshall, his 'publisher', who was still solely responsible for sales and distribution.

Book Three, The Central Fells, came out in 1958 and was dedicated to The Dogs of Lakeland, 'willing workers and faithful friends'. He made it clear on the ascent of Pavey Ark by Jack's Rake that he was not a rock climber, being more concerned 'with a primitive desire for survival' but said that 'walkers who can still put their toes in their mouths and bring their knees up to their chins may embark upon the ascent confidently'. On Ullscarf, he got justifiably steamed up about some schoolboys who had ruined a beacon, describing their inattentive masters as 'brainless idiots, a disgrace to their profession'. His now regular inclusion of himself in one drawing had a backview of him standing looking down over Thirlmere (see page 176).

His Personal Notes at the end of Book Three admitted the possibility that some details in the previous books were now out of date because of new buildings, new signposts, cairns being destroyed, but it was unlikely that he would ever make any revisions to the books. They would therefore be progressively withdrawn, or readers could add their own notes. The good news was that he was keeping the price of the books at 12/6, despite pressure from 'publisher, printer and booksellers alike'. So Henry Marshall did eventually get a mention, if not by name.

Book Four, The Southern Fells, came out in 1960 and was dedicated to The Sheep of Lakeland, 'the hardiest of all fellwalkers'. In describing an ascent of Black Fell, he says it 'may quickly lead to desperate manoeuvres in thick plantations', then he adds a jokey footnote: 'this latter note is also intended for the guidance of walkers, not of courting couples.' He raves about Bowfell, saying it is amongst the best half-dozen mountains in Lakeland, but teasingly refuses to give his other Bests, until he has finished Book Seven.

He has some fun on Coniston Old Man, mocking tourists who squeal with joy as they sight Blackpool Tower or Calder Hall Power Station. 'This book does not deign to cater for such tastes.'

THE SUMMIT

Tourists looking for Blackpool Tower

Boy Scouts

Typical summit scene

Solitary fellwalker, bless him, looking north to the hills

In the Harter Fell chapter, he does a nice drawing of a 'TAKE CARE DO NOT START FIRE' notice, adding that otherwise it will 'waste the effort spent in drawing all the little trees on this map'. He thinks he might have discovered a 35-feet high pinnacle on Pike o' Blisco, but doesn't want to hear from people who have known about it since childhood, or have climbed it blindfold, or stood on its point for hours on their heads.

Scafell Pike merits one of his very few double-page drawings, a magnificent bird's-eye view. In the Scafell section, he includes a drawing of himself sitting staring in awe (*see* page 176). There is also a dramatic spread for the Wastwater Screes. He appears again at the end of the book, under Personal Notes, being pestered by his dog Cindy, which he says is the reason for certain defects in his penmanship. Hard to see any at all, though on the second last page he appears to have corrected the word 'view', which is unusual for him – or was it just a blob?

Book Five, The Northern Fells, came out in 1962. It is dedicated to The Solitary Wanderers on the Fells, and yet when he gets to High Pike he is mourning the loss of the miners who used to be all over the area, feeling sad about the death of their dignified labour. He imagines a conversation between Dodd and Skiddaw which is amusing, and lambasts road widening in Lakeland, cutting off corners, making highways into racetracks. 'Where are the men of vision in authority?' Blencathra covers thirty-six pages in all, the most he devotes to any Lakeland mountain, even more than Scafell Pike which got thirty pages. He does a pretty drawing of Souther

Fell, but admits he has taken a liberty. 'Telegraph poles removed from this view without permission of the P.O. Engineers.'

The destruction of nature by man has become a recurrent theme, the disastrous effects of motors cars and roads, the vandalism of 'slovenly layabouts', yet he is not always consistent in his attacks. Not only has he forgotten about the damage caused by miners and quarries in the past, but in writing about Dodd he also approves of what many people at the time considered a modern abomination – the work of the Forestry Commission.

His self-portrait appears this time on the top of Binsey, describing himself as an Ancient Briton. He is in shirtsleeves and braces, looking a trifle fatter than in previous books (*see* page 176). In his Personal Notes at the end of Book Five, written in the autumn of 1961, he remarks on how few people he met while on the Northern Fells. 'I felt I was preparing a book that would have no readers at all, a script that would have no players and no public.' Coming next, he says, will be the North-Western Fells, 'old Kruschev willing'. Like Calder Hall, that is a reference which has rather dated.

From Book One, Clough Head 7

Haweswater
from the third cairn

From Book Two, Harter Fell 10

Book Six, The North Western Fells, came out in 1964, and was dedicated to 'those unlovely twins, MY RIGHT LEG and MY LEFT LEG, staunch supporters that have carried me about for over half a century, endured without complaint and never once let me down'. No drawing of them, however: 'they are unsuitable subjects for illustration.'

From Book Three, Raven Crag 4

From Book Four, Scafell 9

On the top of
Binsey..........

.......Prehistoric
Tumulus
and
Ancient
Briton

From Book Five, Binsey 7

From Book Six, Grasmoor 15

From Book Seven, Yewbarrow 9

He describes Catbells as having 'a bold "come hither" look . . . no suitor ever returns disappointed . . . No Keswick holiday is consummated without a visit to Catbells.' He is wearing a jacket for his only appearance in this book, sitting on Grasmoor, and the jacket is marked as Harris Tweed (*see* page 177).

When at last Book Seven appeared, in 1966, he reveals he wants his ashes to be scattered on Haystacks. At the time he wrote this he was only fifty-eight, so it was a bit premature. His portrait appeared at the very end of the book, this time wearing a cap. 'First time we've seen him with a cap on,' comments one sheep. 'He must be going bald or something,' says another sheep. An inverted joke because he was always very proud of his thick head of hair, even though it had by now turned completely white (*see* page 177).

At the end, as promised, he listed his Best fells, summits and ridge walks. He boasts that he has completed his thirteen-year task one week ahead of schedule – one week before the end of the summer bus timetable. He also reveals that he had made a small fortune from the books – all of which he is going to give to animals, helping the RSPCA to set up an animal shelter in Kendal.

Harry Firth remembers how surprised he was at the first mention of this. 'We were sitting in a café in Keswick one day, when AW asked me if the books continued to sell, could I guarantee him an income of £500 a year for the next seven years. I think he wanted to do some sort of covenant for animals. I said he certainly could. Sales were going up every year.'

Wainwright had made a fair amount of money by the standards of the day, considering that his seven little books were purely of local interest. They had by now run into many impressions. At the time of the appearance of the fifth book in 1962, Book One had had nine impressions including the first printing, Book Two six, Book Three ten, and Book Four nine. The initial print for each new book was 2,000, while a new impression was usually 1,000. So, with five first printings and thirty subsequent impressions, the total in print by 1962 was 40,000.

Some time in the following year, 1963, sales had reached a total of 50,000, a magnificent achievement when you remember Westmorland Gazette had no sales force, no distribution agreement with any other company, and that all the paper work – orders and invoices – was still being done by Henry Marshall in his back room. Wainwright considered it called for some sort of celebration.

'He told me he was going to take us to Scotland, on a rail runaround ticket,' says Harry Firth. 'Me and Henry Marshall. It was going to be his treat. He'd pay all our expenses. Just before we set off, he rang me to say that Marshall was no longer coming. He didn't explain the reason, but I gathered they'd fallen out. I don't know why. So just the two of us went.'

Harry Firth should have guessed the reason. Some time in 1963, Wainwright had decided that it was time to let the Westmorland Gazette take over the publishing and business side of his books, tired of trying to cope with all the paper work. It was AW's idea, according to Harry, but naturally, the Gazette was pleased to accept.

'We didn't draw up a proper publishing contract at this time,' said Harry Firth. 'I wasn't well versed in that sort of thing. It was all based on loyalty on either side. From memory, I think we agreed to pay him 1/6d a copy on every book sold from then on.'

AW sold them all the books he had in stock, for the sum of £753. A Westmorland Gazette sticker was stuck onto the title page, over the bit that had had Henry Marshall's name, until they had the opportunity of printing their own name as publisher: this began with the next book, Book Six.

Henry Marshall was devastated. It is not known how Wainwright broke the news to him, but it took him two days to calm down. He then wrote a very careful and polite letter, clearly showing how hurt and disappointed he and his wife Edith were.

12th September, 1963

Dear Mr Wainwright,

It has taken me a couple of days to get used to the idea of the Gazette 'take-over'. Although neither you or Firth have mentioned any negotiations it was obvious that something like this was bound to happen.

In the first place, I think the offer a reasonable one. Any firm will jump at a product which has an assured market, particularly if that firm is specially geared to production, a market which has laboriously been built up for them. And so a commercial concern takes over. Inevitable, I suppose, but a little sad and far removed from the original ideas and ideals.

Secondly, my advice, for what it is worth, is to accept. The new arrangement should solve your problems and free you from tedious donkey work. I have no doubt that you will accept the offer and I think that you will be doing the best thing from your point of view.

Now that the books are about to become 'business' and all connection between us is to cease I would like to make one or two comments. Comments which cannot affect the situation in any way but which I think should be said.

Whoever else has or is about to make money out of the 'Wainwright' books I think that it cannot be said to be me. Almost every day for some years I, and latterly Edith, have spent some time, often considerable time (I don't think you have the vaguest idea of just *how* much time) in packing and posting parcels and in conducting correspondence. Here again I don't think you have the slightest conception of just how much correspondence there is. All you see is that which concerns you personally. I think the Gazette will be surprised, too, in due course.

I think it might be interesting (now that the books are about to become 'business' and there is no feeling in it) to check up the cost per annum (i.e. the total number of £12.10.0's you have actually paid out) and spread them over the ten years for the following: –

1. The use of my name and address. Not much, perhaps, but it provided you with an imprint you liked and, even more, shielded you from all unwanted contact with the outside world.
2. The use of a room at Low Bridge, devoted entirely to the books, for ten years.
3. The use of a telephone over those ten years.
4. The packing and posting of all orders except the very large 'wholesale' parcels.
5. The conducting of all correspondence other than that addressed to you personally or dealing with detailed financial matters.

6. Personal attention for all this time to all customers, whether booksellers or individuals. The Gazette won't be able to afford this even if they could do it.

These are bare bones. Work out the cost per annum and I don't think any unprejudiced person would say that I made money out of the Wainwright books.

You will have forgotten by now the early days, and all the work that was put into the launching of the books. It all seems so easy now, so routine. My first negotiations with Sandy Hewitson and others, the problems of production (now routine). The building up of contacts (you were complete aloof and remote from all this) by my contacts with booksellers and individuals and so on. Perhaps all this seems a long time ago to you. But it was a period of hard work over a very long period. You have probably accepted it as the Gazette will accept it when the take-over is complete.

None of these things matter now. The books are a great success. You will be free and happy, with an assured income (*which you very richly deserve*). The Gazette is on to a good thing. All's well that ends well.

There will, of course, be difficulties in the changeover. My name is on every book, my contacts are many. It will probably be years before all traces are removed. We shall cope and I don't suppose that you will suffer any inconvenience, any more than you have in the past.

I am quite certain that you will accept the Gazette's offer, if with modifications. I am equally certain that you are doing the right thing. It is the answer to your problems. For my part I will do everything possible to make the changeover as smooth as possible.

You have my most sincere wishes so far as the new order is concerned. I hope that it will make you happy and that you will have the good health and the strength to complete the series. I am quite certain that you will and that you will have more cause than most to feel a proud and happy man.

GOOD LUCK!

A sad letter. Through clenched teeth he had managed to control his anger and bitterness, trying to be fair and reasonable. Wainwright probably never knew how much Henry Marshall had done as 'publisher' of the Guides, nor how pleased he was that he had helped to ensure their success.

The official handing over of the Pictorial Guides to the Westmorland Gazette took place on 31 October 1963. Wainwright, in his best accountancy handwriting, did a comprehensive statement of the income and expenditure for the eight years of operation and five books completed thus far. The cost of printing the 50,000 books had been £17,511. Stationery had been £170, Advertising £59. Postage and carriage £616 and Author's out-of-pocket expenses £305. There was no mention of what Marshall had received as Publisher, and it's not clear what he meant by the '£12.10.0's per annum, mentioned in his letter, but there was a cost of £600 described as 'Clerical Assistance'. If Marshall had been getting 3d. per book, this would about equal that sum.

All together, expenditure had come to £19,402. The total income from book sales had been £21,801 which left Wainwright with an operating profit of £2,399 subject, of course, to tax. Not a huge amount. The WG's profit must have been a great deal more, but this is not known.

As Marshall said in his letter, they had had ideals, not business objectives, in setting up their little operation. He died the following year, on 7 October 1964, aged fifty-eight, after a blockage in his arteries: just six weeks before his death, he had completed a long-distance climb. 'It's the lack of gratitude that has always upset me,' says his daughter Gillian. 'He worked for years to help the Wainwright books. It's wicked that his hard work was unacknowledged.'

CHAPTER SIXTEEN

Ruth – the Truth?

What was Ruth doing all this time? Being totally neglected, that's one obvious answer, as Wainwright did not leave himself a free moment for her or anyone else during the thirteen years he spent on the Pictorial Guides. But then she had grown used to that, over many years, first in Blackburn and then in Kendal.

On the other hand, you could argue that Wainwright had acted with consideration, taking himself out of the house, keeping out of her way, as they clearly could hardly stand each other, making the best of a bad mistake which they had mutually made and mutually had decided, for whatever perverse reasons, to continue. He had a respectable, responsible job at which he worked hard, always behaving with proper decorum, and in his spare time he kept himself occupied in a healthy, harmless way. A model husband, some might say. He hadn't taken to drink, as he never liked the stuff, apart from the odd half of beer after a long walk, or to chasing other women, not since his Blackburn days, though that idle thought did enter his head from time to time. He never bad-mouthed his wife. No outsider knew about the state of his marriage.

In fact, readers of the Pictorial Guides might have presumed he was not married, for despite a trickle of personal details and opinions – his dog Cindy, his pipe, his hatred of school parties on the fells – there was no clue to his domestic life. It was only in Book Seven, in 1966, that he revealed he was married. This final book in the series is dedicated to All Who Have Helped Me. In this he includes 'my wife, for not standing in my way'. It had taken him a long time to get round to mentioning her, far less thanking her. Had she finally protested? Threatened to do something? Or was it simple guilt that perhaps he might have tried a bit harder to make her life more bearable, more normal, more interesting even? It is unlikely he ever thought that, not for many years at least, because in *Ex-Fellwanderer*, published in 1987, he states that the marriage was a mistake, almost from the beginning.

It was a mistake because I was climbing a ladder to a professional career, but my wife, a mill girl, had no wish to leave the bottom rung. We had little in common and later nothing. If there are any young fellows reading these lines, my advice is to shop around for someone with similar interests and aspirations. Women may all *seem* alike with a blanket over their heads, but they are not.

For a common mill girl, we know she did take interesting holidays, eventually going abroad once a year, with her sister, son, other relatives or friends. She liked going abroad, exploring foreign parts, which her husband never did. We know she sat and read novels, again unlike her husband. She kept dogs and bred them – Cindy was her dog, not her husband's. And she had several loyal, long-standing women friends, one of whom was Beryl Williams who lived in Burneside Road, Kendal, not far from the Wainwright house.

They had met one day in 1948 as Mrs Williams was out walking her dog Bracken, a cocker spaniel. She was sitting on Kendal Green when a slightly older woman, whom she had never seen before, called out to her, asking her if she'd like to come for a walk with her and her dog. The woman had a white West Highland terrier called Cinders. So off they went. They walked through Serpentine Wood, passed the quarry, up to the golf course and round, a walk which took them about two and a half hours, including stops to watch the dogs run around or to sit and chat.

For the next twenty-five years, they continued to do that exact walk, almost every afternoon. Ruth Wainwright had to be home at lunchtime, for her husband always walked back from his office for his lunch, spending exactly one hour, but, after that, her time was her own. She would meet Beryl at two o'clock on Kendal Green, do their regulation walk, then be back by four-thirty. 'Every week day, in all weathers. There were two golfers who used to set their watches by us.'

Beryl was aged thirty when they met, Ruth then being thirty-nine. She originally came from Manchester but her husband, Harold Williams, manager of a local pet shop, was born in Kendal. They had no children. What did they talk about for twenty-five years? 'Oh it was mainly doggy talk. She'd talk about her dog, then I'd talk about my dog. Sometimes she'd reminisce about her holidays. But surely there was some personal chat? 'Well, sometimes she'd talk about Peter, but hardly ever about her husband.'

After a couple of years, they added another event to their afternoon ritual – shopping on Wednesday and Friday mornings. They would meet at ten, then go together to the Co-Op. Neither had a car, so all shopping had to be humped home by hand. After shopping, they usually had coffee together at Riggs. 'Ruth always had to be home in time to make Alfred's lunch. He never apparently said a word. Just ate his lunch, and went back to his office.'

As they became more friendly, they progressed to visiting each other's houses. Beryl started popping into Ruth's for a cup of tea or coffee – but only when her husband was not at home. 'I knew I had to leave before he arrived. But that didn't really strike me as very strange. I always knew he was a bit queer. Ruth sometimes bred cairn terriers, so there would often be puppies around the place, waiting to grow old enough to be sold to new homes. When Alf was out at work, or off walking, they would play around the kitchen, but when he came home, they had to go into an outhouse – he couldn't bear their yapping.

'I did meet him a few times, when I went to the house to pick up Ruth. He'd just grunt at me and mutter that she was getting ready – and then leave me standing on the doorstep. Initially, he did seem to make an effort to say a few words but then even that stopped. He'd just look at me, say nothing and glance away. It was the same if I met him in the town. It was as if he didn't know me – not that it bothered me.'

One Christmas time – Beryl thinks it was 1960 – Ruth invited Beryl round for what she called a little party for three of her friends. The other guests were Beryl's sister Eileen and a slightly older woman, Mrs Wildman. After tea, Beryl offered to do the washing up, but Ruth appeared very relaxed and said she would do it later. 'We were sitting chatting away when I heard these Big Feet going up the stairs. No one else had heard anything and told me I was imagining things. Shortly afterwards, I heard them again – and so did Ruth. She got up hurriedly, opened the door and listened. "Everybody out," she cried, "he's back!" '

Ruth didn't give them time even to put on their coats, but hurried them out of the house. Mrs Wildman was worried about the slippery conditions underfoot, so Ruth gave her a pair of thick socks to put over her shoes and then she and Beryl walked her home. 'I then offered to walk back to the house with Ruth, but she said no. "I'll deal with him. I've had a nice time, so I'm not bothered with what he says." It sounds quite funny looking back now, but we were all a bit scared at the time.

'As time went on, Ruth did tell me odd things about their life, what Alf had said, what Alf liked and didn't like, but she never moaned about him or complained. That was how he was. She was a good walker, you know, but he wouldn't walk with her. I felt sorry for her. She deserved better.

'All the same, I thought they were happy enough – well, to a certain extent, as much as many people are. I knew she couldn't have friends in. I knew she wasn't allowed to make any real decisions. She once chose a new suite, came home and told Alf about it. When it arrived, it was different. She presumed the shop had made a mistake. But they hadn't. Turned out Alf had gone to the shop and changed the order. She was never allowed her own taste. She didn't moan, just accepted it.

'She told me once how she'd collapsed in the night on the bathroom floor. I don't know what caused it. She never told me that, just that it was some time before Alfred found her there. When he eventually did, he went to a neighbour's house to phone the doctor. They never had a phone in their house. Alfred wouldn't have one. When the doctor came, he told Alfred off for not covering Ruth up with a blanket. He'd just left her lying there, on the bathroom floor. She was told by Alfred not to talk about her collapse. He didn't want any scandal. Perhaps she was run down, or worried. Or it might have been caused by something she didn't tell me. I don't know.

'Ruth used to read a lot, going to the library every week and getting out novels. She read in the bath, so she once told me, balancing the book on the taps. And I know she also liked football and went at least twice to watch Blackburn Rovers.'

On her own? 'As far as I know.'

Perhaps she was also visiting relations? 'I think she did visit her sister Doris.'

Was it at the same time as he went? 'I don't know, but I suppose they would have met, if it had been, coming back on the same train, so I suppose they went at different times.'

Beryl always enjoyed her walks and talks with Ruth, finding her friendly, open and cheerful. 'He didn't deserve her. She was grand company and never moody. I'd say she was a good person. And I'd say a good wife. She never complained about him, never asked him for anything, well, except that she was kept short of money. All she had was £10 a week housekeeping for everything.'

According to Harold, Beryl's husband, Ruth always looked older than her years. Her face became wrinkled, her skin sallow, and her hair turned grey. On one occasion when Beryl, who still looks remarkably youthful at seventy-six, was out with Ruth, Beryl was mistaken for her daughter.

'No, I wouldn't say Ruth was attractive,' says Beryl, 'just her plain self. I hadn't noticed the cast in her eye till she mentioned it.'

Ruth might have had no real contact with her husband for the last twenty years or so, but she still had her son Peter. After he left home and moved to Windermere, Peter Wainwright kept in touch with his mother. When, in 1957, he was called up for National Service, he went into the Royal Engineers where he found the square-bashing very easy. 'That was because of all the walking I'd done with my father.'

After National Service, he intended to return to Windermere, but the local gas works had closed. Instead he took a job as an engineer in Bahrain, working with the Bahrain Petroleum Company. He went out in 1959 and stayed there for the next fifteen years. His mother wrote to him regularly. He very rarely heard from his father.

Various Blackburn relatives kept in contact with Ruth, including Alfred's sisters, Annie and Alice, and their children. They always found her friendly and welcoming, although Alfred, as ever, was not quite so sociable.

'I wouldn't say he was grumpy,' says Jack Fish, Alice's son. 'He just wasn't interested. He'd say, "Hello Jack," when I arrived. At the end of the week when I was leaving, Aunty Ruth would say to him, "Jack's leaving now." He would then say, "Goodbye Jack." All he wanted to do was get on with his drawings.'

Annie's grand-daughter Linda Collinge, who now lives near Carlisle, remembers that her Great Aunt Ruth always sent her Christmas presents when she was a little girl, and also sent her a wedding present when she got married – but she heard nothing from Alfred. 'I believe that, in 1956, Ruth wanted a silver wedding party, but Alfred refused. I was told she had it on her own.'

Linda Collinge tells of visiting Kendal and that Ruth was always kind and chatty, but her uncle would disappear and stay in his room working. 'When I went with my husband, Uncle Alfred would often exchange a few words with him about football, but he would never talk to me. I decided he didn't like women.

'We were visiting one Saturday afternoon, and he had stayed in his room as usual. He was taken up a cup of coffee and down came a message for my husband – giving him Blackburn Rovers' half-time score. Almost human. But when I said goodbye, he didn't say one word in reply. I don't think I ever got more than a few words out of him. When I was young, he seemed so surly, but my grandma was very fond of him so I just labelled him an eccentric. He was quite close to Annie. He gave her and Bill some money when Bill had heart trouble so he had a generous streak. Annie always thought of him as her little brother, but she didn't read any of his books. She said she didn't like black and white, she preferred colour.'

None of the relatives had the slightest inkling of any marriage difficulties between Ruth and Alfred. They were accepted as they were, and always had been, although most felt a bit sorry for Ruth, considering Alfred a bit odd, a bit selfish – like many men, pre-occupied with his own interests, but nothing more unusual or more serious than that.

One day, Ruth came round to Beryl Williams's house in great distress. It was some time in 1966, but Beryl's not sure when.

'She told me that Alfred had got another woman. I didn't believe it. I assumed all his walking had been on his own. I was stunned. I told her not to worry, it couldn't be true. Then she said that gossip was flying round Kendal. Other people seemed to know, and she didn't. 'I can't stay in the house,' she said, 'if he has other women there, but what can I do? I've nowhere to go.'

'When I asked her how she knew, she said someone had told her. She'd been stopped in the street by a friend of hers. "Saw your Alfred dropped off in our street again." When Ruth asked her what she meant, she was told that some woman was often seen dropping off her husband at the same place. A woman in a Mini, I think she said, a little car, anyway. Alfred was a big man, so it was awkward for him to get out of a small car. That was how she'd first noticed it was him.

'Ruth then decided to look in his desk in the dining-room. She knew she shouldn't have done this, as it wasn't her nature to be deceitful, but she looked – and found a letter.'

From him to a woman, or vice versa? Beryl wasn't sure. 'But a letter Ruth found made her convinced that her husband was having an affair . . .'

CHAPTER SEVENTEEN

Wainwright and his Women

Alfred Wainwright had several women in his life. On his death, photographs of five different women were found in his wallet, kept in a drawer, but we'll come to them later.

He often made references to women in his books, some oblique, some suggestive, as in the 1938 *Pennine Journey*, and also in his later writings. 'My chances with the ladies were few and far between,' he wrote in *Ex-Fellwanderer*. When sleeping out overnight, so he said, he would think back on the women he might have married. In his letters, he made remarks about his eye for a pretty leg, or a pretty bottom.

These must be AW's jokes, so most people presumed, readers as well as his closer male friends. AW having his bit of fun. For in real life he didn't appear like that at all, being rather buttoned up, shy, old fashioned and prudish. It was on paper, and in his mind, that his fancy seemed to run away, if just to thoughts of Miss D in the Blackburn office, and what might have been. In real life, his relationships with women appeared distant and remote, even antagonistic. Or were they?

He kept up his regular visits to Doris Snape, the widow of his old football friend from his Blackburn days, visits which always worried Ruth. In his Kendal office, he had his devoted secretary-typist, Miss Thompson. A few passing females gave him lifts, when he was going about his duties, taking pity on his car-less, companionless, apparently woman-less state.

But there were also two women, middle-class, bright, attractive and assertive women, each around fifteen years younger than himself, who came into his life and remained firm friends.

Mary Burkett, OBE, was the indomitable director of his local museum and gallery in Kendal, Abbot Hall, which she built up into one of the nation's best, winning countless awards and plaudits. Miss Burkett went on to be a Director of Border TV, a member of the Arts Council and various worthy bodies. She is now retired, still unmarried, living in a stately home, Isel Hall, near Cockermouth, which she inherited from a friend and very distant relative.

She arrived at Abbot Hall in 1962, not long after it opened, having been an art lecturer at Charlotte Mason College in Ambleside. She became Director of Abbot Hall in 1966 and found she had a lot of business connections with Mr Wainwright, in his role as Borough Treasurer and also as Hon. Curator of the other, longer established but smaller museum, Kendal Museum, which she eventually took over, thanks to his help.

'He looked apprehensive when I first went to his office on gallery business, sitting there, puffing his pipe. I'd picked up that he wasn't keen on women, especially professional women, but there was a quiet warmth there and we soon became good friends. It helped that I don't think he was frightened of me.'

She often gave him a lift, if they were meeting on business, or drove him to the beginnings of his walks and expeditions when she got to know him better. In April 1969, she arranged to take him across Cumbria to Ravenglass, on the west coast, which he had never visited. 'I'd told him about the Roman fort which used to be there and because we'd talked a lot about the Romans in Cumbria, he was very excited. Before we set off, he sent me a note which I still have. 'If it's fine, can we go the way the Romans travelled, from Ambleside to Ravenglass – AW.' It's the only way you can go, but he was so keen.

'He reacted liked an intelligent child when we got there, looking round the Roman remains in a sort of naive astonishment. As we were walking round the site, I decided to take his photograph, so I got out my camera, and clicked. 'Did you take my photo?' he asked, glaring at me. I said yes, and laughed, knowing he didn't like his photograph taken, but I knew he knew I was taking it.

No, I never fancied him, not in that way. We never kissed or anything. He was sweet and he had such warmth, but I never had my eye on marrying him.

'He talked a little about his wife, Ruth, but not much. He said she lives in one room, I live in the other. Only the cat goes from one room to another. That was their only contact. He never said anything beastly about her, except that he took to walking the hills to get out of the house. I did once go to Kendal Green, on business, and was given coffee. Ruth stayed in the next room and I never met her. He did sometimes mention his son in passing, but seemed sort of bitter, stilted.'

They did once spend the night in the same hotel, all very innocent, although some gossip did circulate round Kendal. This was in 1966 when he was working on his *Pennine Way Companion*. He had to get near Sheffield, to the start of a section of the walk, and it happened she was going that way anyway, and so offered to drive him there. '"Oh could you, Miss Burkett?" he said. "I'll book the hotel." Which he did, the best in Buxton. I remember I had a headache that day, and felt rotten, but my eyes popped out of my head when I got to the hotel and saw how splendid it was. We had dinner together, and a drink, then I went to bed. There was no question of doing anything further. It was absolutely not like that. Next day, after breakfast, when I went to reception to pay my bill, I was told "the gentleman has paid". I blushed deeply at the time, but looking back it was funny. Goodness knows what the receptionist thought. He went off for his walk during the day, and in the evening I picked him up and brought him back to Kendal.'

Wainwright later did her a big favour, when Abbot Hall was desperate for money, by offering to donate an entire book to the Gallery and Museum. This was *Wainwright in Lakeland*, published in 1983 by Abbot Hall, not the Westmorland Gazette, so that they kept the profits. The book is almost entirely Lakeland drawings, with a few extracts from earlier books. It was dedicated to the memory of Francis Scott (of the Provincial Insurance Company, Kendal) who turned his dream of an art gallery at Abbot Hall into a reality. One thousand copies were printed, numbered and signed by Wainwright, which sold at £15. Today, these fetch around £175 each. There were also one hundred copies bound in morocco leather, which sold for £50 at the time – and now go for £350. Abbot Hall made about £15,000.

Over the years, Mary organized three exhibitions of Wainwright's work in Kendal – and not every art expert thought she should have done. 'I had to justify showing him because he was an amateur, not an RA or an academic. I argued that you had to look at Wainwright in the round. Technically, his drawings were good, but not brilliant, and he did a lot of reconstructing from photographs. They would not perhaps have justified an exhibition on their own, but Wainwright was his own art form which he had created. You had to take into account his words, his layout and his great love of Lakeland – not just his drawings. I don't think he considered himself an artist, more an illustrator, but he was quite proud in the end of what he'd done. He was a stickler for detail, and very scrupulous.

'I always found him funny, in a dry sort of way. I can still hear him saying, "Did you take that photo?" That still makes me laugh. The younger generation didn't find him funny. To them he was very formal and retiring. He *was* retiring, oh goodness. I never ever managed to get him to turn up at any openings, of his exhibitions or anyone else's.

'When he fell out with people, that was it. He was never mealy-mouthed. He saw things in black and white. "People annoy me," he used to say. "You can't go wrong with animals." He hated modern art, so we kept off that subject, and we didn't discuss cats. I'm increasingly anti-cats because of what they do to birds. Cats are man-made bird extinguishers, a menace to nature, in my opinion, though you couldn't tell him that. But I always liked him. You could trust him, because he never passed on gossip.'

Another clever, talented female friend was the writer Molly Lefebure. She made contact with him much earlier, in 1957, around the publication of Book Two, the Far Eastern Fells, at the time when she and her husband, John Gerrish, an oil company executive, bought their farmhouse near Keswick. She went to London University, and worked as a medical secretary to Keith Simpson, the pathologist, before becoming a novelist, biographer, and author of several books about Lakeland, one of which, *Cumbrian Discovery*, is dedicated to Wainwright.

Molly first wrote to Wainwright about Book Two, pointing out some error or confusion, details of which she now can't remember, and Wainwright wrote back and said she was wrong, he was right. They then started a regular correspondence which went on for many years, sometimes once a week, without meeting. 'In one letter he asked if I was broad hipped, as he liked broad-hipped women. I said I was thin, which I was at the time, and my hips were not at all generous. He then started referring to me as undernourished. When he found out I came from London, he called me a guttersnipe. That became his favourite quip from then on.

'He then started leaving chocolates for me, the joke being that I was undernourished and needed feeding. When he was out working on the Guides he would hide a chocolate bar for me, and give me clues where it was.'

In Book Seven, the Western Fells, he announced on one page (Lank Rigg 7) that he had left some buried treasure, all of two shillings, near the Ordnance column, on the top of the hill. It's a witty paragraph, which still appears in every copy, even though the book first came out in 1966.

> **Buried Treasure on Lank Rigg**
> The only exciting experience in the lonely life of the Ordnance column occurred on a gloriously sunny day in April 1965, when it was a mute and astonished witness to an unparalleled act of generosity. In an uncharacteristic mood of magnanimity which he has since regretted, the author decided on this summit to share his hard won royalties with one of his faithful readers, and placed a two-shilling piece under a flat stone: it awaits the first person to read this note and act upon it. There is no cause to turn the whole top over as though pigs have been at it — *the stone is four feet from the column*. If the treasure cannot be found at this distance it can be assumed that a fortunate pilgrim has already passed this way rejoicing. The finder may be sufficiently pleased to write in c/o the publishers and confirm his claim by stating the year of the coin's issue. If nobody does so before the end of 1966 the author will go back and retrieve it for the purchase of fish and chips. It was a reckless thing to do, anyway.

He sent her a copy of the book, hot from the presses, signed 'To Molly, because I like her', with an accompanying note: 'Be quick, Molly, get your boots on. I want you to be the one to find the hidden treasure. Then you can write to *Cumbria* and tell them what a clever girl you are.'

A few weeks later, on 22 March 1966, he wrote again.

Dear Molly,
This isn't a reply to your last letter, not yet. It is written just to tell you not to go rooting about on Lank Rigg. The buried treasure was found by a Seaton (Workington) man and his wife and child at 9.20 am on March 12, after a dawn start from home. I'm downright sorry, love. I wanted desperately for you to find it. You get so little pleasure out of life. Someday soon I'll hide something else, and tell only you where to find it.

At the end of Book Seven, in his Personal Notes, he mentioned three books he was now working on, just in case any of his fans thought he was packing up, now his thirteen-year task was over. There was the *Pennine Way Companion*, which came out in 1968, published by the Westmorland Gazette and done in the same format as the Pictorial Guides to the Lakeland Fells. There was *A Lakeland Sketchbook* which came out in 1969 – the first in a long series, consisting purely of drawings, plus captions.

The first new project, though, was *Fellwanderer*, and Harry Firth stuck leaflets at the end of Book Seven saying it was coming. This told the story of the Pictorial Guides, included some of his own not very good photographs (and, surprisingly, one of himself), plus a lot of his drawings, and around 15,000 words of random recollections on his fellwalking experiences.

He sent Molly the manuscript, asking her editorial opinion, as a professional writer. 'I made a few changes, suggesting he should take out various things, such as boasting that he peed into the Thirlmere streams every time he went near them. This was because he hated the Water Board people for turning the lake into a reservoir. I said it was unwise, encouraging other walkers to do the same, and the Water Board people would object. "Have some people no sense of humour?" he wrote to me, but he took it out. I didn't manage to talk him out of the shape of the book. I thought it was very awkward and would stick out on bookshelves. I said he should do it like the Guides, but he wouldn't listen. He could be very stubborn.'

The book was officially dedicated to 'Fellwalkers, past and present' but in Molly's copy he has written 'For Molly, for helping.'

In the book itself, there's a long section referring to Molly by name, all about her conviction that she had discovered a stone circle on Burnbank Fell. He describes how he tried and failed to find it, mocking Molly, calling the non-existent stone circle 'Molly's Folly' and 'Molly's Shame'. He quotes at length from her letter in reply, adding that the letters between them should be published – suitably edited.

To this day, Molly is convinced she is right, and that the stone circle is there, and still objects to him mocking her in the very book she had been at pains to help him with.

However, they still remained friends and in 1968 he agreed to do the illustrations for a children's book she had written, *Scratch and Co.* This is about a cat expedition to climb a great mountain, on the lines of the Everest Expedition, except it's Scafell in Lakeland. She sent him the manuscript, still without having met him, and he sent some sketches which she thought were very good. Her agent had never heard of Wainwright, nor had the editors at her publisher, Gollancz, but Livia Gollancz herself had heard of AW, since she loved Lakeland, and was delighted that he had agreed. The book was a success, came out in paperback and was sold in the USA and France. Alas, the foreign publishers had not heard of Wainwright, and didn't think much of his drawings, so in their editions they commissioned new illustrators.

Wainwright drew a large map of the cats' expedition, nicely illustrated, which is at the beginning of the book, and several smaller sketches inside of various cats which are amusing. He also did the dust jacket illustration for the British edition, which is not quite so good. The mountain is suitably awesome, but some of the cats in the foreground are rather clumsily drawn.

The cover and frontispiece from Scratch and Co *by Molly Lefebure*

They then did a second children's book, also about cats, called *The Hunting of Wilberforce Pike* which Gollancz published in 1970. Some years later, they started on a third, Wainwright doing some initial sketches, but his eyes were going and the book never saw the light of day.

Wainwright gave away his royalties on both books – the first one to an anti-bullfighting campaign and the second to Animal Rescue, Cumbria. When the Public Lending Right started, he passed his share of the income to Molly.

Throughout thirteen years or so, corresponding and helping each other, they had still never met. She is unsure when she eventually did meet him, but thinks it might not have been until 1970. 'I arrived at Kendal Green with my husband, John. The first thing AW said, when he opened the door, was, "Did you have to bring him?" John didn't mind. He took our pretend Great Romance in his stride.'

In the 1970s, Molly and Wainwright spent a lot of time walking and planning and discussing a book they would do together on the old roads of Lakeland. Molly had been researching these and had dug out numerous old maps which, of course, fascinated Wainwright.

'We went to look at an old drovers' road over Shap one day. He said the old road had gone one way, but I refused to believe him, saying it must have gone another way. We stood there on Shap, yelling at each other. He said I was wrong. I called him a bloody old fool. Oh, we had a right old doo-daa.'

Some time later, Wainwright made approaches to her again. 'You've gone off me, that's why you don't write,' he said in a note when he sent her a copy of his *Coast to Coast Walk* in 1973.

He eventually went back on his own to the idea of a book on the old roads, doing the maps and illustrations, but asked Molly to write an introduction, which she did. 'He sent it back, all corrected, saying it was too long and, anyway, I couldn't write. When I objected to him tampering with my text he said he was only trying to improve it. He said I could be his researcher, not his co-writer. I said no thanks, I had better things to do.'

The book did come out in the end – *Old Roads of Eastern Lakeland* – in 1985, a slim paperback, just seventy pages long. 'A wretched little book, I thought,' said Molly, 'not what we had originally hoped to produce. But we had left it too late. It was really my fault.'

They remained friends, despite the rows and the disagreements, and he visited Molly and John at their Keswick home, but looking back, she thinks it was very much a love–hate relationship.

'I thought he was a good writer. Perhaps a better writer than an artist. He made me laugh. I also respected him as a man. He had great integrity, very loyal, would never let you down, was always honest and honourable – all the old-fashioned virtues. I loved his love of Lakeland. He was a romantic. I admired his wonderful drive, his amazing energy. He lived for his books.

'I once said to him, long before we'd met, that now he'd finished his great series he should buy his wife a beautiful new hat to compensate for having been left alone so much. He never replied to that. No, he never talked about his wife, but I gathered from stray remarks he had an empty married life. He was very lonely, communication with others could never have been easy for him. He felt secure with his pen, his typewriter and the knowledge that the post-box was between him and the recipient of his letters. At a safe distance, he could relax and let himself go. He had a robust sense of humour and you never knew what to expect next. He didn't mind having his leg pulled, though it grew more risky as time passed. When I finally met him, he turned out to be remarkably silent, rather formal and shy.

'What I didn't like about him was his conceit, which got worse as he got older. I don't mean as a person, but as a writer. He did begin to think he was God, or Moses, laying down the law on Lakeland, telling his readers, "You will be treading in my footsteps." He said to me, "Once I've made a route, it will last for ever." He would never admit mistakes, which could make him impossible at times. And he could be spiteful. I also didn't share his sentimentality towards cats. I prefer humans.

'His Guides are wonderful to read, but in some ways I wish

they'd never been written. He's responsible for much of Lakeland erosion, leading people on the same trails. It doesn't matter as much in the valleys as paths can be repaired, but everyone follows Wainwright exactly on the ridges, and those ridges are now seriously eroded and sometimes dangerous.'

This is part of a familiar criticism of Wainwright's Pictorial Guides, which, for as long as they are in print, will probably always be made. Wordsworth had a similar complaint thrown at him – that he was bringing in the hordes who were spoiling Lakeland, the very sort he himself later objected to. Wainwright used to defend himself by saying he never expected so many people to buy his books, but anyway, if he hadn't written them, others would and just as many people would still have come to the Lake District. Most Lakeland book writers like to think they *do* bring in visitors, but it is the national economy, and the price of foreign packaged holidays, which increases or decreases the total of Lakeland tourists from one year to another.

But it is true that, having come to the area, many people do follow the same tracks, as guided by Wainwright. There is therefore the danger of erosion – but there always has been. The old packhorse routes, which Wainwright and Molly were so keen to follow, created enormous erosion in their day. That's why they had 'lengthsmen', whose job it was to fill in the pot holes. Now we have to rely on the National Trust or National Park people to repair the worn patches. The Lake District belongs to all of us, and is not an exclusive domain, to be used only by the right sort of people. Wainwright took it upon himself to help us enjoy it better. That was his real conceit.

CHAPTER EIGHTEEN

Betty

Betty McNally entered Wainwright's life by a side door. They didn't meet through books, as Molly Lefebure did, or through her job, like Mary Burkett, but through a chance letter, one of the many fairly trivial, rather piddling, slighty bossy, official little letters which the Borough Treasurer was wont to send out as he went about his business, chasing up suspected miscreants or possible defaulters. For someone who, in his private life, considered two shillings to be Treasure, then a missing ten shillings, which is what Mrs McNally appeared to be owing, definitely deserved a letter from the Treasurer, commanding her presence before him as soon as possible.

This letter arrived sometime in 1957. Betty is not sure exactly when, and she can't find the letter, but she knows it was 1957 because she took along one of her daughters, Anne, who was then aged six. At the time, Betty was a single parent, a separated woman, living with her two daughters and her parents in a rather grand period house in Kendal.

She was born Betty Hayes in Singapore on 10 February 1922. Her father was working there at the time, representing a Manchester cotton firm but, due to an economic crash in Singapore in 1922, he lost his job and the family returned to England. He eventually settled in Blackpool where he became managing director of a building company specialising in public works contracts. Betty and her younger sister were both sent to Casterton, a well-known northern boarding school for girls near Kirkby Lonsdale. It had originally catered for the daughters of the clergy, including the Brontë sisters.

Betty left school at seventeen and did a Speech and Drama course, becoming an Associate of Trinity College of Music. She taught for a few years, then decided her true vocation was for medicine. She was too late, alas, to become a doctor, so she got a job as Registrar at the Victoria Hospital in Blackpool. She contemplated taking a nursing course, but there was no time before she was swept off her feet by a dashing Irish doctor, Paddy McNally, a pathologist at the hospital, and thirteen years older. They married in 1945, moved to Dublin, his home town, and had two girls – Jane born in 1948 and Anne in 1951. Betty's father, when he retired, and her mother, decided they would also buy a house in Dublin, to be near their daughter and grand-daughters.

'The marriage never worked out,' says Betty. 'Paddy drank too much and I discovered other things about him I didn't approve of. In the end I decided to leave him and return to England, taking my daughters. We got a legal separation, and I decided I would devote the next part of life to bringing up my daughters.'

It was pure chance that brought her to Kendal. She left Dublin with no firm plans, but leaving behind her an added complication – her parents who had uprooted themselves to follow her there. While she decided what to do, she stayed with an old school friend who happened to live in Kendal.

'Kendal seemed a nice place to bring up the girls, so I looked around for a house big enough for us all to live in, my parents included.' Betty found an ideal house in Fowl Ing on the Appleby Road, and they moved there in 1952. Although she was caring for her aged parents, Betty found she had more time on her hands once the girls went to Kendal High School. She busied herself with good works, helping out with local charities. She also decided to do a State Enrolled Nursing course at the County Hospital in Kendal, thus fulfilling her plans which had had to be put on one side when Dr McNally had come on the scene.

The chance meeting with A. Wainwright in 1957 came about through a travelling ballet company, the Ballet Minerva. No, he hadn't gone to see it, nor was she making a guest appearance, petite and agile though she is. The ballet company was giving a charity performance on behalf of the local branch of Save the Children Fund, on whose committee Betty served. It fell to her to book Kendal Town Hall for the show which she did, in her own name, hiring it until ten at night. Unfortunately, the ballet persons got rather carried away, finished late, and took their time vacating the hall. An irate caretaker stomped in, demanding extra money for the extra hours. They refused to pay and next day, they packed up, and moved on.

Betty can clearly remember the strong smell of pipe tobacco, that day in 1957 when she entered the Borough Treasurer's office to explain the matter of the unpaid Minerva money. She also noticed the sun shining on the red hairs on the back of the Treasurer's hands. He, however, was staring at her rather sternly, getting ready his reprimand.

'He said to me, "I hope you don't make a practice of doing this sort of thing. You should never sign a form on behalf of someone else." Anne then started running round his office, which provided a slight distraction. He smiled and I thought he might be human, after all. I'd read one of his guide books and realised he was the author so I decided to venture a personal comment, saying that I'd liked it, or something. I can't remember what he said in reply, if anything. But he struck me as rather endearing. I sensed a gentleness behind a stern front. Then I went home – and forgot about him.'

Seven or so years later, after another Guide had came out, she bought it, thought it was very good, and wrote him a fan letter. 'I didn't really expect a reply, but he sent me a charming letter, saying my letter was like the first primrose of spring. He remembered my earlier visit and invited me to visit his office some time, and talk about the fells. I was a bit surprised by that. I mean, a Borough Treasurer giving that sort of invitation. It seemed rather, well, forward, so I didn't do anything for several weeks, although it lodged in my mind.

'One day, when I was near the Town Hall, I decided on an impulse to pop in and see him. I was just in that sort of mood. He was able to see me and we chatted about the fells and his books and it turned out he was nearing the end of the last one and was thinking about doing something next on the Pennine Way. He told me that his problem was going to be transport. He hadn't a car, and the distances this time were much further and more awkward. I said I'd give him a lift, any time he wanted, as long as I was free . . .'

This meeting, in his Town Hall office, was on 20 September 1965, a date which Wainwright did not forget, feeling something significant had happened, at least in his mind. A day or two later, he asked Betty to pop into his office again, this time by appointment. It so happened that he was about to go on holiday to Scotland, with his cousin Eric, but there was something he wanted to give Betty before he went off. During this second meeting he handed Betty a large envelope containing a manuscript, saying to her mysteriously, 'You are this girl.' He also added a rather elliptical covering note.

Just read the book first, and make sure it is not a case of mistaken identity with me, and mistaken impression with you. Wait a fortnight, please. Then let me know.

How I am looking forward to my journey tomorrow! Twelve hours alone, without distraction, to sort myself out and think tenderly of you . . .

Oh dear!!!!

The 'book' inside was his autobiographical short story, the one he had written in 1939, during the early years of marital angst and bitterness, the manuscript which he had kept hidden, showing it to none of his friends. The running fantasy in this story, you will remember from Chapter Seven, was that one day he would meet his Dream Lady. At the time, he often imagined he already had, that she was with him, that he was talking to her, resting his aching head against her sweet breast.

In 1965, aged fifty-eight and coming up for retirement, Alfred Wainwright decided that at long last he had met this fantasy woman. It had come true. He was about to lay his heart and his head upon her, so he gave Betty the story to read, convinced he had written it for her, although he admitted it could all be a case of mistaken identity.

Betty was forty-three and technically still a married woman, although she was thinking of divorce after many years of separation and living on her own. She was small, petite, cultured, well spoken, attractive, warm and lively, with numerous friends and an active social life. He was tall, bulky, grey-haired and appeared gruff and anti-social, not interested in anything outside his work or his books. And, of course, he was a married man, securely so, as far as most people could tell. He was also very aware of his public position, hence a need for discretion, to keep their relationship, however it developed, as secret as possible.

CHAPTER NINETEEN

Letters to Betty, 1965

When Wainwright gave Betty his autobiographical book, he suggested they should not meet for a while. But on his return from Scotland, he could not get her out of his mind, even though he was hard at work, spending every spare moment of his weekends finishing off Book Seven, the Western Fells. So at the end of September 1965 he wrote to her. He even said she could call him Alfred.

Dear Betty,

I *must* write. An eternity has passed since I saw you. Saturday was a complete non-success. It rained all the time, but I hardly noticed it, and as the day dragged endlessly on it began to suit my mood. Silly me, I looked for you on the bus. I walked the streets of Keswick looking for you, although I knew you would not be there. I walked the streets of Cockermouth looking for you, although I knew you would not be there. I went on to Loweswater for no better reason than that you said you had once been there. I walked by the lake; there was not a soul about. I stood under a tree and listened to the rain on the leaves above. I was wretched. For the first time I was not merely alone, but lonely, desperately lonely. What folly, to have put so much distance between us when every instinct urged me to get closer to you! I wanted you. I *needed* you. I thought of you all day with such tenderness that I feel I was melting away. As for sorting myself out, I couldn't: I need your help to do that. I sighed the three words 'Oh Betty *please*' a hundred times that day, not quite knowing what I was asking of you. Perhaps simply that you should not forget me. Only hours had passed, by the clock, but it seemed to me that an age had gone by without word or sign from you.

I want so much to be with you again.

Forgive me if I should not have written. But I badly need some reassurance that I have not been dreaming, that I was not wrong in feeling some response from you. You seem worlds away at this moment. How cruel a silence can be when it is not explained or understood! You may have disliked my book and be now disliking me. I know I suggested no contact for a month, but that idea has proved a complete non-success too, except perhaps as an exquisite torture. How can I know what a silence means? I want to hear you whisper that you have not forgotten me.

Alfred (to you)

Betty wrote back, saying she had read his book and been 'deeply stirred'. Her letter was addressed to A. Wainwright, Esq. at the Municipal Offices in Kendal and marked Personal.

They managed to meet during that week, but their main contact was in letters. In one letter, Betty said she had decided what she was going to call him from now on – Red. Mainly because of his once red hair, which she had observed on the back of his hands, and partly as a shorthand version of Alfred.

Wainwright replied to this letter after another weekend walking the Western Fells. How surprised his readers would have been to know what was going on his mind, during those last months of his Pictorial Guides.

On Saturday I had coffee at my usual place at Keswick: a nice quiet place of shaded lights and soft music. A lady asked if she could share my table. I said yes, of course. She had a kindly face; she was rather older than I. The background music switched to 'Rose of Tralee', a haunting melody that I first heard John McCormick sing and which always brings me close to tears. I would like this to be *our* song. I wanted to tell the lady that I had found the most wonderful girl in the world. I wanted to tell everybody, even the man sweeping the street. I can tell only you.

I didn't get to the top of Gable. The weather was glorious and I was infinitely happier than last Saturday, but I had your last letter with me for company, and halfway up I thought I would turn aside from the path and find a quiet hollow in the heather and read it yet again. So I did, and then I fell to dreaming and trying to recall every word you said to me last Wednesday. After which it was much too late to go on and I wandered slowly down to Seatoller in a happy trance.

Yesterday I spent on my book, as I always do on Sundays. Sunday is my best opportunity – I can get 10 or 12 hours at it. All day I wondered what you were doing, and ached for your touch again. I have so many

ideas for you, for us. In the evening I watched a film on TV, attracted by
the title 'Magnificent Obsession', which seemed singularly appropriate. I
enjoyed it. The story, a sad one, would hardly bear analysis, but there
were nice sentiments in it. It ended happily, as I wanted it to do. Please,
B., I want to buy you a TV for Christmas. It would be one way of
sharing experiences while apart.

I like the name you have given me. So simple and so appropriate, yet
nobody thought of 'Red' before. Yes, I do like it. Sounds tough! I
always fancied myself as a cowboy riding the lonely ranges, and Red is
just right for a man who sits tall in the saddle. And this is exactly how I
have felt since last Wednesday. Tall in the saddle. On top of the world. A
world that has turned upside down in three amazing weeks. And I like it
so much better the way you have changed it for me!

Take very good care of yourself in Dublin, love. Remember all the
time you are away that there is someone here waiting for you to come
back, and wanting you.

Red

Betty was going to Dublin, a long-arranged plan, to see her
husband Paddy, although she and AW managed to meet again
first. She had already been thinking of divorce proceedings, long
before the bold Wainwright had come along. While she was away,
he carried on with Book Seven, climbing Great Gable yet again,
along with the dutiful Harry Firth, and in his head making
arrangements to see Betty on her return, at some secret and
amusing rendezvous.

Betty dear, I am missing you awfully. We are separated by distance, with
only your sweet letter, received this morning, linking us together. It is a
frail bridge across space, your letter, but a comfort in my loneliness. It
tells me you are safe, and well, and coming back to me.

The wonderful experiences of last Thursday evening, when for a
blissful hour you took me into another world, a world with only the two
of us in it, I shall never forget and I shall never try to forget. Everything
was just perfect, as I have long dreamed it would be, as I have long
known it would be, if ever I found you.

Great Gable was duly climbed last Saturday by an all-British expedition
consisting of Mr Firth and myself, our combined age being 107. I was
not an attentive companion, I'm afraid, my thoughts being very much
elsewhere, and in fact once, in the car, I found myself gently stroking his
knee. However, we got to the top all right, and down again. A thick mist

hid everything. On the summit I found a place to sit facing Ireland (which Mr F. must have thought a bit mad because it was exposed to a drizzling rain and there were better shelters nearby), but visibility was down to 30 yards and never improved. But it was a good day.

Ten hours on my book on Sunday was enough to finish it, except for revision. I was alone with Cindy all day.

I must thank you for understanding so well last Thursday. Telling you my story was the oddest thing! I had been dreading bringing back the old memories, yet you made it so easy for me. You sat quietly listening, so quietly that I felt I was talking to myself. It was a strange feeling, to be talking of things I had always tried to hide, and it could not possibly have happened with anyone else. You gave me your legs to caress, and it was lovely to do this: they were a link between us in the darkness. Today's letter tells me you *did* understand. Bless you, for this and for everything.

I have found a delightful place in Keswick for coffee on the 30th, and next Saturday I shall make a tour of all the ladies lavatories so that I can be the perfect guide. Nothing must be left to chance on the 30th. I want this to be happiest day of my life. I want to feel you are mine, and only mine, for twelve blessed hours, in surroundings I have come to love. All this, and heaven, too!

Red

Betty wrote to him from Dublin, telling him what she had been doing, once again sending her letter to him at the Town Hall. A good job he was always first in the office, but he still had to wait for his own post to be sorted from the hundreds of official letters.

Dear, dear Betty,

My new Monday-morning habit is to scatter all the mail that is brought to me in an impatient search for your now-familiar writing, and read first of all what you have to say. The rest is unimportant, and can wait. For a few moments I can feel you are with me again, and am suffused in a warm glow. I am all tenderness for you.

Thank you for telling me about your weekend. I had been wondering. I am always wondering. How crowded your life is, really! You have the house to look after, a two-acre garden, the children, the car, your friends. You have lectures, meetings, concerts to attend. Is there really room in it for me, too? Am I intruding in the pattern of life you have chosen for yourself? A fear is creeping into my mind, and I want you to kiss it away!

Tonight I have meetings to attend, but my thoughts are all of tomorrow. Another day of waiting and then we shall be together again, really together, in the quiet of the evening. I think of the other nights there have been, of the moments of tenderness, of kisses in the dark, of your heart lying against mine. There is so much still to be said, so much to learn about you – but first twelve days of waiting must be rewarded, twelve days of stored-up affection must be expressed, twelve days of hunger must be satisfied. I want to hold you close. It is five weeks since you called to see me – five weeks today, at just about this hour. It is five weeks today since I fell in love with you. Five wonderful, amazing weeks. I try to think what life was like before. I thought it was a full life, and I was content with it. Only now am I beginning to realise how much better it could have been.

The big meeting in Keswick took place, with Betty driving there in her own car, and on Sunday he wrote to thank her.

Betty my love,

Yesterday was the most wonderful day ever, and although 24 hours have gone by since we kissed goodnight, I am still utterly under the spell. There never was another day like it, from the moment you appeared – or even earlier, when there was the excitement of knowing you would come for me. In terms of geography, our journey covered ground I had covered many times before, but never like this, never like yesterday. How much I prefer your company to my own! How much I admire your competence in every situation, when my own thoughts are floundering in dreams, and your many accomplishments! How I like to hear your sweet voice talking to me – about anything! Betty dear, thank you a thousand times for making yesterday possible and giving me a memory I shall never forget.

It was all too wonderful to be happening to me, and if I seemed a little quiet and sad on the way home it was only because a perfect day was coming to an end. But you have promised me other days, and, much more even than that, you have promised yourself to me, that you will come to me for always if ever I can ask you. Oh, Betty, if only that could happen! Oh my darling that would be the greatest kindness of all . . . Today I am not less happy although you are not with me. My dream of a future together may be proved idle, but it is so very pleasant to think about!

I can hardly believe the good fortune that brought our widely different paths side by side. I am still completely bewildered by the happenings of the past few weeks. If I try to think rationally, nothing makes sense.

Why should you have taken this interest in me, of all people? – Why should the sweetest, loveliest creature I have ever seen prefer to eat fish and chips with me out of a newspaper sat in a car in a scruffy side-street, than to attend a social banquet as a special guest with the nobility? This is the sort of thing that happens on the pictures, but *I* am no film star. Why should it happen to me? Why *me*?

And the incidents in the car, the trembling ecstasies of nearness, the gentleness of your touch, the softness of your lips. Why, of all men, should I be the one so privileged? Not even the gods fared better. But these are questions only you can answer.

Most of the day I have been doing a drawing for you, because I want you to have something of me in your home that others may see, something that has not to be secretly locked away. I like drawing better than writing because the mind can wander, and today it has wandered over every incident of yesterday, and returned to each one time and again – and nothing happened that was not altogether delightful.

Yes, dear, there will be other days, other meetings, other kisses. There must be. Yes, dear, we will go again to Badger Hill, and write our novel. Somehow, we must. And yes, dear, I will come to Fowl Ing. I must. I am riding on the crest of good fortune, and I have a most wonderful feeling that heaven is opening its gates for me, or that you have opened them for me.

Fowl Ing, in the Appleby Road was Betty's home. The novel they had discussed writing was to be a romantic novel, set in Lakeland, which they would live and write at the same time. Very romantic.

On a less romantic note, but bearing in mind his passion for chips, he sent her an official invitation he had received, with her name inserted instead of his, and Cheese and Wine crossed out and replaced by Chips and Vimto. It was the first of many jokey cards and cut-outs which he enclosed with his letters.

A week later, he wrote and said he had finally decided to make a covenant to the local branch of the RSPCA, with the aim of setting up a special animal shelter. Betty had been part of these discussions, and actively encouraged him as she herself had been a long-time charity worker and animal enthusiast.

Like all lovers, young and not so young, he started haunting her house, from a safe distance, of course, noting whether her car was in or out, on her light in her bedroom. And like lovers, he began to be a bit jealous, resenting her having to go to see her husband.

Betty's house, Fowl Ing, drawn for her by AW

Betty dear,

Friday night's meeting was soon over, and I found myself wandering afterwards along Appleby Road, but this was a mistake. I knew you were not at home, but in other company, and quite suddenly I felt miserable and lonely. I wanted you all to myself – I who have no right to you at all! Melancholy set in and I went home, where, at least, I have a right to be.

Today, Sunday. I have finished my book and wondered all day what you were doing. Only a short mile separates us, but when you are not at my side you are a world away. Sunday has become the loneliest day of the week, for it is a day with no contact, when I know there will be no word from you, no sight of you. Sunday has become a day when memories of other days must sustain me. There are many memories now, all of them pleasant to recall, and I like to think back to the 20th September, when you called at the office after I had given up hope that you would, and I fell in love with you; and all this has happened to us since. I try not to think how it will end.

I fear I am growing resentful of anybody being with me if it isn't you. You have sadly spoiled me for anyone else's company! However, I went up Great Gable with Mr Firth and his son Michael and eight hankies, and was in good form (which means I was nearly able to keep up with my companions). On the top, Mr F. produced coffee and mint cake and apples, and this time I sat with my back to Ireland, which is now out of favour with me because I know that Dublin is going to take you away from me.

I *have* been despondent this weekend, and jealous, and hasty with the Firths, and I think you should know that your letter has lifted me up and sent me soaring again. Perhaps it was just my cold that got me down a bit, but this is nothing that the soft lips of my beloved will not cure. Thank you, and bless you for being the sweetest person I have ever known. You will know tomorrow night how much you mean to me.

A few days later, he achieved one of his ambitions – to meet her daughters, Jane and Anne, now aged seventeen and fourteen about whom she had talked so much. The meeting was 'accidental', in their favourite Keswick café, where he just happened to walk in when the three were there, and naturally was introduced.

I loved them on sight, and wanted to put my arms around all three of you and squash you into a struggling lump and hug you all tight. Someday I will do just that. I was home by 7.30, and there was a welcome only from Cindy.

This morning I had to attend the civic Remembrance Service (I remembered it only just in time!) and the rest of the day I have spent sorting out photographs and maps, thinking about you and yesterday and next Tuesday and Saturday, and wanting to love you. I intended to watch Moira Shearer on TV tonight, and pretend she was you but wasn't allowed to. Instead, I am writing this letter.

Today I have been drawing, and imagining you endlessly and uncontrollably eating nuts. I have nothing further to report from home. Mrs W. was out when I got home last night and today has gone to see Peter's young lady at Staveley.

I have read your letter this morning over and over again. You can have no idea how lonely and out of it your account of a happy weekend at Fowl Ing makes me feel, how much I would like to be there, sitting quietly in a corner of the kitchen, watching you all the time and perhaps being allowed to touch you now and then. For this, for the right to sit by your fire in my slippers, I would give everything I have. Ambition has narrowed to this – to be with you, to have you for myself, to be yours, to show you how much I love you. I am so very sure, now, that with you there would be perfect happiness for me: I get a glimpse of it every time I see you in the street, a real awareness every time I hold you close.

The Keswick café – now gone – figured large in their secret life. It was a safe distance from Kendal, as people in southern Lakeland consider any trail over Dunmail Raise as going to a foreign country. AW, on his weekend walks, would always go there in hope, even when he knew she would not be there.

On Saturday I went to Keswick, chasing a 1000 to 1 chance that you would appear to have tea with me. I ought to know by this time that 1000 to 1 chances don't happen, but it was a hope I clung to till 4.30. Such a state am I reduced to that, for a meeting with you, even for no more than a glimpse of you, I would do anything go anywhere. I might not have gone, otherwise, so bad was the weather early on, but it improved magically and transformed the scene. At Low Wood, across a deep-blue Windermere, the mountains looked as though carved in white marble: a picture beautiful beyond belief, and I wanted you there with me to see it. The road was clear, but two miles out of Keswick the bus broke down (the driver said he'd 'lost his air,' whatever that may mean), so I got out and walked the rest of the way.

I had lunch at the George, where our sacred corner was being profaned by a bunch of noisy youths, visited Friars Crag, which was quite deserted, and then walked around the suburbs of Keswick three times, killing time until 4.30 (no climbing, she said – as if I *would* take any risk that might keep us apart!). At 4.30 I entered the Keswick Restaurant to find it completely empty of customers, as it remained for the hour I was there. I listened for the door to open, but it never did. I listened for the patter of tiny feet, but they never came. The peace was warm and cosy, the soft music nostalgic love songs. I pretended you were there with me. Then I went out in the dark and the cold and felt suddenly desperately alone. What have you done to me, dear girl, that I can now find restfulness and comfort only in you?

Red

Their regular secret meetings around Kendal went on each week, plus 'chance' meetings in places like Keswick on a Saturday, when

Wainwright was supposedly off to the Western Fells, finishing the last Pictorial Guide. When he started researching the Pennine Way, where public transport was much more difficult, Betty was able to take him there in her VW Beetle. (Not a Mini, as that neighbour had imagined.) Several drivers occasionally gave AW a lift, others being Harry Firth and Mary Burkett.

Despite his close, nay, passionate friendship with Betty, it took him a while to actually allow her to accompany him on the walk itself. 'I'd collect him from a pre-arranged meeting place,' remembers Betty, 'then drop him off where he wanted to start his walk. He'd point out on the map the spot he wanted picked up later in the day. It was very boring, hanging around. I have always loved walking which was why I liked his books so much. One day I threatened I was going to follow him, walking behind. Eventually he agreed – but on one condition. "As long as you don't talk," he said.'

After their walk, they often had a drink in a pub – no more than half a pint of beer or shandy, sometimes just lemonade. Betty talked about her first marriage, and how unhappy she had been. Wainwright rarely talked about Ruth, except to indicate that they went their separate ways and had no personal contact, but he did talk a bit about Peter.

By the end of December 1965, it had been three months since their relationship had begun, and AW could still hardly believe it had happened to him, after waiting a lifetime.

Betty dear,

The hours pass quickly when I am with you, but how slowly when I am without you! Today has dragged. I have been alone most of the time. I have drawn. I have looked for you on television, in vain. I have checked the proofs for Book Seven. It has rained all day. No bright little face appeared over the garden wall to cheer me up. But I have had our meeting last evening to think of, and I cannot be other than happy when I think of you. So many meetings now, so many places with special memories! I have always been happy with you, from the first moment. I found comfort in your company not after long acquaintance, but from the very instant of our first coming together. I did not then, and have not since, felt any shyness, any awkwardness, any strangeness with you.

It could not be like this with anyone else. You are the one, the only one. Falling in love with you has been the most natural thing in the world: it was bound to happen to me if ever we met. I waited a long time for you to come along, too long. I lived almost a lifetime, missing you and wanting you. I knew you must be around somewhere because you were more real to me than the people I met every day. But the years went by. You never came, and I never found you, until a few weeks ago. And at once everything changed. I had been lonely and now I was lonely no more.

And so the year ended happily, blissfully. Their love letters had turned into a torrent and, on AW's part, were outpourings of released emotion, displaying passions that had not appeared in his life or in any of his writings, revealing a very different Wainwright from the one which his devoted readers had got to know and enjoy through his Pictorial Guides.

Betty in her replies, was equally loving, hoping that 'one day we will be free to express our love'. The romantic novel idea had appealed to her. 'Giving birth to a book, not a child.' While he sent her funny cards, she sent him poems, such as Elizabeth Barrett Browning's 'How do I love thee', or suggestions for novels he should try, classical music he should listen to, and decent Sunday papers he should read, like the *Sunday Times* or the *Sunday Telegraph*. She wanted him to visit her at her home, a social visit, as a friend but he declined, for the moment. Everything seemed perfect in their relationship, apart from the fact that he was a married man, scared stiff of any scandal.

CHAPTER TWENTY

Letters and Problems, 1966

The year 1966 should have looked like being a Good Year for Alfred Wainwright. His Seventh and final Pictorial Guide was all complete and ready for the printer as the year began. He had just finished the first draft of *Fellwanderer* and was now busy in the first stages of his *Pennine Way Companion*. As a devoted football fan and television owner, he had the World Cup in England to look forward to.

And there was Betty McNally, the light of his life, who had appeared as if by magic three months previously, having simmered in his dreams these last thirty-five years. They had hardly seen each other over the Christmas holidays, although he had given her an electric blanket as a Christmas present, a thoughtful but unflamboyant gift, with significant undertones, and he now looked forward to her company, as chauffeur and companion, on his forthcoming expeditions to the Pennines.

Yet when he wrote to her on 17 January he seemed sorely troubled by unknown, unspoken worries. Guilt, perhaps? Or possibly a surfeit of 'happifying', to use his own word, which he didn't quite deserve. So preoccupied was he that he had not realised the significance of the date itself, his fifty-ninth birthday. Or so he said.

Dear Betty,
   Until I saw you in the street this morning, I hadn't realised it was my birthday. It was sweet of you to appear so unexpectedly, and to wish me many more, and to offer me flowers for my desk. I could have kicked myself afterwards for not taking your flowers after you had taken the trouble to bring them, but they would have been too great an

embarrassment. It was a lovely thought, and I spoiled it for you. I'm sorry, Betty, really I am. In fact, I didn't behave at all well this morning. I was unkind. I had much on my mind. A cloud has settled on me and I can't get rid of it.

Your card, and J and A's [Betty's daughters], are the only ones I have received, but Miss Thompson (typist) brought me 20 cigarettes and a box of matches, and Mr Duff bought me a blackcurrant tart which was a beastly thing to eat and squirted all over the desk and my clothes and dripped on the carpet.

I went to Blackburn on Saturday morning (never did your bedroom light shine more brightly!), spent the afternoon with Doris, and came back very disturbed. Things are *not* all right with the business, and I may have to go over again. I told her about you, up to a point, and this was a bad mistake.

Yesterday I sorted out many old photographs, and have put some at one side to show you next Saturday. I tried to sort myself out a bit, too. It was a poor day. I was still disturbed about my visit to Blackburn.

Miss Thompson typed FELLWANDERER for me over the weekend, and I will let you have a copy next Saturday and would value your opinion as to its impact on lady readers. There is a letter today from Molly Lefebure, agreeing to read and criticise it from the point of view of a professional writer. Donald James, Librarian, has agreed to look through it for obscenities. And the fourth opinion, I think, will have to be Mr Firth's, representing the man in the street. I ought really to ask Mr Griffin, but he talks far too much.

Thank you for your charming letter this morning. It did me good to read of your simple faith in me, after a weekend of doubts in myself. I am so glad about the blanket: it must take my place for the time being. Already I am jealous of it!

I am missing you terribly, Betty. It isn't so much that I want my arms around you; I *need your* arms around *me*. Today I feel just a bit that circumstances are getting me down, but I'll be alright by Saturday. If I'm not, Upper Long Churn Cave will cure me, for you can't take worries into caves, and if Upper Long Churn Cave doesn't, you must. Perhaps all I need is happifying, and only you can do that for me. It's been a long long time to have to wait, Betty. Maybe I love you a little too much. I can no longer manage without you.

Red

It's not clear what had worried him, but things ticked on happily for the next three months, Wainwright meeting Betty as before, writing regularly as before, but on 14 March 1966, something dreadful happened.

Betty dear, I am terribly and wretchedly sorry for behaving so badly. The very last thing I ever wanted to do was to cause you any distress at all. You must believe that.

But things have gone tragically wrong. I ought to be right on top of the world, but find myself suddenly in the bitterest depths. I am in bad trouble, and must find a way out of it myself. Nobody can help me in a positive way (although I wish someone would show me how to fry an egg!) and, in the circumstances, you least of all. Thank you for your kind letter, but please do not try. You can help only by being there when it is all over.

I am grateful for six months of the most wonderful happiness. I was not entitled to this, and now, for a time, I must pay for it.

I am too confused in my mind to explain anything yet and sorely troubled by a conscience I had forgotten I had.

I feel like a man who has been betrayed, but in fact know I have been caught in my own betrayal.

There have been dark passages in my life before, but I have always emerged in the sunshine. This will happen again. In the meantime you will not hear from me, but Betty please, you must trust me to do what I think is right.

Red

What had gone wrong? Had someone told Ruth about his new friend and driving companion? This would explain it, and tie in with Beryl Williams' story that Ruth had discovered one of Betty's letters which he had been silly enough to bring home from the office to read once again in secret. In his letter to Betty of 14 March, he did not spell it out, but the reference to frying an egg makes it clear that his wife of thirty-five years had gone off somewhere or downed tools. For the next few weeks he would have to take care, or behave himself. Or perhaps get some other kind person, preferably female, to give him a lift on his Pennine jaunts. Which is what happened, and on 18 April 1966, Wainwright wrote to Betty from the Palace Hotel in Buxton.

Dear Betty,

I am in Room 72 in this very palatial establishment – and guess who's next door in Room 73? Yes, you're right. Destiny has played another of her tricks. It's Miss B. I can, and will, explain everything when I see you.

The drive down was O.K. – no touching, positively! – but we ran into bad weather, mist and rain, before arriving here at 9 o'clock. Prospects aren't too hopeful for tomorrow.

Wish you were here.

Miss Mary Burkett, Director of Abbot Hall Gallery and dear but platonic friend of AW had, as we know, proved to be a brick in driving him to Buxton, and had also provided a perfect cover.

All the same, it looks as if his wife Ruth still continued to absent herself from the house. This might have enabled Betty to make a secret visit, except for the fact that son Peter happened to be home on his annual leave from Bahrain.

AW then had another chance to cover his tracks and his relationship with Betty. A correspondent from America called Ade Meyer, a wealthy widower, one of the earliest fans of the Pictorial Guides, was staying at Grasmere and was desperately keen to go walking with AW. So it seemed a good idea, perfectly safe and respectable, for Betty to join them and make a threesome.

Peter was over to see me on Saturday, and has been here again yesterday, all day, and today morning. He intends to come tomorrow and Friday, so I have had to tell him I shall be away both days. He has bought a tape-recorder and is building up a library from my records, which will make his visits frequent. His appearances are not likely to follow any pattern. He has hired a car (110 pounds for 10 weeks). On the 25th of this month a friend is coming up to join him, a youngish man I have met and like, and I have suggested that he can stay here with me: I have found some more blankets. The ulterior motive, not yet disclosed, is that he can pay for his keep by Hoovering the house.

Saturday is definite; it must be. Mr F. is back at work and has promised to help with his car. Ade is still keen, and will pick me up at 9.15. Please be ready at 9.25. You will need your boots.

See you then, love.

Red

And so it came to pass that all three had a delightful walk. Ade from America proved a charming companion. He got on very well with Betty, and she with him, which made AW start thinking of plans for them to do things, all together.

Betty dear,

The days I spend with you are the happiest I have ever known. They are, to me, like days on parole from prison; days in the sunshine after long confinement in the darkness. Saturday was such a day, a wonderfully happy and (in spite of everything) carefree twelve hours. The unpleasant things didn't seem to matter while you were with me, and I could forget them. You are a constant delight to me. Perhaps it was as well that Ade was with us.

I *want* you to go out with Ade, as much and as often as you like. He is hard work at times, I know (he reminds me of an old St Bernard dog), but really a delightful man and I greatly admire his determination and independence. Quite obviously and understandably he is fond of you. He is a stranger in a strange land and has need of friends. Yes, please go with him, and make him happy – up to a point (there must be no sprigs of heather sticking in your jumper when you come back to me!). Show him your home, your daughters. Krishna ... [Betty's cat]. Besides, I have the idea of suggesting a pact – that the three of us do the John Muir Trail together in 1968, and I'm serious about it. For you and me this could be a heavenly holiday. But it depends on how well you and Ade get along during the next few weeks. It depends on nothing else. The barriers are falling.

Thank you for your letter. I have today spoken to the Lancaster solicitor on the telephone. He sounds very nice. He will start the ball rolling by asking T. & B. [Ruth's solicitors] to submit a draft agreement, incorporating their client's wishes, and then I will have to go to see him.

Ruth had departed from the marital home and AW had been persuaded to press for a divorce. With this in mind, he had contacted a firm of solicitors in Lancaster, not Kendal. He well knew that in a small town like Kendal, gossip could too easily spread.

That looked like one awful problem about to be settled when out of the blue, a complication arose from a quarter he presumed was safe and respectable, and which he himself had created.

Sunday evening
[18 July 1966]

Betty dear, this letter will be the most difficult I have ever written. I don't like writing it, and you won't like reading it. But, after yesterday, there are some things that must be said, and quickly. I am sorry to have to say them in a letter, when you have no chance of immediately replying, but you happen to be in Dublin and I am sitting here in a lonely house, with a heart turned to tears, and cannot wait until I see you again.

It concerns Ade and yourself, of course. Nothing I say must lead you to think that I have changed my opinion about Ade in any way. He is the most generous, most considerate man I have ever known. A gentleman, as I always wanted to be – and never made it. Nor have I changed my opinion about you. You are the sweetest woman in the whole world, and always will be. Yet yesterday, Ade and I came near to having a blazing row.

As I expected, our Saturday walk was all 'Betty this' and 'Betty that' (except that I *do* wish he would say Betty and not Beddy!), and at first I was wagging my tail, mightily pleased because there are so few people I can talk to about you and because compliments about you always make me feel so proud. But then he went on to tell me about his more personal relationship with you – the late evenings you had had together, the telephone calls, the places you had visited in his company, your calendar of future engagements and I could feel my innards shrivelling up. He was brutally frank and open about everything, brutally so only because he did not know my feelings for you and may also have assumed that you may have mentioned these events to me anyway already. Betty, this affair has gone much further than I imagined from the very little you have told me. With pleasure he reported that after Dufton ('I don't want him to come home with me,' you said) he was with you until 11.35.

Ade told me all his plans for you, more than he had yet told you. You are to have dinner with him at the George in Keswick. He intends to see you, or at least speak to you every day during the remaining seven weeks of his stay. He is going to insist that you visit San Francisco this autumn. He has suggested you have a few days with him in London.

Oh Betty love, why didn't you tell me? What is going wrong between us?

I don't object to what you are doing (because I asked you to see him as often as you wanted, and make him happy), and can't (because in Ade lies your best chance of happiness). I had no idea you and he had become so close.

He has wonderful plans for you, and is absolutely convinced and absolutely sincere. A really wonderful new life is being offered to you, by a generous man who loves you. You should accept it.

I ought not to be in the picture at all, not even in the background. The solicitors are meeting on Tuesday next to consider figures that will leave me £5 a week to live on (after meeting commitments such as tax, mortgage etc) plus what I can get from my books (they may want some of that, too). And smoking costs me £2! There is clearly no future for me and certainly none for you with me.

Saturday was a bonny day, but Ade took all the sunshine out of it for me. After hearing him, how could I tell him that I loved you more than he ever could, that I had known you in dreams long before we ever met? Nor could I tell him of my own troubles. I had very little to say all the way back. There seemed nothing I could do but tell him I would pull out of the trinity, leaving the two of you to sort yourselves out. This I did when we got to Grasmere, and he was dreadfully upset (still not realising why) and in fact we spent the evening in the car park at White Moss (of blessed memory), arguing about it.

I enclose the photographs. Ade has ordered more enlargements. He wants me next Saturday to take a picture of him kissing you, so you see how impossible things have become. He may get his kiss, that's up to you, but it will certainly not be recorded on *my* camera.

Please don't worry. I will see you on Saturday at 9.30, as so often before, but for the first time I shall not be looking forward to it. I will bring the drawing of Fowl Ing: I have been working at it since 8.30 this morning, and will finish it before then [*see* page 212].

As for the Pennine Way, I don't know. The spark has gone . . .

I didn't bow out very gracefully, did I? I'm terribly sorry now. I had a rough bringing-up, and the grittiness still comes out at times.

Betty, you don't have to reply to a letter that should never had been written. If I do not hear from you at all, I will get the message, perhaps better than if you tried to tell me.

Let's end it romantically, as it started, please, love. Let my farewell present, very appropriately, be this record of the theme music from Dr Zhivago. Please play it when the house is quiet, and mark well the words, for these are the words I wanted you to hear from me. I was clumsy and cruel. Do try to forgive me.

With all my heart, dear. I hope you find the happiness you never found with me.

Red.

Betty wrote back, saying he was being silly, there was little between her and Ade, he was imagining it all. AW was suitably contrite, yet deep down still very worried and perplexed.

Betty love, your reply filled me with remorse, but did me a world of good. It has needed Ade's intervention to teach me that I could not face a future in which you had no part. I love you, and only you, and always shall. If you had to take a whip to me you could not alter that.

I am sorry for some of the things I implied in my letter. I was always a bad loser. But last Saturday I was given the impression that you had encouraged Ade in his hopes. Betty, it was a nightmare experience. I was having to listen to the last things I wanted to hear, and there was no escape. The man was gloating all day over his conquest (so quick and easy!) and I took a very bad thrashing.

I don't blame Ade. In his position I would have been in seventh heaven of delight, too, and wanted to enthuse about you to others.

I am not offering you love. I am giving it to you, as I have for the past thirty years, and I always shall: I can't help it. It is you I want, not any woman. Just you.

Over the summer, they continued meeting, all three of them, but Betty also continued to go out with Ade, on his own, which greatly worried AW. Yet he found himself unable to tell his friend Ade the true relationship between himself and Betty, which had been going so smoothly until Ade came along. Then on 3 August, Betty rang AW at work, saying Ade had proposed.

Betty love, listen. You are worrying your pretty little head over a problem that does not exist. A man has offered marriage. You do not love him. You know, and I know, that you never could. Why can't you see the answer as clearly as I do. It must be no.

You confuse a simple issue in your mind by thinking that I am involved. Love, I am not. Your answer to Ade has nothing to do with me.

Ade is ready to settle for marriage without love. He has suffered a rebuff (which he is not accustomed to) and his instincts are in revolt. He had a business arrangement all planned. Of course he won't like it. He wants a wife (preferably, but not particularly you), and just see if he doesn't get one within the next year or so. And then you lecture me about his strong moral fibre! Snap out of it, love. Moral fibre, indeed!

Once again, Betty calmed him down, telling him he was being melodramatic, and they started their regular Saturday meetings again. But on 12 September, after a day out in the Pennines, AW returned to Kendal Green to find something different about his house.

Sunday afternoon

Dear Betty.

ON LIVING ALONE

Well, of course, my spirits took a nose-dive as I watched you drive away through the rain. I felt bleakly that you were leaving me for ever, leaving me in a sea of troubles of my own making. I was depressed, and frightened. Yours was the hand I wanted to hold, and I no longer could. You had gone.

There was a bus waiting for Settle, so I went there and had a meal big enough to last me until Monday in the dining-room of the Golden Lion, where you and I dined last November after a visit to Haworth.

I was in a bad state of mind on the journey home, naturally, and extremely apprehensive as I approached the house. Surprisingly the lights were on and the lady of the house in residence. Supper was served and nothing was said.

Nothing had gone from the house. A busy day's work had been done. In addition to the week's washing, the summer curtains had been taken down and the winter ones put up. The television set had been moved to its winter position, nearer the fireplace. Everything was neat and tidy.

This morning I carried on with my book (Wythes Hill to Middleton) while a busy morning's cleaning and cooking was going on. I had an excellent dinner, and returned to my book. The dinner plates were washed up and put away, and Cindy prepared for going out. THEN, at 1.30, she announced her departure to her new home in Kentmere and there ensued a fairly rational conversation, at last. She has rented School Cottage, just by the church, for a few months, furnished, at the reasonable rent of £3 a week. The cottage is the converted school-house, and very attractive. Peter will stay there when he comes. I offered to pay her £10 a week while she is there (which she accepted, but protested it was much too much) and gave her £40 for the next four weeks. Her intention is still to go to Blackburn to live, and I then asked whether she would say how much a week she would want from me then, after I had retired. Would she not agree a figure with me now, and save all the unpleasantness and expense of solicitors? Yes, all right, £7. All right, I said, £7. We are to inform our solicitors accordingly, but ask them to leave the matter in abeyance until she has discussed her position with Peter.

Had she kept a key? Yes. Would she come in once a week to do the washing? Yes, if the solicitors said it was all right for her to do so, she would come every Saturday (the only day when there was a bus) and wash and bake for me.

I felt dreadfully sorry for her. She is obviously in a state of extreme nervous depression, probably ill, and confused and unhappy. Off she went, in the rain, after doing everything she possibly could for me in the house and writing out full instructions about the milk and newspapers and coal arrangements, on how to de-frost the fridge, and so on. She has gone to a place where she will be desperately lonely, where the winter months will be severe, where there are no shops and no link other than the Saturday bus. She has no TV, but hopes Peter will provide one.

She has gone, a tragic figure, a faithful wife who can no longer live with her husband because of his conduct. I have driven her to this.

I am relieved that we have reached an agreement, and grateful for the further delay. It seems there will be no scandal now for people to gossip about, that I need not now have to explain what has happened, or if I have to, can tell a plausible story that she is away for a time for reasons of health.

Selfishly, my first concern is for myself, and I am pleased I have come out of this trouble fairly satisfactorily, or look like doing. If I had anything of my conscience I should now be in a desperate state of mind, but I honestly haven't, and I am not. I am deeply sad that she had found it necessary to go, particularly so because Kentmere is not a place where she will find happiness, but only an awful loneliness that, I am sure, will not bring the improvement in health and mind she badly needs. These things she can only find amongst her many friends in Blackburn.

So that's it, love. Next Saturday I shall go out with Mr. Firth, or if he is not available, to Gargrave alone. I cannot see you just yet – it would be quite wrong. I will write again next Saturday.

A funny thing – this conversation I have reported interrupted my notes on Kirkcarrion! I am not feeling too good, but, as you said, I am resilient. I will get over it.

Red

The next day, AW got a letter from Ruth, saying she could after all not be his housekeeper on a once-a-week basis, and offering to deduct £1 from the allowance he was giving her. She enclosed a list of essential information about the house. She had gone for ever.

Sheets & pillow cases & towels in top drawer of dressing table.

More towels in bottom drawer of tall boy. Extra blankets in tin box in cloakroom.

Coal will come once a fortnight unless you cancel it, its the National Coal Board, offices where Whartons used to be on the Market Place. Coke from Gas Board.

Milk is 10^d a pint

There is nothing owing, papers are 5/4 a week at Kendal Green Post Office

You can get groceries delivered from the shop next to the Post Office, if you leave the order before Saturday, also a loaf on Sat.

> My address will be
> School Cottage
> Kentmere

Defrost fridge once a week, lift everything out turn off at the switch & leave for one hour, then empty water out of tray & wipe out then switch it on again.

If electric clock stops turn the little nob [sic] at back at right hand side, switch it to spare room when you use the electric blanket. If you want the alarm pull out nob on top & push down to stop.

CHAPTER TWENTY-ONE

Obsessions, 1967–70

Alfred Wainwright retired as Borough Treasurer of Kendal in January 1967, aged sixty, earlier than he need have done, but he had had a long working life in local government, serving it well and conscientiously since the age of thirteen. He realised the days of pen-and-ink accountancy, in which he excelled, were over for ever. Computers and calculating machines and other so-called labour-saving devices and methods were coming in, which he did not understand or approve of. The most modern machine he had managed to master was a typewriter, and he asked for a new one as his leaving present. He never returned to the Town Hall, not even on a brief visit, despite living only a mile away.

'Three weeks before I left the office for good,' so he wrote in *Ex-Fellwanderer*, published in 1987, 'my wife walked out of the house also for good, unable to tolerate any longer obsessions of mine that had left her out in the cold, and I never saw her again. I was not greatly concerned. I had planned a very full literary programme for my years of retirement.'

Ruth had in fact left three months earlier, as those letters show, but that's only a minor economy with the truth. More important are 'his obsessions' which finally made her leave. Most readers of that book would naturally presume he was referring to his grand passion for walking in Lakeland rather than his grand passion for Betty McNally. In *Ex-Fellwanderer*, he also gave the impression that he met Betty *after* his wife had left. 'An angel without wings appeared, offering transport.' The simplification is understandable, trying not to hurt the feelings of all concerned.

Ruth did not at first tell her son Peter all the reasons why she had left home, perhaps sparing his feelings for his father. When she first broke the news to him in Bahrain, she did not mention her suspicions about another woman but told him something else her husband had been doing behind her back.

'What first made her leave my father,' says Peter, 'was discovering about his charity donations, least that is what she told me. She went into the town one day and three people stopped her and said, "Oh, isn't it wonderful what your husband's done". She didn't know, until she was told. He'd donated £7,000 to the RSPCA to build a shelter. It wasn't just that he hadn't told her, but that she'd been scrimping all those past years on £10 a week. And he had shown little affection for animals. After all, Mum was the one that looked after the dogs and loved them. She couldn't understand that bit. All the same, I must say the news came as a bit of a shock.'

Yes, but not a complete surprise?

'No, they'd never got on. But I don't remember any rows or quarrels – just silences. Silent hatred on her side – silent ignoring on his side. Perhaps it was also connected with his retirement coming up. She couldn't stand the thought of him being at home for twenty-four hours a day.'

Why do you think she hung on for so many years, when she was clearly unhappy? 'Where could she go. She had no money.'

Peter thinks his father was unfair to Ruth, giving the impression later on that she was totally working-class, uneducated, and not interested in improving herself. 'She could have expanded her social circle, given the chance. She was the one who travelled, the one who read books, unlike him. She was a Labour supporter in their early days. Her father had been a big Labour man, but later she became Liberal. He was always Conservative.

'She used to say she would never have married him if she'd known he had red hair. When they first started going out, they only ever met in the dark at night – and he always wore a cap. His red hair came as a bit of a shock.'

Was the breakdown of the marriage totally his fault? 'Mostly. She would have been willing to talk, if he'd been willing to listen.

There was no compromise between them, so they each went their own way. She concentrated on looking after him, keeping the house clean, making him gooseberry pies. I don't think there was any love between them, not after 1939. But in those days, people stayed together, whatever the situation. There were a lot of unhappy marriages.'

There is little doubt that suspicions about an affair made Ruth finally leave home, as she'd told her friend Beryl. In the subsequent legal correspondence over the divorce, she alleged he had been philandering. She did not name any other woman, and it would appear she did not know Betty's name at this stage, suspecting someone else instead. Wainwright denied philandering. His explanation to his lawyer for the 'love letter' she had found was that it was part of a romantic novel he was writing. True, and yet not the whole truth.

Peter, when he next came home from Bahrain, visited his mother at her rented cottage at Kentmere. He says she did then talk about another woman, and continued to be upset by the donation to the RSPCA. 'She believed the other woman had not only stolen her husband, but had made him give away his money to animals, which was a bit rich since she had always been the animal lover of the pair.'

Correspondence with various animal charities, and the dates of donations, show that Wainwright did help animals long before his marriage ended – although it is perfectly possible he never told his wife about such things, considering it his money to do with what he wanted.

On his leave, Peter also visited his father, although this upset his mother. 'She didn't like me having any contact with him. She did get a bit bitter and twisted at times. It didn't upset me because I'm fairly thick-skinned – like my father. She had never argued with him, because I think she'd been scared to, so she moaned to me. I felt sorry for her, but I felt sorry for him too, living on his own. He was so damned helpless. He was living on tinned potatoes.'

He had let the garden become overgrown during his Lakeland

Guides walking years. Now with Ruth gone, the house was equally neglected, becoming run down and charmless. He still had no telephone and no central heating, and often ate out in cafés. He had no close male friends, the nearest being Percy Duff, but he never revealed to Percy or anyone else, apart from Betty, what had happened to his marriage. Twice a week he went to the Kendal Museum, the little museum near the railway station. After his retirement as Borough Treasurer he had remained the Hon. Curator and used the place as his office, meeting people there while he worked on cataloguing and also on his own books.

Fellwanderer had come out in 1966, and attracted several poor reviews, readers preferring his hand-written, hand-drawn guides, not his photographs and printed prose. *Pennine Way Companion*, which he was still working on during the first half of 1967, was going to be in the Pictorial Guide format, but was proving a struggle to complete. Betty had been so helpful during the first stages of research for the *Pennine Way Companion*, and he had decided to dedicate it to her, but anonymously. 'To the one who helped most of all.'

He was still seeing her occasionally, by appointment, and writing letters, but he was taking care to keep their relationship as secret as possible while his divorce proceedings continued, in case she might be named.

Ade had gone back to America, so that was a relief, but the first careless raptures of AW's romance with Betty seemed to have lessened. All the same, she still wrote to him from time to time, as his good friend. And he hoped she might pop into Kendal Green, from time to time, to see him at home.

July 3 1967
Monday afternoon.

Betty dear,

Thank you for your letter. I think I ought to reply at once.

Yesterday was completely wasted – except perhaps that in the morning I cleaned the house, even doing some Hoovering, and changed the flowers – in anticipation. From 2 o'clock until 10 I did nothing but pace the house, waiting for you. I had such a lovely tea ready, every item personally selected for your delectation in Carlisle on Saturday.

The endless hours of waiting did, at any rate, give me plenty of opportunity to think about you and about us. It is now perfectly clear (to both of us, surely) that there can be very little, if any, room for me in your crowded life. You must devote yourself to the essentials – work, home and family – and ration such leisure hours as you can afford between your older friends and older interests. You must set your priorities and work to them. Time has become very precious and you cannot afford to waste any on non-essentials, such as me. There is now a real danger that you may make an appointment with me that, when the time comes, you wish you had never made because of something else you would rather be doing instead. I would never want you to spend time with me that you prefer to be spending elsewhere. I should hate to feel this was happening. I don't want to be a friend on sufferance.

I am writing to let you off the hook. You have no duty to me, and you mustn't feel you have. I have sensed a change in your feelings recently – one or two things you have said. They were happier days for me when we saw or wrote or spoke to each other almost every day. When you kept a light in your bedroom window . . . Sometimes I wish I hadn't such a good memory. I remember I was Priority No. 1 then! Now, if I am only going to be allowed odd minutes with you, always with an eye on the clock (and I can see no other way) I really think you would be kinder to me if no further promises were made, at least for the present.

I will manage fine, and always be grateful for all you have done for me. Nothing will ever alter my esteem: you are the most wonderful woman, the only one for me, the one I have always wanted. I will keep myself busy, and get on with the book. I will get a divorce, and then see how you feel. If any emergency arises, of course I will let you know, and if you want me for anything at all, you know I will always be at home in the evenings, alone, and glad to see you.

Betty wrote back, nicely, but rather surprised by his tone, and he responded in turn.

July 6

Dear Betty,

Thank you for your card. I hadn't meant to shock you, and if my words were clumsy, I am sorry.

I had a dreadful shock myself on Tuesday, when I was unexpectedly served with fearful-looking papers to attend High Court in connection with a petition for judicial separation. So either I have been double-crossed or someone has bungled matters. The charge is cruelty, and the allegations are so grossly untrue, exaggerated and misleading that I must defend the case. It is unfortunate that those that are untrue deal with aspects I cannot disprove, but they must certainly be denied.

It is very important that you should be kept out of this, for your own sake more than mine, and therefore better we should not meet. To your friends 'in the know' you can quite truthfully explain that your business arrangement is now ended and I am doing those sections of Pennine Way beyond the reach of a car, on my own; and that, in any case, your new circumstances give you no time to help further.

I am naturally very upset, but trying to concentrate as much as I can on the book. I am making good progress and have got as far as Thirlwall and should be glad if you could kindly send it when you write.

I want desperately to get away for a few days and may go up to Bellingham next Tuesday to distract my mind, if I am allowed to. Tomorrow I am going to Lancaster to see my solicitor.

This is the worst crisis yet, but it is one I must face alone. I have a host of wonderfully happy memories to sustain me, but these are not enough. Without you, I shall be utterly desolate.

Take very good care of yourself until we meet again. It is forever.

Red

The dramatic news about Ruth had indeed shocked him. She was now going to fight the divorce case, not give in meekly and accept a modest amount of money as she had at first appeared to agree. The tables had now turned. Wainwright had, for some reason, believed he had a case against her, that he could charge her with cruelty for leaving him. Now she was going to charge him with cruelty and make a case of it. It had been bad enough having to trail to Lancaster to see his lawyers. Now a barrister from Manchester had been briefed, had to be visited, and official responses and explanations given.

Betty's 'new circumstances' mentioned by AW in the last letter refer to the fact that in the summer of 1967 she fulfilled an earlier ambition and started a nursing training course in Kendal which was to last almost three years.

July 10
Monday afternoon

Betty dear,

I do not want to weary you with letters, but must thank you for returning the guides and writing so sweetly.

You ask to be kept informed of events. These are likely to be harrowing and I would not wish to sadden you with details nor cause you anxiety. I saw the solicitor only for a few minutes, my call not being convenient, but felt rather better for the visit. At least he was a friend, when all others seem to have fled. His attitude was 'Not to worry'. It is for the opposition to prove their case, and we have a good barrister. He asked me to let him have my replies to the charges, a marital history and any other observations.

These I prepared on Saturday, a most distasteful and disagreeable task that made me very unhappy. The day was a nightmare of self-reproach and indignation confused together. I felt completely wretched. I wanted you to come and tell me what to do. The enclosed envelope contains the specific complaints, my replies, a marital history and one or two other observations: bad copies through a worn carbon, but all I had. Love, you need not look at these if you don't want to. You can say to yourself that it is none of your business. You will not like me any better for what they contain. Please return these papers. If the envelope is unopened I will understand.

I think I will go to Bellingham on Wednesday, staying in Tuesday to take in the groceries. I hope this outing clears my mind. I am very depressed and miserable. This wretched affair has knocked the heart out of me. I have collected the gooseberries and forgotten what you told me to do. The electric fire has broken down. The house needs cleaning, but what the hell? who is to see it? I am alone, a recluse on parole only on Monday and Thursday mornings. I have even felt like putting 'P. W. Companion' in the dustbin, but then I have remembered from past experience that I recover quickly from a stunning blow and that the present bleakness of my existence will be followed by happier days, happier perhaps than any I have known in the past.

Absence, they say, makes the heart grow fonder, but absence long continued can make the heart forget. Betty love, be fair to yourself. As I said, I know you have lost the first rapture, which was only to be expected, and if you find in your heart that it has not been replaced by something more enduring, then it's curtains for me. In due course I shall ask you, and you must tell me, honestly. And don't worry. I'll get by!

So Wainwright sent Betty a copy of his 'marital history', the one he had to submit to the lawyers, a most depressing document, which must have caused him much anguish to write. He had to tell the truth, as he saw it, but at the same cast himself in the best light, as he was now engaged in a fierce and expensive legal battle. One of the illuminating admittances was his explanation why his wife had left him, taking Peter with her, just before the war. 'He became involved in the formation of the Blackburn Rovers Supporters Club as Secretary and Treasurer,' so he wrote, talking about himself in the third person, 'which not only took up much of his spare time but introduced him to many friendly people with a very different way of life, these new contacts leading to many late nights out. Because of this, his wife left him for a short time.'

He also suggested that in recent years his wife had become mentally depressed, considering her life empty when their son Peter got a job overseas, but all the same, he was 'utterly shocked' when his wife suggested a separation. She then became hysterical, so he alleged, and clearly unwell, finally leaving the house, against his wishes, on 11 September 1966. Summing up, he said the marriage had broken down because his wife did not want to share his life. 'Never did she say she was proud of her husband's achievements . . . their sexual relationships had always been unsatisfactory.' He admitted she had always been a 'devoted mother and an excellent housekeeper, but a disappointing wife . . . the only welcome the husband got on coming home from work was from the dog'.

Wainwright had obviously written these words himself, and they appear in his typing. Ruth, for her part, gave her side of the story through her lawyer. In it she accused her husband of having affairs, which he hotly denied, and claimed he was 'selfish, withdrawn, sullen, refusing to converse for long periods of time . . . had shown scant and increasingly less interest in her, her happiness and general well-being and who has regarded her as being but a housekeeper, domestic worker and convenience'.

There was also the matter of money. Originally, she had appeared content with £10 a week. But as soon as she told her lawyers that 'she had always been in the dark' as to her husband's financial affairs, they began pressing for a much larger settlement – a lump sum, plus a much higher weekly amount. This argument went on for many months. The lump sum started at £1,000 then rose to £4,000.

Wainwright worried that Betty would think the worse of him, having to read all these confessions. So he wrote to her about the trivia of his life, while waiting impatiently for her reaction to his marital statements.

Not much has happened today. At the Museum two boys called to have books autographed and then Mr Firth appeared with my cheque for royalties for the first six months of the year (£562) and discussed details for printing 'Pennine Way Companion': in particular the colour of the Rexine cover. This I had intended to ask you to select, but I think you will approve my choice of turquoise. It is *your* colour. It will match. You will be able to sit in your turquoise car, wearing your turquoise dress and turquoise earrings (inter alia), with a turquoise book on your lap, and you will look right bonny.

This afternoon I did a full page of drawings in 3½ hours, which is good fast progress, and am now only six miles short of Byrness.

Tuesday evening
Your letter arrived this morning, and was more welcome than a cheque for a fortune. It was Magna Carta: it freed me from my worst fears. Not only that, it transported me, made me feel good again. Oh B, it was sweet, and charming. I had deserved reproach, but reproach there was none – only kindness.

Over the summer and autumn of 1967, while the divorce proceedings continued, becoming nastier and more vindictive, Wainwright started wondering why Betty still seemed so remote and detached, not the passionate woman he had courted the previous two years, who had once appeared to be the lady of his dreams, as eager as he had been for an intimate relationship.

I always read your letters over and over again, squeezing every ray of hope out of them but without gaining much comfort these days. Now you promise soon to explain your 'rather complex feelings'. There you go again, hurting me! Have I become a problem? See, love, the issue is dead simple, not complex at all. Either you do or you don't. That's all you have to decide, and you don't have to do it right now. It's nothing to get all mixed up in your mind about. It isn't, anyway, a matter for the mind to work out; it isn't a matter of cold calculation, it's an affair of the heart. If there are complexities, there are doubts. If there are doubts, commit yourself to nothing. That makes sense, doesn't it? Anyway, forget I asked. We drifted together and we can drift apart if you want it that way. It's just up to you. You have a very full life now, lots to do, lots of friends. If your new life, besides being full, is also happy with things as they are, well then, why take on a bad risk? Spare me an explanation of your rather complex feelings, please: it could only make me unhappy.

I'm sorry if I seem peevish. I have just been reading that last bit again. It sounds like sour grapes. Maybe it is. I am not rebuking you, or being unkind, not intentionally. Oh Betty, *please* understand! I am deprived. I am sick of an old passion. I have grown used to you and miss you terribly. I, for one, still do. I, for one, always will.

The privations of these past months are taking their toll on my tummy. I'll be lean and slender and more distinguished-looking than ever when you see me again. And hungrier!

Betty now had to tell him that it wasn't possible for her to complete her nurse's training at the Kendal hospital. Instead, it would mean going to London for a while, where there was a course at Whipp's Cross Hospital.

Yes, I understand now, perfectly. I will not ask again for too much, to have you wholly; but you will not mind if I go on dreaming my favourite dream, without ever mentioning it again? Yes, love, we will have it the way you want it, for as long as you want it. You put your case with sweet reasonableness and I have no counter-argument. You win. Your intention to work for your own security is admirable, and, because there is really no compulsion to do so, noble – but please don't ever again suggest that your life up to now has been wasted or unfulfilled. It is a fine thing to be independent, but it is also a fine thing to have others dependent on you, knowing they can rely on you, and this has been your position these past nineteen years. This is really the fundamental role of a woman and a mother, and surely there is more fulfilment of life in this than in being concerned only with a career? Don't be *too* humble and penitent. You have made a lovely and intelligent woman out of the little frightened girl who went to Casterton School; you have made a charming and devoted mother; you have failed in nothing. Feel *proud* of your accomplishments, as you ought.

Yes, love, we will do anything you say and everything you want, see each other, be loving companions, walk together. We must.

Wainwright became resigned to Betty's decision, but being forced to spend all his spare time alone made him more depressed. He didn't mind working alone or walking alone when engaged on a project, but being totally alone, without the Lady of his Dreams, was very hard to bear.

Friday evening

Dear B,

Today I have been to Morecambe, a place that depressed me, especially when crowded with visitors. To escape the glare of the promenade, which hurt my eyes, and get away from the Lancashire dialect, which offended my ears, I took a ride on the Sand Trail Express, a daring thing for me to do –

Then I went to see 'The Sound of Music' and was no longer depressed but quite wonderfully uplifted. There were only two other people in the balcony, and nothing to distract attention from a very beautiful, very happy and yet very moving film. It was *fab*. If I could make a film like that I would consider it my life's work. At times the screen went misty and tears rolled down my face, and it didn't matter because there was nobody to see; but mostly I was enthralled by the wonderful happiness of the story and the glorious scenery. Julie was magnificent: She was *you*, when I have seen *you* happy. I enjoyed it tremendously. I sat transfixed, it did me a power of good. I felt a heel for having written to you as I did. I knew now that I had said things that were hurtful.

On other days, he sat at home, feeling soulful.

It has been a cheerless day, with the rain lashing the windows and the hills obscured in a fall of wet mist. I have badly wanted you to call; I listen for the gate opening, but it never does. On a miserable day like this, when I am housebound and rather lonely, the Pennine Way is a blessing: without it to pass the time I should feel completely lost. Where is my life drifting? What aims have I left? What is to be the end of it all? These are the questions I ask myself. I do not know the answers.

Bedtime now. The electric blanket is operational again.

In October 1967, he hit upon a new idea. He decided to address her indirectly – pretending to be her Dutch Uncle. So he sat down and wrote her a long letter, as if from her Uncle Hans, someone who had known her all her life. He went over all her problems, analysing them, covering six pages and then came to the obvious solution.

Utrecht, Holland. Thursday evening Oct 23

My very dear child,

You will be greatly surprised to hear from me. I have played no part in your life, living as I do in another country. You will have heard of me, a long time ago, from your father, but your recollection will be vague, if indeed you remember me at all. I am old now, and long retired from work, but, thanks be to the good God, I keep very well. I have my garden, which keeps me busy, and now and again I still win a prize at our annual show with my flowers.

I have always taken a great interest in you. I have on my writing desk (you will hardly believe this) a small framed photograph of you when you were at school – must be over thirty years ago. It has always stood there, between the two inkwells. Your father sent it when you first went to boarding school. I love that picture. You were so small in your new uniform, so neat, so tidy. The expression on your face always brings a smile. You look so serious, my dear! And just a little fearful, as might any child at a new school. There is an elfin wistfulness about you that is very appealing. And, if you don't mind my saying so, your ears did stick out a bit, didn't they?

You grew into a beautiful woman. You were talented, intelligent, charming, but never lost the bubbling curiosity of the young girl. I heard of your marriage with profound pleasure and my heart warmed towards your husband for his good taste in choosing my favourite niece for his bride . . . I was shocked when, a few years later, I learned that you had left him and returned to your parents with your two babies.

You are not entitled to say that life has given you a raw deal and you must find happiness where you can get it. Can you look at Jane and Anne and truthfully say that life has given you a raw deal? Can you think of the hundreds of women in your own town who must envy you the opportunities and achievements and experiences you have had, and still say that life has given you a raw deal? Of course it hasn't. You have a better life than most. It is not complete, but it would be folly to wreck what you have and opt for anything less permanently satisfying. You are approaching the age when you will want only to be peacefully settled in your own home, to enjoy the security you have earned and have the love and respect of your children and friends. You won't want men throwing pebbles at the window. The present unrest you feel will die, and when it does you must not find yourself stranded in strange surroundings. To embark now on a voyage of endless drifting with no harbour in sight, to jettison dignity and pride and self-respect as you go, is asking for shipwreck. Please don't do it. If you hurt yourself you hurt Jane and Anne and all of us. You are a limb of the family tree; when you are distressed so are we all. We love you.

Stay with old Red. He's dotty about you, we know. But at least he's harmless.

Your devoted Uncle Hans

Betty replied in the same vein, as if writing to her long-lost uncle, and it slowly all came out, all the misunderstandings. She had never meant to encourage Ade. That was due to being an outgoing person who liked people, and Ade was kind and interesting, and she felt sorry for him, losing his wife so tragically. She'd also been upset that Red had not come clean, had not told Ade right from the beginning that he himself was in love with Betty.

Then there was her bigger, more nagging worry – maintaining her independence. Now that her girls had grown up, she didn't want to jump from one restraining relationship to another one, which was why she wanted to remain free and not commit herself for the moment. She was still career minded, desperate to finish her training. It was nothing to do with her feelings for AW, whom she still loved dearly, but because she did not want to become too dependent on someone else. She hoped Uncle Hans would understand all this.

What she didn't spell out in her reply was a worry about AW's obsessive qualities, clear enough to anyone reading all his letters to her over the last two years. These had revealed a vital part of his character, which had been a strength and virtue when tackling a thirteen-year book project, but must have appeared to Betty a trifle alarming. He had, of course, waited thirty years for her to appear, so to him his passion seemed reasonable. But to her, his obsession had become almost frightening. Hence her hesitations. In the guise of the sweet niece, confessing all to her Dutch Uncle, she managed to convey these hesitations, without upsetting him, she hoped.

Betty love, it was a beautiful letter. You chose your words with great care and you meant exactly what you said. It was written at some cost in anguish of mind, and not without some heart-burning. I know, love, I know. You had to refer to past episodes that must have been painful to recall and relate. It was courageous of you to write so openly and frankly. I could not but regard it as an expression of your trust and confidence. I am humbled and contrite. Betty love, I understand now. I didn't before. I'm sorry I whipped you. It has been a bad time for both of us, because when I hurt you, I bleed too.

Each of us has something to forgive. I cared for you more than you wanted me to. You cared for me less than I wanted you to. I was roughly forging ahead too far while you were gently applying a brake. We have been pulling apart.... Of course you are right. It is a matter of balance and adjustment. Somewhere midway we had found a common ground of respect and friendship and affection. We have both strayed from it recently and lost track of each other in a lonely and frightening wilderness. It has made me realise that a life in which you have no part is a life without meaning. You too found, in lesser degree, that you were losing a friend you valued. Now you have called me back, and I come gladly.

Yes, we have our differences of character and outlook and, above all, background. I think you are shallower and more superficial than I, more cautious, but only because you are afraid to venture, to risk a mistake. You don't permit yourself dreams. You are capable of great depth of feeling, but lack the sense of security that would let you express it freely and fully. I too like to keep my feet firmly planted — you have seen me climbing a wall — but that does not stop me from indulging the most heavenly flights of fancy. My dreams become very real, and for two years they have been centred on you. Your influence on me is too profound, I know. I ought not to be so obsessed, I know. But I have liked to have you in my thoughts all the time. When we are friendly, this helps a lot to make a lonely life tolerable; it keeps me happy and inspired even when I am not seeing you. When we are not friendly it makes life hell for me, for I have lost the knack of shutting you out. You are everything to me. I would give my life to save yours. There are social differences of which I am acutely aware: you belong to a class where the common term of affection is 'darling', overworked until it becomes meaningless; in my world we say 'luv' and mean it. Yes, of course there are differences between us, but one complements the other. What I lack, you have. What you lack, I have. Together we are complete.

Please let me see you soon. Please use the enclosed letter card to tell me when — it is designed to save you time in correspondence. Any time, any day, but soon.

I have no other news, except that I have bought a new pair of braces and go to the Palace on November 23rd. I am not given an alternative. Ordinary suit will do. Wish you were going with me to make sure my flies were buttoned up.

In my darkest hours of depression I kept recalling a saying I heard when I was a boy, and have never forgotten:

"Keep a green bough in thy heart,
    and God will send thee a singing bird."

He has, with your letter and gift of books. Bless you.

Red.

Sunday,

ITINERARY:
    The Glens and Waterfalls of Ingleton.

DAY: Saturday next

DATE: 11th Nov. '67

TIME: ——— ——— at but wait. I may be a few minutes late.

PLACE: Ingleton Town Centre near the church.

I WANT
(a) WEEKEND
(b) BLACK MAGIC
(c) LIQ. ALLSORTS
(d) KISSING + PERHAPS
(e) BURNT ALMOND.
} Delete any three.

THERE WILL BE a little TOUCHING / NO TOUCHING } Delete as applicable

I LIKE YOU A BIT - wait + see / LOVE YOU A LOT }

ANY OTHER COMMENTS OR ABUSE.
Thank you so much for replying as you did. + for the diary. I am overjoyed at the prospect of seeing you - bless you Red.

Love. B.

Betty filled in his enclosed card, agreeing to meet him again, and re-start their relationship. He then sent an extra note, nicely illustrated, with a dash of colour in it, something he rarely did. He had a really exciting thought – suggesting a detour to Morecambe, after their walk, to see 'South Pacific'. Not exactly a cultural feast for someone who loved poetry and ballet and read the posh Sunday papers. Betty politely declined, saying she had already seen it.

REMEMBRANCE DAY
NOVEMBER 11ᵗʰ 1967
Wednesday.

Thornton Force, Ingleton

BALI HA'I

I'm thrilled and delighted about Saturday.

I've had an idea that might please you. Would it be possible for you to get a late pass (11.30) so that we could go to Morecambe after our walk, to see SOUTH PACIFIC? If not, O.K — you'll be home by 6.

Be seeing you, love. Only 64 more hours to wait. I'm excited!!!! Put a hatpin in your rucksack, and bring a skirt.

Red

WHAT DO YOU MEAN,

PERHAPS?

ARE YOU GOING FRIGID, LOVE?

BE QUICK, LOVE, FOR CRYING OUT LOUD, IT'S COLD STANDING HERE.

Ingleton Church

Wainwright's mention of his trip to the Palace did not refer to one of Morecambe's other cinematic attractions, but Buckingham Palace, London, England.

During the summer he had been mightily surprised to receive a letter from Harold Wilson, the Prime Minister, inviting him to accept an MBE. No reasons were given, but presumably it was for his seven Pictorial Guides rather than his Borough Treasurership, distinguished though that had been. The Guides were selling very well, although mainly in the north and his name was by no means known nationally. He wrote later, in *Ex-Fellwanderer*, that he'd been told that a Southport man, unnamed, had taken it upon himself to station himself on the summit of Great Gable for a whole day, collecting signatures in praise of Wainwright, which had then been sent to Downing Street.

The invitation to the Palace had arrived during a period when he and Betty were not quite best friends, so on one of his visits to Blackburn for the football, he had asked Doris's advice. She said he might have to wear a morning coat and top hat, but he said he wasn't having that. He'd wear an ordinary suit, that was all. In that case, said Doris, he'd need to get a decent hat, not his flat cap. She also offered to accompany him, if he wanted someone to be with him. Wainwright told Betty about her offer, slightly to tease her, showing he did have other female friends, but in fact he had said no thanks, he would go alone.

It so happened, however, that the day before he went to London, Peter announced that he was also due to travel from Kendal to London, en route to Bahrain since he had just finished his annual leave.

'So we went together,' says Peter, 'with my father carrying his rucksack. When we got to London, we booked into our hotel and then set off on the Tube to the West End as he wanted to see the film "Camelot". I had to help him on the Tube escalator. He couldn't understand how it worked. At the top, he just stood there, not knowing what to do next until, of course, his body was thrown forward. After we'd seen the film, he refused to go on the Tube again, so we had to walk all the way back to our hotel.

'Next day, he set off for the Palace alone. He never asked me if I wanted to come with him, and I didn't ask. I thought I'd say nothing. I wasn't bothered. He set off on his own while I headed for the airport. A year later, when I was next home, I asked him what it was like, meeting the Queen at the Palace. "She's very small." That was all he ever said.

'I didn't know why he'd got the MBE because I didn't know much about his Guides, or their success. I was in Bahrain all the time. My mother wrote to me every week. He wrote once a year, if I was lucky. He did show the Guides to me once when I came home, but I can't say I was very impressed. Nice enough, but I was very surprised to hear they were selling so well.'

On the way home from London, travelling on his own, Wainwright sent Betty a picture postcard of Buckingham Palace, telling her how it had gone.

Over the next year, they got back together again as best friends, seeing each other as often as they could, considering the divorce wrangles were still rumbling on. Wainwright was now not quite so obsessive and possessive, allowing Betty some independence and freedom. He realised, perhaps, that he had been over-zealous, over-powering in the past. She was able to continue with her nursing course in Kendal, and did not, after all, go to Whipps Cross in London.

Wainwright's divorce finally came through on 24 June 1968. He was the loser in the case, being found guilty of mental cruelty, and had to pay a lump sum of £4,000, plus £500 a year to his wife during her lifetime.

Ruth had by now moved into a house in Windermere, at 8 Upper Oak Street, a little terrace house which Peter had bought for her, handy for the shops. She started making new friends and joined new organisations, twice going to Tenerife with a new woman friend she'd met locally.

Beryl Williams, her old friend from Kendal Green, visited her once every two weeks, going on the train from Kendal to Windermere. 'She liked living alone without Alfred – just her and her dog.'

After his divorce was official, Wainwright asked Betty if she would go with him to Scotland for a holiday in November 1968. 'I said yes, at once. I'd recently got divorced.' Betty drove him all the way to Ullapool where they booked into a little hotel – and slept in separate bedrooms. 'Oh, it was purely platonic in the sexual sense, but it was very romantic.'

The idea of marriage came up a year later, while she was helping him with transport and research and companionship on his next book, *Walks in Limestone Country*. This was again in the style of the Pictorial Guides, describing in words and drawings thirty-four walks, just over the border in North Yorkshire. When it came out, in 1970, it was dedicated 'To Betty, a charming companion on these walks'. She also appears in some of the drawings.

'It was in Ribblesdale that he finally proposed', says Betty. 'Well, not quite in so many words. He sort of skirted round the subject. He felt he couldn't be direct. He said something about my friends would think I was marrying beneath me, if I married him. I said don't be silly why should that matter. I then made it clear that if he asked me such a question, I wouldn't say no. We'd each known, of course, for some time, without speaking about it.'

In January 1970, Betty got a call from him one bitterly cold morning, saying he was in some trouble. 'He told me he'd been sitting all night on a chair, spitting blood. I'd only ever been to his house on short visits, for a few minutes, having a cup of coffee. He was always worried about me visiting him there, guarding me from any scandal. But I knew his house was very cold, with no proper heating, just a coal fire. He was trying his best to keep the house clean and make proper meals for himself, with little success. He could never manage the simplest machine or follow basic instructions.

'I drove over to see him and he had big bowl beside him, full of blood. I rang his GP at once who summoned an ambulance. He was in hospital for three weeks altogether, suffering from bilateral pneumonia. When he came out, I persuaded him to come and stay in my house, along with my parents, until he had recuperated. He stayed about five weeks. During that time I insisted that some proper heating should be installed in the house at Kendal Green.'

Betty McNally and Alfred Wainwright were married at Kendal County Hall on 10 March 1970. Betty's uncle and aunt were the witnesses, Peter being in Bahrain. Their honeymoon was spent in York, three nights at the Viking Hotel. 'He deliberately chose a big hotel. In a little place, he was worried people might recognise and bother him. In a big hotel, he could hide behind pillars. He also wanted a big bedroom, with a big bathroom.'

Betty moved into Kendal Green, and their long and rather fraught and complicated courtship ended happily. Alfred Wainwright had achieved his fantasy: the woman of his dreams, through so many decades, had become reality.

Why had it taken so long? After all, from those first passionate months of his early meetings with Betty in 1965, when AW at last felt he had met the woman he had been looking for, there was a gap of almost five years before they finally married. 'Yes, it does sound like a long time,' says Betty, half surprised herself to look back and realise the gap. 'You have to remember that in those five years, a lot of things did happen, a lot had to be overcome, a lot of things had to be solved.'

There were two divorces for a start: Betty's decree nisi absolute was on 29 August 1968, and AW's on 27 September. His was stormy and messy. Hers, in theory, should have been simpler, as she'd had a legal separation from her husband since 1952, but he was a Catholic, living in Dublin where divorce is not possible. She had never contemplated it, because of these problems, until she finally decided to marry AW. Unlike him, she also had a responsibility for two elderly parents who were living with her when she first met AW (her father did not die until 1975 and her mother in 1984), as well as two teenage girls still at home. The mix-up over Ade knocked things back for a while but probably the most important element in the delay was her determination to retain a degree of independence, and not tie herself totally, once again, to a man. This was why she had started her nursing course. During those three years, from 1967–70, her course took up thirty-two hours of every week. Even after she married, she carried on nursing for another year.

On her arrival at Kendal Green, one of the first things she suggested was that he move his writing and drawing things out of the living-room, where he had sat at a card table beside the fireplace for so many years, and go upstairs to the little study where he could work undisturbed. She also made him give up using Brylcreem, which she never liked. His mutton chop whiskers, which became a feature from now on, happened more by accident. He had cut the side of his face shaving one morning, and it wouldn't heal. Betty suggested he shouldn't shave there for a while, nor the other side, to even it up. The whiskers appeared, and he decided he liked them.

Was he different in any way as a person, once married life began, living with him from day to day? 'I was surprised how active he was.'

You mean he had great physical energy, still able to do all those long walks, even at the age of sixty-three?

'Yes, all that. But he was always so loving and tender. I had never expected that.'

CHAPTER TWENTY-TWO

Books Galore, 1970s

The 1970s were very productive for Wainwright. The combination of being happily married and happily retired acted as a combustive force, inspiring him to twenty-two new books in one decade. A remarkable achievement for a late starter who did not have his first book published until he was forty-eight.

If he'd met Betty earlier, and found true love and marital bliss at thirty-three not sixty-three, how would his life have been different? Perhaps he would have walked far less and written nothing, throwing himself into family responsibilities, content to make a success of two things – marriage and his accountancy career – without striking off and becoming obsessed with a third and rather solitary activity.

What if *Pennine Journey* had been published in 1938, when he wrote it? His writing career would have begun much earlier, and perhaps would have gone in another direction, producing more literary material rather than pen-and-ink illustrated guide books. Guesses, guesses.

The facts of the matter are interesting enough – even more interesting with hindsight, now that we know the turbulence of his life at the end of the 1960s which, of course, he revealed to no one at the time. *Pennine Way Companion*, which was mainly written in 1966 and 1967, was a prodigious piece of work, a long-distance walk of 270 miles, but in his Personal Conclusions at the end, he appeared not to have enjoyed it very much, saying he was glad it was finished, feeling sorry for the reader about to follow his footsteps. 'You won't come across me anywhere along the Pennine Way. I've had enough of it.'

"Please can you tell me where the Pennine Way is?"

From Pennine Way Companion

In the book, he put his disappointment down to the weather. It had rained most of the time and he'd got stuck in the Way's notorious bogs and it had been very cold. On Cam Fell, he reported that 'a freezing east wind near to gale force, so shrivelled some of the body organs necessary for a full and enjoyable life that I feared they were perished forever, but happily their use returned in full flower after a brief rest.' Knowing what was going on in his private life, we can now read a bit more into this statement. We also know he did contemplate packing in the book a couple of times, not just because of the weather but when feeling depressed over the divorce wrangles and his relationship with Betty.

By comparison, *A Coast to Coast Walk*, which he worked on in 1971 and 1972, and is a follow-up book to the *Pennine Way Companion*, positively bounds with joy and happiness. The route was his own creation, from St Bees Head to Robin Hood's Bay, so that was one good reason for satisfaction, but throughout the book he is smiling and beaming, even writing 'yippee' on one drawing. He raves about the beauty and variety of the scenery, much preferring it to the Pennine Way.

There are various references to girls in his *Coast to Coast Walk* which, in some quarters today, might be considered sexist. His running joke is that the object is to get to Robin Hood's Bay where there will be 'ice cream, girls and all that'. As usual, he assumes his readers will be male. He includes a tip for getting over barbed wire by placing a coat on top. 'Better a torn garment than impaled testicles or what have you.' At Richmond, thinking of the sweet lass of Richmond Hill, he instructs readers to 'tidy yourself up a bit' in case any are met.

At the end of the *Pennine Way Companion*, he promised a free pint to all walkers who had genuinely done the whole route, telling them to put it on his bill when they got to the Border Hotel at Kirk Yetholm. The landlord had been instructed to send him the account, at regular intervals, but at the end of *A Coast to Coast Walk*, he said there would be no treats this time. 'No, sonny, that game won't work here. Pay for your own. I'm skint.' Hard to believe he was, as the seven Pictorial Guides had by then sold about 200,000 copies.

He summed up the charms and beauty of the Coast to Coast Walk by saying it had feminine characteristics whereas the Pennine Way was masculine. 'If there happens to be something in your temperament that makes you like the ladies the odds are that you will prefer the C. to C. You may not meet any but you will be reminded of them. On the PW you never give them a thought . . . well, hardly ever.'

It's always dangerous to read into an author's books what you know about his or her personal life, and vice versa, although critics do it all the time with novelists and poets and composers, but the influence of his new wife, Betty, is pretty clear in *A Coast to Coast Walk*. He does thank her in his Introduction, if not this time by name. 'Everybody has a car these days, even me (and, in my case, a good-looking, competent chauffeur to go with it).'

Betty proved much more than just a chauffeur. She organised his domestic life which had been in chaos during the three years or so he had lived alone, and helped with the research on the new walks he was now starting. She was his constant companion on every trip, keeping quiet when she knew she had to. In his books, he still glorified the spirit of the Solitary Walker, maintaining that only he 'truly identified with his surroundings' and 'achieved the most satisfaction', but in reality he himself had a companion from now on.

Is his theory totally true anyway? If you are in a group, or even with just one other person, there is always the temptation to chat and miss the scenery. And it is true that if you are working on a project, making notes, taking photographs, then the fewer distractions the better. On the other hand, there are benefits in beauty shared, an experience mutually remembered. A companion can see things you might miss, contribute knowledge and observations. Wainwright had in many ways made the best of his own circumstance. He did try, in his younger days in Blackburn, to organise walking groups, to go off with his chums, male and female, and would have liked their company, but for various reasons they didn't always want to go with him. Then when his marriage collapsed, he chose to walk alone.

One of the advantages of travelling alone, especially if you plan to write a book about it afterwards, is that you meet more people. Being with someone limits the new relationships you can make, the conversations you can strike up, the chance meetings you can capitalise on. Whereas on your own, people tell you things. This, of course, never mattered to Wainwright. He was not writing books about people. He was getting away from them, inspired by landscape, not human contact. In only one of his books does he describe people he met along the way – and that is *Pennine Journey*, the one not published until almost fifty years after it was written.

Well over half of those twenty-two books he published in the 1970s consisted simply of drawings and captions, which explains how he managed to produce so many. He completed a series of Lakeland Sketchbooks, doing five in all, and then six volumes of Scottish Mountain Drawings, plus sketchbooks on other areas, none of which needed as much time or research as his guide books. Some of the sketchbooks repeated drawings which had appeared elsewhere.

But there were several new books in the Pictorial Guide format – *Walks in Limestone Country*, *Walks on the Howgill Fells*, *The*

Outlying Fells of Lakeland – which took quite a bit of time to research, draw and write. *The Outlying Fells*, published in 1974, was the first book he wrote by request – i.e. readers had suggested it to him, as opposed to his writing it for his own amusement. He described it as a book for old age pensioners which he himself had become, and in his Introduction said it would be useful for three sorts of people – those whose legs were perhaps rickety, those who had smoked too much, or those whose 'over-indulgence in sexual activities may have robbed the limbs of energy'. He made it clear, nudge nudge, he was not in this latter category, and that his problem was the second – half a century of pipe smoking. On one walk, he mentions a kissing gate, and then adds, in brackets, '(it seems a little nostalgic to be talking of kissing gates at our age)'. Another double bluff from old Wainwright.

In the 1970s, he also did a couple of more ambitious books, bigger in size and format than anything he'd done so far, each about his local area. The first was *Westmorland Heritage* in 1974, a requiem for the passing of the ancient county of Westmorland which became part of the new county of Cumbria on 1 April 1974. The idea was sparked off by a request from the Lord Lieutenant of Westmorland to do a map of the county. In the book, he described in words and sketches the towns, villages and main places of Westmorland. It was an expensive production, 504 pages long, handsomely produced with some of the best drawings he had done so far, and it required him for the first time to do quite a bit of historical research. Westmorland Gazette, as ever, was the publisher, but because it was felt there might not be many readers, Westmorland being sparsely populated, it was decided to produce the book in a limited signed edition of one thousand copies. The retail price was £11, and it sold out at once. Two years later, copies were changing hands at £85 each. Later on, there was a Popular Edition.

In 1977 came *Kendal in the Nineteenth Century*, another big book, but not published as a limited edition, being priced at a more modest £5.40. For the first time, AW worked from other people's photographs, not his own, copying and converting some nineteenth-century photographs which he had found in the collection of the Kendal Museum where he was still Hon Curator. Many of them are street scenes, full of people and activity. In order to explain the background, research was also needed, for which he hired help, and also used Betty.

There was one exceedingly small book, published in 1978, which was little more than a booklet, just thirty-two pages long – *Walks from Ratty*. This described, in words and sketches, ten walks to be done from the Ravenglass and Eskdale miniature railway – or Li'l Ratty, as it's called. This was the first book since the days of Henry Marshall not to be published by the Westmorland Gazette, thus establishing an important if very minor precedent. It was published by the railway itself, and they received all the proceeds.

Despite the ever-growing sales, the increase in book titles and the widening of his reputation and recognition of his name, his face was still unknown to the general public. Harry Firth at the Westmorland Gazette had to field all calls and enquiries about him, and was not allowed to give out any photograph or reveal his address. He did no personal publicity for any new book and made no public appearances. His head was down, concentrating hard on the next project, working ten hours a day, seven days a week.

He did take an annual holiday, usually going to Scotland, Wales or Yorkshire, often to an area he was thinking of writing about next, and he and Betty got into a routine of going in a foursome with Harry Firth and his wife, Kay.

'If it was a pure holiday, with no book research,' says Harry, 'then we'd pay our own expenses. I remember AW stopping Betty's housekeeping while we were on holiday. He said he was paying her holiday bills so he was not paying her housekeeping as well.'

Betty agrees this was true, as he always did keep a close eye on day-to-day expenses. However, she did manage to get a new car out of him on one occasion, arguing that she needed it for her job as his driver.

Harry always called him AW or Mr Wainwright, even on holiday together. 'As the years went on, he did start to refer to me

as Harry when talking to other people, but to my face, I was
always Mr Firth.'

During fifteen years or so of regular holidays with AW, he
must have learned a lot about him? 'Not really. In the evenings he
would pore over his maps or go to his bedroom and prepare the
route for the next day, leaving Betty to stay up and talk to us.' Did
you like him? 'By and large, yes. Kay and I had some nice times
with them. We wouldn't have gone hill walking in Scotland and
Wales if it hadn't been for AW's expert guidance.'

Was he surly? 'No, I'd say unsociable.'

Now and again AW would go on holiday just with Betty,
especially to Scotland, which they both loved but he would always
send Harry a picture postcard, all of which he has kept. From
Plockton in Scotland in 1975, he has a card which says 'WARNING
– Prices have rocketed – 2/10 for a moderate three-course meal!'

They also had regular habits and routines in their working life,
with Harry going to visit AW at his home twice a week to bring
proofs, letters, requests. Harry has a memory of several big London
publishers beginning to sniff around in the 1970s, trying to buy
over Wainwright, but they were sent packing.

One of Betty's aims, when she married Wainwright and moved
into Kendal Green, was to look after his health. He always boasted
that walking had kept him fit and that he was never ill, which was
not strictly true. Betty indulged his morning passion for bacon and
eggs, but tried to restrain him during the rest of the day, limiting
his intake of biscuits and puddings which had been Ruth's speciality. He was sixteen stone when she married him but gradually she
managed to get him down to twelve and a half stone. 'I found he
was puffing up the hills, which he thought was due to smoking
but I knew it was also his weight, so it was best that he should cut
down. He later found he had mild diabetes, so he had to watch his
diet from then on.'

Most evenings he watched a bit of television, especially 'Coronation Street', and any cowboy films. 'He loved those for the
scenery, but worried about the horses being ill treated. John
Wayne was his hero.' He also watched football, and took down the

scores, betraying no emotion unless it was Blackburn Rovers; then he might smile if they scored. He was never interested in politics or current events. Betty took the *Daily Telegraph* while he preferred the *Daily Mail*, but only to read the Fred Bassett cartoon strip.

While he worked, he had his pipe in his mouth, filled with Three Nuns tobacco, but he wasn't always smoking it, often just sucking. 'There was utter consternation if he ever lost it.' (*See* plate 23.)

He never answered the telephone, even if he was in the house on his own, letting it ring as though unaware of its existence. 'When we first got married, and I had to go away somewhere, visiting my daughters perhaps, I used to ask him if he'd answer the phone, just in case it might be me. "I don't think so," he'd said. Eventually I got him to promise that if I rang at a certain time, say nine o'clock, he would answer it. He agreed to that, but if I rang at five past, or five to, he just let it ring. He never liked talking on the phone, no matter how urgent it was.'

They never entertained. Dinners were never given nor parties held. No one, in his whole life, in either marriage, remembers being formally invited to his home for a meal or a drink, although family friends sometimes stayed the night and visitors might be offered a cup of tea and a biscuit, provided by Betty. Wainwright himself very often never put in an appearance when visitors were present, staying upstairs in his room. Some of his Blackburn relations remember being asked to leave, to their faces, if he felt they had stayed too long, such as over half an hour.

'I would have liked more of a social life,' says Betty. 'I enjoy talking to people who are interesting. But he didn't like people coming to the house and resented any interruptions. He wouldn't meet my friends, and had no desire to enlarge his circle. "I'm not a peep show," he always said, or "I've got too much to do." I suppose he was selfish, like most men.'

Wainwright never went abroad, never flew in an aeroplance or sailed the sea in a ship, apart from ferries between the Scottish Islands. He restricted himself to short holidays in Britain, usually Scotland. 'He felt people who went to Spain to sit in the sun were wasting their time, were without any purpose in life. I would love to have taken him to Switzerland or Norway as I thought their mountains would interest him, but he always refused. We once did discuss a visit to Ireland, but then he said no. "I'm not meeting trouble half way." '

Until her marriage, Betty had had a full social life, with numerous friends, meetings, concerts and fun activities. Perhaps it was his anti-social streak which was part of the reason she hesitated after their first year of passionate courtship. She says his lack of interest in a social life did not worry her too much. She still had her two daughters, although they did not find AW quite the caring and involved step-father they might have hoped for.

'I didn't really object because I was very happy with him. We had a lovely life together. I was able to keep many of my old friends, as long as they didn't come to the house too often. He himself was very happy. He never got depressed or bad tempered. He was very philosophical and accepted everything without complaining.

'We never had rows, though he was difficult to argue with as he never answered back. If he'd been particularly unhelpful and selfish, I'd start fizzing and say this is a one-sided marriage, I do all the work in the house etc – then he'd just walk away and not talk. If I was really fizzing, he would let me say it all, then he'd lean down and put his hand on my shoulder and say, 'Have you done?'

'If I had been born later, I think I would have been a feminist. Women do have a raw deal. But, on the whole, despite being totally different personalities, he never really irritated me. We got on very well. I didn't even mind that he was so untidy. His room was a mess. I don't know how he could find anything. His clothes were always full of burn holes from his pipe, yet he wouldn't throw them out. He had one good suit, the one he bought for his visit to Buckingham Palace, which he kept for funerals. He hated wearing a tie and usually refused. He didn't even have a proper anorak for walking until I bought him one.

'He answered all his fan letters himself, letting them pile up beside his desk until they toppled over. He could be very rude in some of his replies. There was a man who sent his son's essay on travelling, which the father thought was very good and should be published. Red wrote back and told the man his son should go back to school and learn grammar. If you asked Red a question, you always got the ghastly truth.

'He was abrupt with people and rather gruff, which could appear to be rudeness. I met him too late to put any frills on him. He thought it was of no consequence what people thought of him. He had confidence in himself and didn't care. He also had confidence in his work and didn't want any of his guides updated. Above the intake land, nothing would change, he said, and if below that, new gates or stiles appeared, he felt readers should use their nous and work it out for themselves. He later admitted that in *A Coast to Coast Walk* he'd led people once or twice across private land, thinking they were public rights of way, but that has now been corrected.

'He wasn't religious. He thought there might be something up there, but didn't know what. He was pantheistic. I was quite surprised when I married him to find how right wing he was. I'm always less certain. He was a hanger and a flogger, but he wasn't racist. I remember we gave a lift to a boy from Bangkok hitch-hiking in Scotland and he was fascinated by him.

'His growing fame meant nothing to him. He just wanted to be undisturbed and allowed to get on with his work.'

The nature of fame is such that anyone who prefers to remain reclusive becomes even more attractive, with the media competing to get the first interviews, the first foot across the doorstep, the first face-to-face meeting. The extraordinary sales of his books, from a little publishing firm in Kendal no one elsewhere had ever heard of, which still had no reps or sales force, encouraged regional and then national radio, TV and newspapers to ask constantly for an interview, but they were all turned away. All requests came through the Westmorland Gazette, who didn't employ such persons as PR or marketing managers, leaving Harry Firth to say sorry, Mr Wainwright does not give interviews.

I got through to him in 1978. I wrote to him, via the Westmorland Gazette, saying I was doing a walking book around Lakeland, which would include bits about notable locals, such as Joss Naylor the runner, the owners of Sharrow Bay Hotel, the Wordsworth experts at Dove Cottage, and could I talk to him. Fortunately, he had read a walking book of mine about Hadrian's Wall, and agreed on one condition – that nothing ended up in a newspaper.

His house in Kendal Green was a surprise. I had expected something rural and quaint, an old farmhouse on the fells perhaps, not a modern building in a rather suburban setting, but there were good views of the fells from the back. He was taller and burlier than I had expected – but what did I expect, having seen no photographs of him? – with thick white hair and a soft Lancashire accent. He was seventy-one at the time, and looked pretty fit. The furnishings were modest and chintzy, with no sign of the wealth I presumed he must be accumulating from his book sales. There seemed to be a lot of cats around but very few books, mostly presentation copies of Lakeland books by other authors, which he hadn't yet read. He explained that his long years of study to qualify as an accountant had killed any instinct for reading or research.

Once he settled down, and started chatting, he proved to be an interesting talker, very slow and deliberate, considering every thought and fact. I now know that on paper, in letters particularly, he was fluent and effortless, making good jokes and producing fine, polished prose, but verbally he was hesitant, awkward, ill at ease. I remember thinking he wouldn't be much good on radio or TV, and presumed that was one reason he had avoided them, knowing his own limitations.

I had four hours with him, while Betty was out, with the telephone going continuously but being ignored. He went over some of his early life in Blackburn but mainly we talked about Lakeland and the Pictorial Guides. I couldn't get over how he'd done everything by public transport, trundling across Lakeland for sometimes up to four hours, even before he could start his day's walk, but he said he had loved the buses. 'I never missed the bus home in the thirteen years. I was always at the road end twenty minutes before it was due, just in case my watch had gone wrong during the day. The slower the bus the better I liked it. There's nothing more restful than a stopping bus.' I didn't know, of course, that in those years he'd never been in a hurry to get home.

I congratulated him on the success of his Pennine Way guide, which had reached the 100,000-mark in just under ten years, so the Westmorland Gazette had told me, and that started him moaning about the increase in the price of beer. The previous year, the publican at the Border Hotel had sent him a bill for £400. 'Back in 1968, beer was only 1/6 a pint. Now it's four shillings. It's quite shocking. But I don't really regret the promise. If you've walked 270 miles, a free pint is a nice thing to have at the end.'

He revealed that he had turned down several honorary degrees. He had accepted a Hon MA in 1974 from Newcastle University, and had quite enjoyed the occasion, but was now refusing. A Salford MA had recently been rejected and even a D.Litt. from Lancaster. What he did, when offered some university honour, was write to their biology department, asking if they experimented on live animals and, if so, he could have nothing to do with them.

Betty eventually returned to the house. She then had to go to Abbot Hall where an exhibition of his drawings from *Kendal in the Nineteenth Century* was about to go on show and she was supervising the hanging. I went with her and was so impressed by the AW originals, which of course I had never seen before, that I went mad and bought three of them. Well, they were only £10 each, a snip, even in 1978.

When I came to sign the cheque, I started writing the name A. Wainwright but was told by an attendant that that was wrong. I had to make it out to Animal Rescue Cumbria. Didn't I know he gave away all his money to animals? I didn't, actually. And that, to me, was perhaps the biggest surprise of all.

19 & 20 AW and Betty McNally during their early courtship, 1965: after waiting and wondering for thirty years, his Dream Girl appeared to have entered his life at last . . .

21 AW at Ulverston for the exhibition of his drawings for the Furness Sketchbooks

22 AW after receiving his honorary degree from Newcastle University, 1974: more were offered but all refused

23 AW at home working on one of his sketchbooks

24 AW and Eric Robson below Darwen Tower, filming for the BBC, 1985

25 AW and Eric Robson resting on location in Glen Brittle, on Skye, 1988: after
    Lakeland, Scotland was AW's favourite place

26 AW and Eric Robson in front of AW's birthplace, Audley Range in Blackburn, 1990

27 AW, co-founder of Blackburn Rovers Supporters Club in 1939, filming at Ewood Park, 1990. The television series was not completed, nor did AW live to see Rovers' finest hour

28 AW relaxing at home

29 Unknown
woman

30 The desirable Betty
Ditchfield

31 Peter Wainwright, AW's son

32 Ruth Wainwright, his first wife

33 Doris Snape, faithful friend

34 & 35 Two photographs of Betty McNally, later Betty Wainwright

The photographs found in Wainwright's wallet after his death, 1991:
who is the unknown woman?

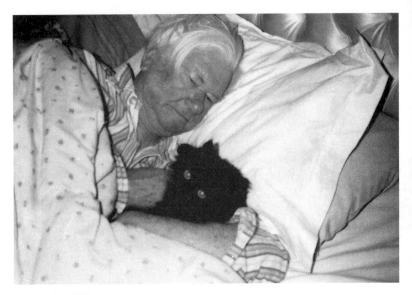

36 In bed with Totty

37 The memorial slate in Buttermere Church

CHAPTER TWENTY-THREE

Of Animals and Books

Ruth had left the marital home with her dog, taking it with her on the bus to her rented cottage in Kentmere. Betty arrived with her cat Krishna. 'I've always had this feeling for animals, and always tried to help animal charities when I could. Red felt the same.'

Very soon they were taking in other cats – homeless cats, strays or ones which had been ill treated. One Christmas, they had a total of twenty-four homeless cats living with them, which was fairly exceptional but it proved to them that there was a need for some sort of animal refuge in the Kendal area.

Wainwright's favourite cat was Totty, a stray they took in when she was three weeks old. They called her Totty because she tottered when she walked. She became a permanent part of the household, sitting on Wainwright's desk when he worked, watching him write and draw, watching him puff away at his pipe. 'Totty eventually suffered from passive smoking,' says Betty. 'She had an awful chest in the end. Sometimes she would plonk herself on his work in progress, making it impossible for him to continue. I often used to come into his room and find Totty sitting on his papers. He would just be staring at her, puffing away. "Why don't you move her," I'd ask. "She thinks I need a rest," he'd say.'

Totty slept beside him at night, back to back, on his side of their twin beds pushed together. 'I'm sleeping with a strange woman at the moment,' he often told visitors. Betty worried that he'd turn over in his sleep and kill Totty, as he was so heavy. In cafés, when Wainwright ordered his usual fish and chips, he would always put a piece of his fish in his pocket to take home for Totty.

'Then he'd forget about it – and the smell was terrible'. Totty died aged seventeen in 1993.

The formal giving of money to animal charities by Wainwright, which he revealed to his readers at the end of Book Seven, began on 11 November 1965, a few months after his important meeting with Betty. That was when he wrote to the local branch of the RSPCA.

I am prepared to enter into a covenant to pay to the Westmorland Branch of the Royal Society for the Prevention of Cruelty to Animals the sum of one thousand pounds per annum for seven years, the first payment to be made on 17th January 1967, for the purpose of providing a headquarters for the Society in Kendal. The annual payments would be made out of income that has already been subject to income tax, and the Society would, therefore, as a registered Charity be able to claim a refund of tax on each annual payment. In round figures the tax refund over the period would amount to about £4,500, and with interest accrued from investment of the annual payments as they are made, I estimate the value of the gift to the Society to be around £12,000 by the end of the seventh year.

This amount should be enough, I think, to erect and equip a small building with office accommodation for the Inspector (sufficiently large to be used as a Committee Room), a waiting room, clinic, surgery, store, and inside kennels and cages, opening on to an exercise yard or compound. I have in mind a central site, quiet and remote from private residences, which I hope it may be possible to acquire.

Apart from providing greater convenience for the Inspector, and freeing him from the present need to use his home as an office and animal shelter, the primary object would be to make available a 'hospital' where sick animals and birds could be brought for care and attention without charge, but voluntary contributions would be invited. I feel confident that there would be no lack of voluntary helpers to staff the building, but would expect the professional services of veterinary surgeons to be paid for in accordance with their normal charges.

I should be grateful if you would kindly arrange for your Committee to consider this offer and let me know their decision in due course. In the meantime I should be obliged if the matter could be treated in confidence.

Yours faithfully,
A. WAINWRIGHT

He had chosen 17 January 1967 as the starting date because that would be his sixtieth birthday, the day he planned to retire as Borough Treasurer, and would then have his municipal pension to live on. He made ten copies of his letter, sent it to various committee members, and waited for their reaction, ecstatic or otherwise. By return he got a letter from the Hon. Secretary, saying she was 'utterly overwhelmed', though she confessed that she had never realised that the Mr Wainwright with whom she corresponded as Town Treasurer was the same as the author of the wonderful guides to the Lakeland Fells. Nor did she know he was a lover of animals.

Over the next two years, there was a long drawn out series of meetings, discussions and letters from various RSPCA people, local and national. Mr Wainwright's Animal Hospital idea was a bit too ambitious, said one expert, as that would need a proper clinic, surgical equipment, animal wards and it would cost £20,000, far more than he was offering. Then there would be the problem of getting professional staff, plus enough voluntary help. In addition to these problems, many other obstacles were pointed out. In fact, it would be much better if they forgot the whole idea of an Animal Hospital and had a simple Animal Refuge. Best of all, why not just buy a field with the money. That would be easy to look after.

Wainwright was furious. There had been some publicity about his offer in the local paper, as well as in Book Seven, and it had figured in his divorce row with Ruth. On 3 May 1968, he sent off an aggrieved letter to the RSPCA formally withdrawing his offer and threatening to make public their behaviour, although he never did.

Betty says that the main problem was that there were too many timid people around and too many moribund committees who couldn't cope with such an exciting idea. And so the Wainwright connections ceased with the RSPCA.

'Some animal lovers can be a bit eccentric,' says Betty. 'They're not quite balanced. You need to put a hoop of steel round them to keep them in place.'

Nonetheless, they gave generously and worked actively for a year or so for a newly established animal charity in Lancashire which had been receiving some publicity in the national press. This was the Bleakhold Animal Sanctuary near Ramsbottom which specialised in helping old or invalid donkeys. Its Patron and President was Margaret, Duchess of Argyll, and its list of Hon. Vice Presidents dripped with aristocratic names. In July 1969, Wainwright and Betty made a three-day visit to the Sanctuary. They were pleased by the work going on, and how their donations were being spent, but appalled by the financial state.

Wainwright wrote a long and detailed report on his visit, beautifully laid out. He found the account books of the Sanctuary 'not merely hopeless – they didn't exist at all.' He went through all the problems, point by point: how it would be impossible to submit accounts for their first year of operation, no proper records having been kept. He then made a long list of recommendations for their future activities, such as putting some of the money from his £200-a-year covenant towards hiring proper accountants.

They also became involved with another local charity, Animal Rescue Cumbria, which had been founded in 1972 by a group of local ladies. Betty became a committee member. 'There were various changes going on, and various disagreements, and in 1974 Red was invited to become chairman, to pull it all together, sort things out.'

That is Betty's memory of what happened. Several disaffected founder members believe the Wainwrights made a takeover bid, and are *still* upset. (One of them wrote to me, on hearing a biography was being written, threatening legal action if I did not make it clear that the Wainwrights were not the founders of Animal Rescue. So there. I've said it.)

Their inspiration was the need they had felt for some time to have a proper refuge centre, rather than members taking strays into their own houses while new homes were found, which is what was then happening. To achieve this, they realised efficient management, accounting and clear leadership was necessary, with the minimum of petty squabbles.

'It was vital to have a permanent building so we started to raise the money and it took many years. Red donated a lot of the money, but we also had other fund-raising activities.' Betty explained that that was why I had signed the cheque to Animal Rescue when I had bought three of his drawings at Abbot Hall. It was the beginning of their campaign to buy their own site and build their own animal shelter.

Wainwright started giving away almost all his royalties to Animal Rescue, keeping very little for himself, content to live mainly on his pension. Hence that reference to being skint at the end of *A Coast to Coast Walk*. He had always been careful with his spending anyway when it came to his own comforts, preferring the cheaper hotels and guest houses, but now he had another reason for doing it, even though it might appear to outsiders he was penny pinching. Fans who wrote to him about his books often found him moaning about money. To one correspondent, who had written about his *Scottish Mountain Drawings* in September 1975, he replied that on his next trip to Scotland he had booked a caravan in Glencoe. 'Hotel charges are really getting out of hand. I shall know later whether the suffering is worth the saving.'

In order, therefore, to help Animal Rescue as much as possible, he was keen to see sales of his books increase, and to keep up his output of titles. At the same time, he was still refusing to do any personal publicity or agree to any of the marketing methods most publishers use to push their books. However, sales were continuing to increase steadily, much to the pleasure of the Westmorland Gazette.

Bill Mitchell, editor of *Cumbria*, noticed how well they were doing every time he went to the print works. 'I had to pass between white cliffs of paper earmarked for the Wainwright books.' By the early 1980s, new impressions of Book Three, The Central Fells, had reached the 100 mark. Eventually they stopped changing the impression number.

Harry Firth retired from the Westmorland Gazette in June 1982. A dinner was held in his honour at the Wild Boar Hotel and Wainwright, who normally avoided all such social occasions, turned up to bid him farewell. Firth had been involved in printing and supporting Wainwright from the beginning, as well as becoming his holiday friend.

Andrew Nichol, who had been Production Manager, took over as General Manager. The previous year, the company had suffered a blow when they lost the printing contract for both *Cumbria* and *Dalesman*.

'The two magazines had been our biggest single printing job,' says Andrew Nichol. 'When they went, at a stroke, we lost a third of the general printing turnover. It made the publishing part of the firm, i.e. Wainwright, even more important. At this point, the tail was wagging the dog. We were printers who'd become dependent on publishing.

'When I joined the general printing side in 1974, publishing was a fill-in sort of activity, done when we had the space or time to spare. The books we published often ran out of stock, or ran out of covers while we concentrated on the general printing side of the business. But by 1982, thanks to Wainwright, it was publishing which kept us going. It provided two sorts of income, because we made a profit as the printer, but also as the publisher. We sold the books direct to shops and wholesalers, and did all this without ever having any reps, the way normal publishers do. We had always relied on orders just coming in. So my job in 1982 was somehow to try to increase the Wainwright sales, in order to keep us afloat.

'His books were a joy for a printer to handle. There was no typesetting, so we saved expense on that. And there was no proof reading either. I couldn't believe it when I first saw his pages, justified at each end of the line, and each page ready for same size reproduction. I was also surprised by the passion his readers had for him. Just after taking over, I got a phone call from a couple in London, wanting to send one of his books for AW to sign. I said I'd do my best. They could either send it to me, or drop it in next time they were in Lakeland. They said they'd drop it in. I said in that case they could have a look round the works, see where the Wainwrights were printed. They arrived next day! They'd immediately taken a day off work, and come straight up to Kendal. I couldn't believe it. But that sort of thing happened so often that I was soon no longer surprised.'

Andrew Nichol was taken by Harry Firth to meet AW soon after he took over. 'Harry told me to come in behind him, not to speak till he speaks to you. It was like meeting the Pope. AW asked me if I did much walking, and I said not a lot, I haven't got time. I only walk to my car. I thought that may have upset him, but he didn't seem to mind. We wouldn't always agree on things, but he never wasted time or words.

'From then on, I went to see him twice a week – Fridays at 10.30 and Mondays at 2.30. I would take his post, any queries or requests, bring him proofs, discuss any new business.'

Many of the requests, so Nichol found, were from newspapers, radio and TV companies wanting to interview AW, so naturally he passed them on, and naturally AW said no, certainly not. 'I suggested that things like Desert Island Discs sounded good to me, but he still refused. I knew if only he would do a little bit of publicity, we would double our sales. Television was my main aim, but he wasn't interested.'

In 1983, Animal Rescue, thanks to Wainwright, had raised a total of £30,000 towards their dream of a permanent animal refuge. 'We needed at least double to purchase a suitable property,' says Betty, 'and it was Andrew Nichol who suggested a way we could get the money.'

'It was about this time I raised the question of copyright with the directors of our parent company, Westminster Press,' says Nichol. 'I outlined my plans for expanding the book publishing side, to create extra work for General Printing through increased sales of the books, but could not be confident about my plans in the long term unless we owned the copyright. At this stage AW was saying publication of his books should cease on his death. The Directors, and in particular our Chairman, the Duke of Atholl, responded quickly and within a day or two I was given permission to offer AW £40,000 for the copyright. He would also continue to receive royalties.

'I went to see him next morning and he was delighted. I've never seen him show so much emotion. He was absolutely beaming and called the news through to Mrs Wainwright who was in the kitchen. She was pleased and said they would be able to start looking at properties for Animal Rescue and invited me to help them find somewhere suitable. Of course, publication had to continue after his death and I expected him to co-operate with publicity.'

Betty now thinks it was a mistake. 'Red didn't argue or bargain. He took their first offer. I said at least we should get a lawyer to check the contract, but he just signed, without properly reading it. He trusted people to do the fair thing. On the one hand, he used to say that seventy-five percent of people were not worth bothering with, but on the other hand he always acted honourably. I do regret he ever did it.'

Wainwright still received all his royalties, as in the past, but he had also realised a large capital sum for Animal Rescue (and soon afterwards the charity was able to buy a $4\frac{1}{2}$-acre property in a village not far from Kendal). The Westmorland Gazette had in a sense only bought an abstract asset, the Wainwright name. What was the drawback?

'It entitled them from then on to market and promote Wainwright's name, without consulting us,' says Betty. 'That's what upset me.'

'It's true we gained control of all reproduction rights,' says Mr Nichol. 'We had already been handling permissions to reproduce as requests used to come to us in the first place, but it meant we didn't in theory have to get his permission for the use of his drawings on cards and that sort of thing. However, we still always asked him. In 1984, we did some prints which he signed and we paid him a royalty. In fact we got no additional income out of buying the copyright. It was purely to protect our investment in him.

'Before then, all we had with Wainwright was first refusal on his next book. He could have left us at any time, taken his books, old and new, and gone elsewhere. We would have been sunk. It would have been the end of our publishing department. So £40,000 was worth it to us to safeguard our future.'

The contract was signed on 11 October 1983, and lists all the Wainwright books which the Gazette had published so far – forty-two titles in all. The sum of £40,000 for the copyright seems to me not too unreasonable, but as a full-time, professional author, which AW was by then, I would have got my agent, not a lawyer, to read the small print concerning future sales. The royalty was set at a rate of 7½%, regardless of how many were sold. I would have expected it to start at 10% on the first 3,000 copies sold, which is normal with hardbacks, and then on a sliding scale, going even higher. Those are the rates a London publisher would have paid. Wainwright was by then a bestselling author, but of course he was still being published by a small regional company.

Some time in 1985, thirty years after Book One of the Pictorial Guides first appeared, the Westmorland Gazette did some interesting calculations. They worked out that the one millionth copy of the seven guides was due to come off the presses. Time for some celebration, surely.

It's hard to calculate exactly how much money the Pictorial Guides had generated by then. They had started at 12/6 each in 1955 which had risen to £3.45 in 1984, so total revenue by 1985 must have been well over £2 million. Then, of course, there were his forty other books by 1985, some of which, like the *Pennine Way Companion* were approaching the 200,000 mark. Altogether, Wainwright had sold around two million books, making him one of Britain's bestselling but least known living authors. Time to wave the publicity flag, well, just a few inches.

Andrew Nichol, ever on the look out for a way of getting Wainwright to agree to some publicity, brought the subject up at one of his weekly visits. He said they must celebrate the event in some way. One million copies of a series of local guides, from a local publisher, was worthy of some commemoration. Not necessarily fireworks and a grand party but some modest marking of the occasion. After a great deal of discussion beween them, it was decided the millionth copy would have one vital but subtle distinguishing mark. Whoever chanced to buy it, would be suitably rewarded. Nothing vulgar or lavish. The lucky owner would simply be offered a free holiday for two at the Langdale Time Share and a meal for two with Wainwright himself. A modest publicity campaign was mounted, announcing these delights.

'The book would also be re-bound in leather and gold lettered,' says Andrew Nichol, 'stating it was the millionth Wainwright. One enthusiast rang to say that he would be prepared to pay £500 for it, if whoever got it was prepared to sell.'

The one millionth guide turned out to be a copy of Book Six, the North Western Fells, and the distinguishing mark they decided upon was to be placed at the end, on the page before his Personal Note. In this particular book he would write his name, in handwriting, A. Wainwright, not have it printed.

Betty thought it was a good idea to celebrate the one millionth copy but thought marking the book in this way was silly. 'How would anyone recognise it was different? I don't know whether it was Red's idea or one of Westmorland Gazette's poorer marketing ideas, but I told them it was stupid, and then let them get on with it, playing their little boy printing games.'

Andrew Nichol watched the marked book leave the print works, noting that it went in a batch to a bookshop just outside Manchester. He told no one except AW. There was no reaction for a week. Then two weeks. Then six weeks. Still no one came forward to claim the prize. It had either not been sold or not identified, despite the fact that Wainwright fans were trying to find it, though without knowing precisely what they were looking for, or indeed which book.

'I then got a call from AW, a big event in itself,' says Andrew Nichol. 'I don't think he'd ever rung me before. He said he'd had second thoughts and gone off the idea. He wanted the book back. He was going to Manchester himself to buy it. I thought it wisest to go with him. I suppose I could have rung the bookseller, made up a story and got him to send it back, but AW wanted to do it himself, right away. So off we went, in my car. The book *was* still there, so he bought it.

'On the way home, the real reason emerged why he'd gone off the idea. "I don't want to eat with strangers," he said. So it was only the meal he was really against. When I discovered that, I talked him into continuing with the prize but with changed rules – no meal with Wainwright this time, but still the free weekend, plus the winner would have his book specially bound.

'We then decided to place the book in a faster selling outlet somewhere in the Lake District and re-publicise the benefits for the book's buyer minus the meal with AW. As I was going to be on holiday the following week, the book was left with our Order Processing Clerk, Mrs Cooke, who included it in an order for Chaplins of Keswick, one of our best customers. A couple of weeks later AW and I went to Keswick and I went into Chaplins and checked the stock. It wasn't there. We returned to Kendal and next day circularised the national press with the details, but to this day it has never turned up. I can only think it was bought by one of the many thousands of foreign visitors who come to the Lake District each year, and returned home unaware of the search.

'I have one suspicion about who just might have got it – AW,' says Nichol. 'I wouldn't be surprised if he changed his mind again, and when I was on holiday, went to Keswick and bought it himself. It would have been his sort of joke.'

CHAPTER TWENTY-FOUR

Bestselling Fame 1984

In March 1983, Jenny Dereham of Michael Joseph Ltd, the London publishing house, was looking for an author for an illustrated book about the Pennine Way. It was to be the latest in a very successful series they had produced about various parts of the British Isles, all with colour photographs by Derry Brabbs. Not quite coffee-table books, as the term was now being used rather dismissively, but celebratory books about well-loved parts of the country.

One secret of their success was that the writer should be not only well known, but also well loved, though not necessarily in the field of lovely landscape writing. The writers of the three books in this series published so far had made their names in rather different fields. James Herriot was a vet and an author, while Wynford Vaughan-Thomas and Angela Rippon were both broadcasters. They had written respectively on Yorkshire, Wales and the West Country.

James Herriot's Yorkshire, the first in the series, had been a mega-bestseller, selling 650,000 copies in hardback and paperback – not surprising really when one remembers that his books, films and television series 'All Creatures Great and Small' had been international bestsellers for over ten years. It was Derry Brabbs, the photographer for all three books, who had suggested a Pennine Way book as the next in the series, having noticed that 1985 would be the twentieth anniversary of its official opening.

The problem for Miss Dereham – brought up in the Hampshire countryside, educated at a boarding school in Sussex, started at Michael Joseph as a secretary in 1965, and now a Director – was to find a suitable author. One of the early ideas in her mind, trying it out for size, had been Brendan Foster, the celebrated middle-distance runner from Gateshead, but she had not pursued this idea when she reckoned that writing the text of a coffee-tablish sort of book might not be his forte.

She turned to a friend, Victor Morrison, who had been Managing Director at Michael Joseph and who had masterminded *James Herriot's Yorkshire*, for advice since she knew that he had walked the Pennine Way a few years previously. His immediate suggestion was Wainwright. Jenny Dereham had heard of his name, indeed she owned one of his books and had used it when walking in the Howgills in 1974. But she had been told that Wainwright was wedded to his local Cumbrian publisher. 'It will only cost you the price of a stamp to write and ask him,' Victor Morrison pointed out.

On 11 March 1983, she wrote a long letter to Mr Wainwright, care of the Westmorland Gazette. She realised from reading his *Pennine Way Companion* (smartly acquired) that he had loathed some parts of the walk, so her proposal was that they should only concentrate on his favourite bits. 'We are not envisaging a book covering the entire Way. After all, your *Pennine Way Companion* is the walkers' Bible and we know we can't compete!' She also enclosed a copy of *James Herriot's Yorkshire* – 'to remind you of this marvellous book – which is reprinting yet again!' It was a neat letter, although she was possibly a trifle fortunate in that AW had never been a hater of exclamation marks.

Other London publishers, over the years, had tried to tempt Wainwright away, but with no success. The nearest he had come to a London publisher was very occasionally contributing illustrations or maps to other people's books. Apart from Molly Lefebure's children's books, already mentioned, his most notable contribution was to Richard Adams's novel *The Plague Dogs*, set in Lakeland and published by Allen Lane in 1977; this contains eight diagrams and twenty of his drawings.

What Jenny did not realise, when she wrote, was that Wainwright was in the throes of wondering how to raise extra money to buy a property for Animal Rescue. (At this stage, in 1983, it was a few months before Westmorland Gazette had made their offer to buy the copyright.) So Wainwight replied to Jenny by return to Michael Joseph's Bedford Square office, suggesting a meeting a few weeks later, not in Kendal or London, but in Buxton, Derbyshire, where he happened to be heading, working on *A Peak District Sketchbook* for the Westmorland Gazette.

The night before their meeting, Jenny was at a nephew's 21st birthday celebrations until two in the morning, partying on the Thames, so she had only a couple of hours' sleep before rising at five to drive to Buxton and get there by nine, the time Wainwright had decreed. Derry Brabbs, driving from Harrogate, arrived slightly late. AW, becoming impatient, muttered dark questions about whether people who arrived late could really be trusted to take photographs.

Eventually they all gathered and sat down to talk in the hotel's sun-lounge. Jenny presented the project and Derry talked about the photographs. Betty asked a few questions, and AW just listened. Jenny was wondering whether he was really interested in providing the text for the book on the Pennine Way when he suddenly spoke – and took her and the others by complete surprise. Yes, he would do the Pennine Way book but since the anniversary wasn't until 1985 there would be time to do another book first.

Jenny was naturally enthusiastic at the prospect of *two* contracts, but Derry paled slightly at the thought of having to get all the photographs done in a very short time. Wainwright suggested the first book should be a collection of his favourite Lakeland walks – *Fellwalking in Lakeland* it could be called. The advance for each book was agreed at £10,000 – shared equally between Wainwright and Brabbs.

Jenny later wrote to Wainwright suggesting a 60/40 split as he was the major player, but AW insisted on 50/50, saying that Derry was the famous person, having secured his name through the photographs for *James Herriot's Yorkshire*.

The business having been done, Betty drove them in her car to

Edale. During the drive, Jenny fell asleep, suffering severely from the lack of sleep the previous night. That could have been a loss of house points but they all got on well and walked for about a mile up the beginning of the Pennine Way from the Old Nag's Head. Jenny remembers that no one gave Wainwright a second glance – just a big man walking steadily along the boot-scarred path, his old macintosh looped over his arm, his pipe firmly in his mouth. Just A. Walker.

Discussions took place by letter over the next three months about both books, sample pages written and first photographs submitted. A Michael Joseph designer, Susan McIntyre, got working on layouts, while AW carried on with the words and Derry on the photographs.

In July, Jenny wrote to AW about their production plans, as a good publisher should, and received a furious letter back. So upset was AW by what Michael Joseph appeared to be planning that he issued a threat.

Dear Jenny,

I must thank you for your letter of the 3rd, but must also say that my reactions to its contents are of surprise, shock and even horror. Here am I, getting along like a house on fire, and then you suddenly explode a bombshell that stops me in my tracks.

Surprise

I am amazed to learn that you have pre-determined the number of pages in the Pennine book and presumably of the Lakeland book. Surely the number of pages should be that required to contain the full narrative and the photographs needed to illustrate the text? If you were publishing a novel or a biography you would let it run its full course even if it was over-running the number of pages you earlier had in mind; you wouldn't cut out a chapter or two because it proved to be longer than you intended. Similarly I think that the narratives and photos of our two books should be given all the space necessary for the production of complete and unabridged books.

Shock

I have been working under the impression that you wanted books to match the Herriot book in size, format and printing area on each page, and my layouts have been prepared with this in mind. You now say that your designer plans to make the Pennine book slightly smaller than the

Herriot. Slightly smaller? The proposed reduction in printing area is dramatic. Herriot has a printing area of over 50 square inches per page. Susan plans 35 square inches only. That's why my layouts don't fit her drafts. As a matter of fact I have been intending all along that each book should be of 224 pages, as you suggest, but they were to be pages having a similar printing area to the Herriot, and my layouts would have slotted into place very nicely had they been adopted.

Susan wants her bottom smacking for implying that some passages should be cut out and some photographs omitted. This is unfair both to me and Derry. As for counting the characters and spaces of my typewritten lines, how can you assume that my typewriter characters and spaces between lines are going to coincide exactly with the printer's type and spaces? As for single or double columns for the text, I rather favour single: your letter to me, and this one to you, have lines about the same length as a single column, and of course are quite easy to read as well as easier for a printer to set up, and fewer hyphens would be needed.

Horror

I am horrified at the emphasis being given to the cost of publication, by the counting of pennies. Your intention should be a perfect book, full stop, not a book as perfect as finances permit. By cutting costs you could lose the sale of 10,000 copies. Where's the saving?

Please turn over;
I haven't finished yet.

In general, I think I know from long experience what fellwalkers and Pennine wayfarers like to read and the sort of photographs they like to look at, and it is with their preferences in mind that I have been working. They are outdoor people: they like spaciousness around them and they prefer books that have the contents spaciously arranged, not cramped. They prefer large photos that make them feel they are out in the open, not pictures reduced to snaps and crowded in restricted space.

You have knocked the stuffing out of me. I like to feel free to do as I think best, not to work in harness imposed by designers who may never have been out on hills and have no feeling for them.

I am sorry to be so forthright but am sure you are on the wrong tack. I have no interest in doing a book I cannot feel proud of. If you persist in taking advice from your staff, and not from me, I am afraid I must consider pulling out of our arrangement, much though I need the money for a good cause.

I think now that we are not going to produce bestsellers. Just books.

Despite all this acrimonious argument, please be assured that you still have my very best wishes.

It can be argued, very easily, that the Westmorland Gazette had been paying him short all these years, and that a good literary agent could have secured him almost double his royalties, but at the same time Wainwright had evolved into an unspoken, unwritten law unto himself. His success over thirty years, doing things his way, and being proven almost always right, had allowed him to dictate layout, size, pagination, price and title. It had enabled him to produce one or two books WG were not very keen on, but could not risk rejecting, and had allowed him the privilege of never having to visit their office or the chore of addressing sales reps or the bore of attending signing sessions. AW, and Betty in particular, did later castigate some of the Westmorland Gazette's methods and procedures, but it has to be said that they did fit themselves to AW's moods, talents and personality, to the advantage, convenience and profit of all concerned.

Jenny rang him at once, which was a mistake, not knowing his phobia about telephone conversations, and was told to put her reply on paper, if you don't mind. She wrote a long explanation, beginning with the problems of a Production Department but her main point was simple and to the point – abject apology. 'Please go ahead as you are, and we will re-think our design accordingly.'

He replied, thanking her, and gave her the benefit of his own wit and wisdom in the design field acquired over thirty years. His letter makes some interesting points about his books, which most of the one million readers of his seven Guides might well have missed, showing how careful and calculatingly professional he had always been in creating pages which appeared at first glance to be charmingly natural and amateurish.

My ideas on layouts are that they should be informal and not all be to a set pattern, which tends to become monotonous and even boring. The reader should not know in advance what the next page will be like when he turns over; let it come as a surprise and so maintain his interest. I have never in all my books had two pages together that look exactly alike. Every turn of the page is fresh and exciting. Further, the narrative on every one of my pages ends in a full stop, so that each one is complete in itself and gives the reader a chance to pause and study the illustrations on that page, these being closely related to the narrative. I dislike intensely sentences that run from one page to the next, or overleaf, as in a novel, which tend to keep the reader's attention on following the text rather than on the equally important illustrations. This is the way I plan our two books, and you will be simply thrilled to bits when you see what Derry and I have done to uphold the proud traditions of Michael Joseph Limited.

Each book will be of 224 pages, including eight blanks at the beginning for the titles, a publisher's foreword and a list of contents. A final index will not be necessary for the Lakeland book but may be advisable for the Pennine one.

Only innate modesty has prevented me from suggesting the inclusion of a few small black-and-white drawings instead of photographs to fill awkward spaces, and I am therefore glad to learn that you have the same idea. I am all for large photographs only. Colour photos reduced to cigarette card size never give the effect desired, are unfair to the photographer, and are a needless waste of money, but small drawings are not only more likely to attract the eye of the reader but can be quite decorative and much less costly to reproduce, and moreover they can show detail that the camera cannot capture; for example the view from High Street with all the distant features named. I have in fact sprinkled a few of my own illustrations in the chapters I have done so far in cases where the subject is beyond the scope of the camera but needed to illustrate the text. So I agree absolutely.

It's you who doesn't need to worry, not me. Derry and I are providing you with books that will be highlights in your publishing career. You'll see! So don't worry. Everything will be alright.

With best wishes,

Yours sincerely,

Derry, who agrees with me in all things except in the matter of pipe versus cigars, tells me he is visiting you shortly and has craved my permission to smack Susan's bottom on my behalf. So that no further misunderstandings will arise in Bedford Square I think I should confirm to you that I have given him such permission if, after seeing Susan, he still wishes to exercise this rare privilege.

And so began a partnership which over the next eight years produced nine colour books in all from the pen of AW, seven of them with photographs by Derry Brabbs.

Derry was born in Sheffield in 1947, studied photography at Leicester College of Art, then worked for the *TV Times* in Manchester and London. He had returned to Yorkshire, and was working freelance from a rented studio in Leeds when a call out of the blue asked him if he would submit his portfolio. 'Michael Joseph got my name out of the Yellow Pages. They were searching Yorkshire, looking for a local photographer. Luckily my name began with B and they telephoned me first. That's how I got the Herriot job. It was the first book I had ever worked on. I just happened to be in the right place at the right time, and that led eventually on to Wainwright.'

When he arrived for that first meeting in Buxton in 1983, Derry had never heard of Wainwright before. He cannot remember being late, but doesn't deny it.

'My first impression of AW was that he was physically imposing. I'm six foot three but he always seemed to have half an inch over me, but then he was a bit bulkier. Fluent conversation was not something he appeared to indulge in. I naturally wanted to create a good impression but I didn't know whether to babble on like an idiot or keep silent. I soon picked up his preference – if nothing needs to be said, don't say it. I am used to working alone, and in silence, so we got on fine.'

They never walked together, during the production of their books, but then AW was in his late seventies, and had done all the walks anyway. The procedure, with all their books – dictated by AW, of course, having won his battle with Michael Joseph – was for him to write ahead, typing out his own words, then he would sketch the layout of each page, marking where a photograph would go, its shape and size and content.

'That has never happened to me before, or since,' says Derry, 'and it saved me such a lot of time, especially in the early years when I didn't know anything about the place. I had never set foot on a Lakeland mountain. He practically dictated the actual pictures, telling me the view I should look for, such as High Stile from a certain point on Buttermere. He knew the best views, and had drawn them, and I didn't know one rock from another when I started. Sometimes he would add pen drawings of the photograph I should take, perhaps just in silhouette. He was a fantastic help.'

Four spreads taken from Wainwright's original manuscript for Fellwalking with Wainwright: *the key folios and ticks are Derry Brabbs' marking, everything else is AW's. It is worth comparing the pages to the finished book to see how AW's vision was interpreted by the designer.*
Above: pages 20–1: High Street and Harter Fell
Below: pages 38–9: The Fairfield Horseshoe

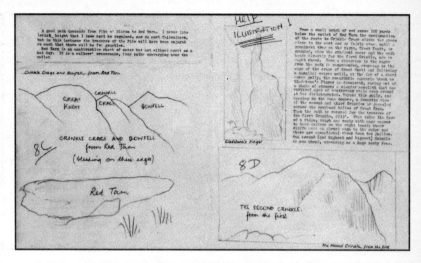

Above: pages 102–3: Crinkle Crags – note Derry's cry of help when he could not find Gladstone's Finger to photograph; AW's drawing is taken from the imprint page of Book Four of the Pictorial Guides.
Below: pages 190–1: Great Gable

After Derry had completed the pictures for each chapter, or each walk, he would arrive in Kendal with his projector and transparancies and show them all to AW. They would then edit them together, and pick the best. (A job which is normally done by a publisher's art editor.) 'He had a very good eye – even when his eyes were failing, he could still somehow see enough to identify every shot.'

Derry never stayed the night at Kendal Green. He fitted in his visits when going to or from Lakeland. 'I couldn't have stayed. They always seemed to have a million cats, and I am mega allergic to all cats.

'My first visit was just after I'd completed chapter one of the first book, covering High Street. I was absolutely shattered. I couldn't believe anyone climbed those mountains for pleasure. I found it very hard going. We sat in his garden on a wooden bench and he was intrigued to hear how I'd got on.'

Over the eight years or so, Derry got to know Lakeland well, plus Scotland and the Pennines, but did not always enjoy the climbing parts. 'A lot of the time I was pretty scared. I was never happy on ledges, mainly because I'm a coward. It was always a personal challenge – me against the elements. I had to talk to myself, make myself brave. One winter I was on Bowfell, going through the Climbers' Traverse, trying to find the Bowfell Buttress, when the path I was on, which was covered in snow, started to move. I realised I was on some scree. I could hear this rumbling sound. I absolutely froze. I had a long conversation with myself, wondering what to do. Should I stay put, will it start moving again? After twenty minutes standing still in total panic, I decided what to do – run like hell.'

He did sleep out overnight once, on Crinkle Crags, taking a small tent with him, but it burdened him down too much and he didn't do it again. Carrying his camera, a 35 mm Olympus OM 4, a heavy tripod weighing 8 lb, four lenses and four filters, plus food and drink and bad weather clothes, was already more than enough for him. 'The main battle was with the weather. It is so fickle in Lakeland. If you don't get the right light, the mountain you want is in black shadow and it can make it unrecognisable. With experience, I got to know when to wait, hoping it might clear, and when to pack up for the day.'

He got into a routine of ringing the Lakeland weather forecast in Windermere the night before, then if it sounded reasonable, he would leave his home in Harrogate at three in the morning and drive in pitch black across the Pennines. 'As I got near Lakeland, and dawn was breaking, I would usually see thick clouds mustering and think, oh God . . .'

Looking back, with hindsight, he feels a bit disappointed with his photographs in the first book but he was working against the clock in a strange area. 'Given a second chance, I wouldn't try to do so many in summer, but I thought I should take advantage of the long hours. I now know that autumn and spring are best for colour. That's when you can make the landscape sing.'

His finest work, he thinks, is in *Wainwright in the Valleys of Lakeland*, published in 1992, because it has a variety of seasons, atmospheres and a mixture of high land and low land. His 'best' book, though, probably has to be *Wainwright's Favourite Lakeland Mountains* (1991) because, for him, it was the hardest to shoot and therefore the better achievement. Derry is not ashamed to admit that he doesn't have the best head for heights: he avoided the Cuillin ridge on Skye when doing the photographs for *Wainwright in Scotland* and the section was illustrated with AW's line drawings instead. In response to Jenny's slight worry about Derry's safety whilst taking the photographs for *Mountains*, AW wrote to her: 'Don't worry about Derry injuring himself. This is bound to happen, probably several times. Our concern is that he should not kill himself and leave the book in limbo.'

Did you like him? Without hesitation, unlike many friends of AW, Derry immediately said yes. 'After my initial shyness, I always felt at ease with him. He could be very dogmatic, on things like cruelty to animals, but his brusqueness was a front which never worried me. I recognised bits of him in me. I'm happy in my own company, and prefer peace and quiet. When I heard him on Desert Island Discs, I was in stitches, listening to his deadpan comments about hiding behind rocks to avoid groups of people. Very Wainwright.'

Fellwalking with Wainwright, their first book together, was published on 20 August 1984. Despite the fact that AW was a new 'national' author, appearing for the first time from a well-known London imprint (some of whose directors had never heard of him until Jenny signed him up), and still refusing to do any publicity tours or any promotional interviews, the book jumped into the bestseller list and remained there until Christmas, selling over 60,000 copies in hardback at £12.95 a copy in just four months. Friends in other publishing companies telephoned Jenny to ask who, or what, is Wainwright? (The book's total sales to date come to 129,000 in hardback and 50,000 in paperback)

In writing the second book, *Wainwright on the Pennine Way*, AW revealed he had done an earlier Pennine book which had lain, unpublished, in his drawer for forty-five years. Jenny asked to see it, was delighted by the contents but not too thrilled by the black and white photographs which AW had taken all those years ago. It was published without illustrations, by Michael Joseph in 1986 and then in paperback by Penguin in 1987. (By a complicated series of coincidences, Penguin took over Michael Joseph in 1986, having themselves been bought by the Pearson Group in 1970, who already owned Westminster Press, who already owned the Westmorland Gazette – which meant that the books by A. Wainwright, both his old and the new, ended up belonging to the same organisation. I hope that's clear.)

All the big, glossy Wainwright books were deservedly successful, including one with photographs by Ed Geldard. The pictures were stunning and the prose professional and informative, but many old Wainwright fans, either of the purist, romantic or hairy-kneed variety, were slightly disappointed that he appeared to have sold out, lending himself to London publishing values, glamorous production and clever marketing, not knowing of course that his purpose was not self-promotion or personal gain but Animal Rescue.

None of these illustrated books explored new territory, except perhaps *Wainwright in Scotland* (1988). He had been there many times on holiday, in fact, almost every year for forty years, and had produced six volumes of *Scottish Mountain Drawings*, published in the 1970s by Westmorland Gazette, but they had contained little writing, apart from captions. *Wainwright in Scotland* did have a lot of new writing. All the other photographic books repeated old material as well as geographical territory, never in exactly the same words, but re-working old information and observations.

In *Fellwalking with Wainwright* he bemoans, once again, the loss of Mardale village, the advance of man in Lakeland and his concern for material advantage, and extols the joys of solitary walking. 'For a man trying to forget a persistent worry the top of Haystacks is a complete cure.' In *Wainwright on the Pennine Way* – which was published on time to celebrate the twentieth anniversary of the Way's opening – he tells about his worst walking drama, when he sank in a bog, and in *Wainwright in the Valleys of Lakeland* he remembers Winnie the waitress in the Keswick café who used to shout 'One plaice and chips' the minute he appeared. All of these thoughts and memories were familiar to readers of his previous books.

It is, of course, hard to find new adjectives for the same views once you've said they're lovely, superb or of 'international renown' which, anyway, was stretching it a bit, even first-time round. Lakeland mountains and lakes, however wondrous most of we British think they might be, are not, alas, known to every man in the street in Africa, Asia or America, where they have their own wondrous, awesome sights.

AW also repeated his liking for anthropomorphism – giving mountains human attributes, saying they are male or female, with the appropriate qualities. Even within the series of photographic books, there was a bit of re-working. In *Wainwright's Favourite Mountains* he describes Blencathra as a 'Jekyll and Hyde mountain', which was exactly the same phrase he used about Helvellyn in *Fellwalking with Wainwright*.

The inevitable re-treading of some old paths and old topics did not upset all the true believers because along the way we did acquire some new memories of his old travels, especially in the Scottish book. Personally, my only complaint was the lack of much humour in these picture books. There are few jokes along the way, few of the little asides which are such a feature of the Pictorial Guides, but when doing those, he was on his own, creating the words and drawings, and so able to drop little bits of himself into the odd space or corner of a drawing. In the later books, there was also, now and again, a slight pompousness creeping in, boasting that he had been where 'surely no man had trodden before', taking himself a little bit too seriously, laying down the Lakeland laws.

He was aware that some people thought he was overdoing Lakeland, as he said in a letter to Jenny at Michael Joseph: 'Although *Passes* has been generally favourably received, there has been mild criticism from two reviewers who suggest we are over-killing the Lakes: one snide comment is that my next book is likely to be *The Lay-bys of Lakeland*, another that I will probably soon be doing a guide to *The Rabbit Warrens of Lakeland*.'

However, these undeniably well-produced books were aimed at a newer, wider audience and they certainly succeed, bringing in thousands of fresh fans. Altogether, in hardback and paperback, the ten illustrated Wainwright books published by Michael Joseph (including those which appeared posthumously) have sold over 600,000 copies, and are still selling.

Jenny Dereham, his editor throughout, became a close friend, staying with Betty and AW when she visited them in Kendal, a rare honour. She thought she had killed him once, when she took him out for a meal at a Little Chef (his choice), when Betty was out somewhere. 'He insisted on having gooseberry pancakes – and went on to have three in all before I remembered he had diabetes, and might not be allowed them. I thought he might collapse before I got him home. I got my wrists gently slapped by Betty.'

Did you like him? 'Yeh-es. I became enormously fond of Betty but perhaps I was always a bit in awe of AW. He knew so much about Lakeland and did not suffer fools. He was an extraordinary person, with so many talents. I got used to his ways and became content to sit in silence with him, perhaps reading a newspaper until he spoke. I think he liked me because I'm fairly methodical and efficient. He hated inefficiency.'

It wasn't just Jenny's editorial efficiency, or Michael Joseph's marvellous publishing methods, that made the books so successful. They had a vital stroke of luck, just after the first two of their books were published, which made all the difference to their sales and to Wainwright's national fame.

CHAPTER TWENTY-FIVE

Television Fame 1986

In 1969, Richard Else was a schoolboy in Leicester, doing his A levels. He came to Keswick on a Geography field trip and fell for Wainwright, the words and the drawings of the Pictorial Guides, imagining he must be long dead, probably Victorian. He returned to Leicester, went to university at Lampeter in Wales, then got a job in local radio and TV in Cardiff. In 1982, he engineered a move to the BBC in Newcastle to work in TV Features. With the express purpose of doing a TV programme on Wainwright. So he says. All those years, you were waiting to do AW?

'It's true. Well, there was more to it than that, but Wainwright was one reason for my move. I'd become fascinated by him. As in all great works of English Literature, you learn more about the author by careful study. In those seven guides, he revealed himself as he progressed. His views on women, for example. He seemed to become more vitriolic as the books went on. By Books Five and Six he appeared to me to have become very anti women . . .'

In Newcastle, he was told that AW refused to appear in any TV programme. They'd all tried. As for getting him to answer questions about his views on women – no chance. Even harmless stuff on Lakeland walks, he had said no, umpteen times, including a request on behalf of the well-loved TV personage and Lakeland lover, Melvyn Bragg.

Richard spent five months reading every book AW had written, researched his life, discovered his passion for animals, and decided to make a TV programme about Wainwright – without, ah ha, using Wainwright. He wrote to AW care of the Westmorland Gazette, saying I am not asking you to appear in the television programme, as I know you will not, but could I have your permission to quote some bits from your books? AW graciously agreed, much to Andrew Nichol's pleasure, hoping for any extra publicity for the Wainwright books.

Filming then began. The plan was to get a feeling for AW by talking to his friends, such as Percy Duff, Harry Griffin and Andrew Nichol, and to review his books. It would be a half-hour feature, for showing locally in the North-East Region.

Reports on its progress filtered back to AW who began to think they were working on his obituary, as if he were already dead. Very smart, on Richard Else's part, as of course he was hoping all the time that Wainwright would agree to appear. It was Percy Duff who finally secured AW's agreement – on condition that he would be seen for only a minute or so at the end of the programme, proof enough that he was alive. (For his troubles, and his own contribution, Percy received the magnificent sum of £25 from the BBC.)

'Percy took me to Kendal Green and introduced us,' remembers Richard Else. 'AW's first words to me were: "I think you've got a scoop, young man."'

He then discovered AW had his own ideas on what form his brief appearance should take. There will be a cloud of smoke, he said, which will clear to reveal him sitting on a bench, puffing his pipe. 'I think he got the idea from one of the cowboy films he loved.' The programme was well received locally. Richard Else had achieved his life's ambition.

A couple of years later, he approached AW again, this time with a more ambitious idea. How about a series on the Lakeland landscape, with you as our guide, taking us round, being as true to the books as possible. 'He took some persuading. He said he didn't want the programmes to be about him, more on the landscape. I agreed to that. Then he didn't want to film in Lakeland. I think he thought he would start being pestered, with too many people suddenly recognising him, so we agreed that only two of the five proposed programmes would actually be in Lakeland. I also promised him the same crew as before and a sympathetic interviewer who would walk with him.'

AW had been worried that some smoothy London TV presenter would be used, so was very pleased when he heard that his companion would be a Cumbrian sheep farmer, living in Wasdale on a sixty-acre National Trust-owned fell farm. Eric Robson still lives there today, but he also happens to be a very experienced broadcaster, currently chairman of Radio 4's 'Gardeners' Question Time'. He was educated at Carlisle Grammar School, one of the best starts in life anyone can get, and worked for several years with Border TV, before joining the BBC in Newcastle.

Just before filming began, in the summer of 1985, Eric and AW had lunch to get to know each other. 'It was some caff in Kendal, nothing smart. I had a ham salad, while AW had fish and chips. As I was eating, a hand came across the table and stole a slice of the ham from my plate. It was AW's hand. He put the slice of ham in a bag, and said nothing. It was only later I discovered from Betty that he'd taken it for Totty.'

On the first day of filming, Eric discovered AW had insisted on another condition – he wanted them to film the script *he* had written, and assembled on odd scraps of paper. 'Richard had tried to talk him out of it, but failed, so the idea was that we'd humour him by appearing to follow his script, but do ours as well.

'In his script, I meet him first at the top of Penyghent in Limestone country. He's there with his Thermos and sandwiches and I sit down and chat with him, pulling out Wainwright's *Walks in Limestone Country*. He then says, "Not a bad book. I know the chap who wrote it." We then walk down the mountain, chatting away, and get to the car park at Horton-in-Ribblesdale where someone comes up and says, "Hello AW, good to see you after all these years . . ." I'm then supposed to say, "You're not *the* AW – you must sign my book." Close up of AW's hand, shaking slightly, signing my book, and that's the end of the first programme.

'It was a terrible idea, and would have taken Alec Guinness at least to have carried off that final bit in the car park. So on the way down the hill, with both of us miked up, I tried to chat to him as naturally as possible. I wanted to get him talking about himself – he wanted to talk about sheep. He was fascinated that I was a sheep farmer and kept asking about every sheep we met, was it a man, was it a woman, why did it have only one horn. I was getting nothing usable at all out of him, so I broached the subject of his early books, asking how he'd started. "You can't ask me that," he said. "You don't know who I am yet." Richard and the sound man were listening to this, and naturally had hysterics.

'He never did get the hang of things being shot out of sequence, or the idea that conversations could be put over different shots, or the fact that when he was pointing out something, the camera didn't have to follow his directions. He did seem to enjoy that first day, though we didn't get much out of him that we could use and Richard had to post-sync his words. We were, of course, handling him with great care, trying to do everything to please him. He told me that he'd had a nasty experience with television in the past. A camera crew had surprised him somewhere in Kendal, lying in wait to film him, and that had made him very wary. The main problem was that he was a very shy man.'

The series was shown locally in the north-east in November 1985. The following year, in May 1986, it was taken by BBC2, for national showing. AW even agreed to go to London to give a little press conference. It was his first visit for twenty years, not having been there since going to collect his MBE. Richard Else went with him from Kendal by train. 'At the last moment, he tried to get out of the trip. That was typical of him. He would agree to something, then get worried and tense and regret it. We only spent three and a half hours in London.'

During that time, he managed a quick visit to Michael Joseph, the only time he ever visited his London publishers, but the main object was to talk to about twenty TV journalists who were invited to meet him at a little room near Broadcasting House. On the train home, sitting in First Class, Richard suggested they had dinner, but he said he preferred to wait to have fish and chips when they got back to Kendal.

The programmes received good coverage, although the reporters hadn't got much out of him. They said he had come for the day from his 'modest Kendal stone cottage' and that he had given over

£200,000 to animals. They quoted him on animals – 'No animals have chips on their shoulder, unlike all the people I have ever met.' And on solitary walking – 'Walking alone is poetry, walking in a group is only prose.' Each programme was watched by three million viewers, an excellent audience for BBC2, and with a high Appreciation Rating of 89%. Most programmes get nearer 70%.

Wainwright turned eighty in 1987 – and found himself a TV star. Over the next three years, Richard Else and Eric Robson, plus the same crew, completed another two series, of five programmes each, in Lakeland, the Pennines and Scotland. They usually filmed in the summer, shooting with AW for five days every month. Betty would go too.

They all stayed in the same hotels, sometimes quite luxurious, sometimes humble, depending on the nearness to the next day's filming. 'He'd always ask, "How much is this meal costing?"' says Eric, 'then shake his head and say, "Really, really." He'd buy a round for the camera crew, though he never drank more than half a pint himself. We had to be back in the hotel each evening for his favourite TV programme, which was 'Coronation Street'. If we happened to film on a Saturday, there would be all hell to pay if he was not back in time for the football results. He didn't like talking about himself, and he'd dry up if the conversation came round to him, but he liked hearing about television, how programmes were made, and he loved hearing about my farm in Wasdale.

'He couldn't walk as far as he used to, so we had a Land Rover to take him up to the fells. He seemed fascinated by the exact degree the Land Rover could lean to without tipping over. This was just to tease Betty, who was a fairly timid passenger.

'Filming is ninety-seven percent hanging around, waiting for the light, the soundman or whatever, so most of my time was spent as his minder, keeping him amused when we were having a long wait. Sometimes we'd just sit on a rock. I'd read a paper and he'd puff on his pipe. Now and again I'd mention things from the paper, so we'd chat about topics of the day. He got very interested in the Common Agricultural Policy, for some reason. He had some very right wing views – on hanging, chucking out foreigners, castrating criminals, that sort of thing. I got off those topics when they came up as quickly as possible. He was a strange contradiction. He bemoaned the loss of Lakeland industries, like the slate quarries, yet he hated Sellafield. There were so many things he didn't know about and he could appear like a man from a different planet. Once he suddenly asked me: "What are schools like today?"'

The success of the television programmes was surprising when you consider how slowly Wainwright talked in them, how little he gave away, how leisurely they moved. Richard, however, thinks this was part of their strength. 'We found a silent majority, we appealed to viewers who like slow, thoughtful people. TV is filled with people with verbal diarrhoea. AW never liked speaking off the cuff. I think deep down he was afraid of being made to look foolish.'

Eric thinks he was simply single minded. 'He knew what he wanted to say, and wouldn't budge. He was certainly the most difficult interviewee I've ever had to deal with. TV is a game, with two partners who agree to go through the ritual dance. You ask things you know the answer to, and the other person knows you know the answer, but he wasn't prepared for any of that. The maximum he'd talk for at any time was forty seconds – and that was him being garrulous. If you asked a supplementary question, he'd grunt and say, "That's all I'm saying." Some days he'd say hardly anything, just puff on his pipe. If you tried to push him, he clammed up. Richard had a terrible job making it all work, stringing half-sentences together. We used a lot of voice-over, with an actor reading from his books.

'I agree we didn't get a great deal out of him, not anything personal, but we captured his presence. The rotund old gent, standing in his landscape. We deliberately tried to capture that image, though he didn't like us doing it. He thought we should be filming the view, not him. "Why is the cameraman moving?" he'd ask.

'He would do retakes, once, if requested, because an aeroplane had gone overhead or something like that, but otherwise he expected us to capture him first time. He expected us to be as organised as he was. Richard had a plan in his mind for each day, of what points he would like AW to make, and at which situations, but over breakfast AW would give us *his* thoughts on what he was going to say. Sometimes he didn't tell us and we wouldn't know until he started talking. But when his mouth opened, his brain was engaged – which is something you can't say about some people, such as politicians. It wasn't talk for the sake of talk.

'He wore the same clothes from week one to the very last programme, so there was no problem with continuity. Same boots, rucksack, trousers, pullover. I think it was a new pully when we started, bought by Betty, but as the years went on, it got more holey from his tobacco burns.'

One of the problems with his new-found television fame was that he was increasingly recognised. 'He used to say he was half-blind, his eyes were failing,' says Eric, 'but he always seemed to realise when he'd been spotted and a blue anorak miles away was making a bee-line for him. His main trick, when someone got close, was to announce loudly, 'I think I'll have a pee.' It is very hard to go up and try to shake hands with someone when they're peeing.

'We took him up onto Haystacks on a really terrible day, torrential rain and mist. We used a caterpillar truck to get us right up, but it was shuddering so much that we had to get out to walk the last bit. We arranged we'd all meet at a certain cairn on top, but the crew got lost. I got lost. Richard got lost. When we found each other, there was no sign of AW. I thought he was going to get his wish, actually dying on Haystacks. When we eventually got to the rendezvous, he was already there, puffing his pipe. "Where've you bin?" he asked.'

In Scotland, he was taken to Cape Wrath which he had never visited before. 'It was a real epic to organise,' says Richard. 'It was out of season so we had to get the ferry to run especially for us. I got Eric to ask AW if he was pleased, standing on Cape Wrath for the first time in his life. All he said was, "I'm glad I've been."'

'He could be grumpy and uncooperative during the day, then have us rolling about in the evening, complaining about a menu written in French. I liked him, oh yes, and admired him. He stood his ground and made no concessions. In the end, I felt very protective of him. He might be sitting silent, but his mind was always working. I was once in a Little Chef with him and after a long silence he said, "I wonder where their gooseberries come from. You never see them being delivered." '

It seems clear that AW grew to like both them and making the programmes, despite his supposed shyness and hatred of publicity. One attraction was more money for Animal Rescue who received all his fees. The programmes themselves didn't pay much – £500 each, plus repeats – but they greatly helped the sale of the Michael Joseph books, who made the most of his television fame, as well as the Westmorland Gazette books.

'I remember him asking us to change the "Barring clause", ' says Eric. 'This is common in TV contracts, stopping you for a year from doing a similar programme for a rival channel. He wanted it extended to four years. Not because he was going to desert us for ITV. It gave him a good excuse when he was pestered by other people.

'I think in the end, though, the real reason he did so much filming was that he enjoyed it. He went to places he thought he'd never see again, fells he was too old to climb. It was all organised for him; we got four-wheel-drive vehicles, helicopters, booked the hotels, did everything. We cocooned him and he liked that. He could use us as an excuse for refusing other offers – not just other television programmes, but anything at all, saying he had to stand by for the BBC helicopter.

'He also found out that fame wasn't as horrible as he feared. He'd had visions of reporters door-stepping his house, but the fame he got through the TV series was quite pleasant. People liked the programmes – and he liked them being well received. His fan mail was enormous. Betty said the programmes were honouring him, and he had not to be churlish.

'In the first series, we had a terrible battle over music. He didn't want any music – and threatened he wouldn't do another series. He wanted just to say his bit, then we'd have five minutes of lovely pictures, with silence. He said that if people couldn't concentrate for five minutes on nice pictures, that was their loss. But by the second series he had forgotten his objections when he realised the first series had been well received. Or he decided to give in on that argument.

'They were a success because of him. I don't honestly think we introduced many new people to the fells. I think most viewers were already Wainwright fans. That's why the videos are selling so well to this day. His fans like to have them as a memory of him.'

There was also an important radio programme which added to his media fame – Desert Island Discs. Over the years, Andrew Nichol had been forced to turn down their approaches, back in the days when Roy Plomley was in charge. 'They tried again when Michael Parkinson arrived, but AW didn't think much of him. When Sue Lawley took over, I thought this time he might be talked into it. He always had an eye for a good pair of legs . . .

'He only agreed to do Desert Island Discs', says Nichol, 'because he had never been on the M62 and I promised that if he did the programme, I would take him afterwards from Manchester, along the M62, through Bradford to Harry Ramsden's fish shop and after fish and chips we would come home through the Dales and stop somewhere for an ice cream. "Would you?" he said. "All right then." I just hoped and prayed that Gillian Hush, the Desert Island Discs producer at that time, could arrange for Sue Lawley to do the interview in Manchester as he was adamant that he would not go to London. Fortunately she did.

'Just before the recording, Sue talked to him for a few minutes about Blackburn Rovers. That put him nicely at his ease and the recording went without a hitch.'

In the programme, he talked a bit about his early life, the early books, praised the Westmorland Gazette for being a good friend to him, but was pretty abrupt when the subject of his first marriage came up.

'Nothing mattered to me except getting these books done,' he said. 'I had a single-track mind. It ended finally with my wife walking out, taking the dog, and I never saw her again.'

'Did you blame her?' asked Sue Lawley.

'Not at all – I don't know how she stuck it for thirty-odd years. Right, what's your next question?'

According to Sue, her mind then went blank, confronted by AW's blunt description of his marriage collapse, so she took refuge in the programme's format, and asked for his next record.

His choice of records was fairly lightweight and sentimental, from 'The Happy Wanderer' to 'Oklahoma!'. He declined to take any books, including the Bible and Shakespeare, saying his eyes were not up to reading anything, but requested a mirror as his luxury. It had always been his ambition to grow a beard, so he said, and he'd like to watch it growing.

Afterwards, he and Andrew Nichol had a snack in the BBC canteen, where AW complained about the sandwiches, then they got lost trying to find their way out of Manchester.

'AW made me return to the BBC car park and start again, following the directions we'd been given. He navigated this time, saying which was north, which was south. It was an overcast day so I didn't know how he could tell with no sun. "Aye, but that's where it would be if it was out."

'He wolfed down his chips at Harry Ramsden's, twice as fast as me, then asked the young waitress what was for pudding. It was ginger pudding; he asked if it came with custard. "Is it hot custard?" The waitress nodded. "Does it come up to here, over the pudding, right up to the side of the bowl?" The girl nodded. "All right then, I'll have some."'

Desert Island Discs, which was broadcast on 4 September 1988, was more of an accolade than a sales boost. It was the television exposure which always resulted in increased book sales. According to Andrew Nichol, the Westmorland Gazette found that the Wainwright titles were selling three times as many once television came along. In 1982, when he was still a blushing violet, unseen by the public, unwilling to expose himself, the Gazette sold 28,284 of their Wainwright titles. In 1986, the year he became a household name, they sold 87,378 copies and still without employing any reps.

Cumbrian animals were suddenly doing very well. The separate Wainwright Animal Trust had been set up which gave financial assistance to animal charities in the north of England, but the main beneficiary of Wainwright's years of fame, receiving royalties from his books, radio and television programmes, was Animal Rescue Cumbria. Its Chairman was A. Wainwright, and the Hon. Sec. and Treasurer, Mrs B. Wainwright. Their accounts for 1990 show at the end of the year the balance in hand was £353,643. That was cash, unspent, lying in the bank. Lucky animals.

DESERT ISLAND DISCS: AW'S CHOICE

Tales from the Vienna Woods (J. Strauss II) – Richard Tauber
Smoke Gets in Your Eyes – Tommy Dorsey and His Orchestra
There's an Empty Cot in the Bunkhouse Tonight – Rex Allen
Come Back to Sorrento – Luciano Pavarotti
Oh, What a Beautiful Mornin' (Oklahoma!) – Gordon MacRae
The Happy Wanderer – Berkshire Boys Choir
Skye Boat Song – Kenneth McKellar
SOMEWHERE MY LOVE ('LARA'S THEME' from DR ZHIVAGO) –
JOHNNY MATHIS

Luxury: A mirror (to watch his beard growing)

Book: No book, but two photographs – one of the 1928 Blackburn Rovers football team, the other of his wife, Betty

CHAPTER TWENTY-SIX

Pen-friends

One of the insidious aspects of media fame is that personalities are simplified, people summed up in black and white snapshots, characters reduced to shorthand, the cartoon version becomes the accepted image. Wainwright was that grumpy old man with the muttonchop whiskers, great walker, written some lovely books, shame he doesn't like people.

It was his own fault, of course. It had been one of his constant themes, from the very first book, this disillusion with modern life and the modern passion for more and more money. Better to stick to nature rather than humanity. Mountains and animals, they won't let you down. In *Ex-Fellwanderer*, his second and final attempt at some brief, personal reflections (published by the Westmorland Gazette in 1987), he declared that cruelty to animals, by vivisection and other means, had caused him to lose his faith in the human race. Religion had failed and money was the root of all evil. The Lake District was now overrun with 'noisy, ill-mannered people' who were incapable of appreciating beauty. The world was sick, people were getting worse, and the only hope was for criminals to be 'birched until they squeal for mercy' and football hooligans to be castrated. And much more in the same vein.

Little wonder that AW was perceived as a people hater. On his own, increasingly extreme admissions, he appeared out of sympathy with almost everyone. His public face was one of antipathy to the human race, not approving of our conduct, and certainly not wishing to meet us in the flesh. All he seemed to have time for was the animals, the only way he spent his money, the only way he appeared to express any love. It must be true, because he himself declared all this, repeatedly. And yet it was not the whole truth, nor anywhere near it. Why did he persist in giving this one-sided impression? It amused him, presumably. Just as it had amused him to appear prim and austere when deep down he was seething with sexual passion.

In his private life, there are countless examples of Wainwright being kind to people, warm towards total strangers, generous to those in need, helpful to those who were struggling. But there was almost always one important proviso, one common denominator in these examples of his brotherly love to his fellow humans. Friendship and intimacy was best kept to paper.

Wainwright loved writing letters. That's when he expressed himself best. Did he not say that his Pictorial Guides were love letters? Throughout his life, he had at any one time twenty correspondences on the go, twenty people in regular contact with him, to whom he gave his time and attention, sometimes money and help, keeping them amused with accounts of his own thoughts and activities and at the same time being genuinely interested in what they were doing. Ordinary people, a proportion of whom he never met, but to whom he devoted an extraordinary amount of time.

First, there was a group of old friends and contacts, people he had known in the past, mainly from his Blackburn days. In a 1965 letter to Bob Alker, whom he did remember well from their years together in the Treasurer's department, he reverted to a saucier mode, reminiscent of his office magazine days, when he considered himself a young blade, still making jokes about women panting for him, and including cartoons of himself.

Dear Bob,

I am a little ashamed to note that your letter, to which this is a reply, was dated as long ago as Sep. 10th, but you cannot expect priority on the strength of past acquaintance. (Now if you'd been a soft, juicy woman it would have been different.) What happens is that I maintain a cairn of unanswered letters on my desk and when it collapses I answer one and build the rest up again. In fact you have been fortunate. I know there are some in the heap dated 1963 and 1964 still awaiting attention, but, of course, none from women, who form the majority of my correspondents. It is my ingrained gallantry (which you remarked in earlier years) that makes me give them immediate attention, nothing else. I offer them no inducements (as a rule), but they keep coming running back for more. All I need to comment is that my knowledge of women's anatomy is derived purely from hearsay, and they cling like leeches. I like them clinging like leeches. I always did.

Well, thank you for all your kind comments. It wouldn't be me if I didn't say they are well deserved. Last time I heard anything about you, you were dying, so that I am doubly pleased to hear from you and to learn that you had started fellwalking. Good lad! After fifty wasted years! You must look out for me – a tall, distinguished-looking figure (to quote one source) recognisable by the long tail of females straggling along behind. How they hate each other! It's funny, really.

Two pages is as much as any male correspondent gets from me. If you want to write again and expect an earlier and fuller reply, get your missus to write instead and address me as 'Dear Alf'.

You have been warned.

AW

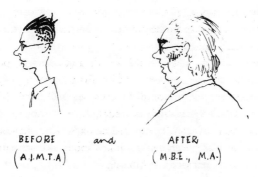

BEFORE   and   AFTER
(A.I.M.T.A)   (M.B.E., M.A.)

He kept up his letters to Bob for many years, in the same sort of tone. In a 1975 letter to him he wrote: 'Tell your missus to let me know when you die. I might be able to attend the funeral, but I doubt it. I fear I will be much too busy.'

Then there were new friends he acquired purely through correspondence, fans who wrote to praise him, thank or pick him up on a point, who somehow edged their way out of his cairn of impersonal letters and established a relationship. This often happens with writers. On a certain day, in a certain mood, chords can be struck by a totally unknown person and a lifetime of letters ensue.

One of his earliest and longest running correspondents was Len Chadwick of Dobcross near Oldham. He first wrote to Wainwright in 1960 who replied on Henry Marshall notepaper – so that's a collector's item in itself.

Len described how he was a member of a local club, charmingly named the Kindred Spirits Fell Walking Society. In one letter, he happened to mention he and some members were planning to climb the Munros – the 277 Scottish mountains over 3,000 feet – during their two weeks' holiday in the summer, and enclosed their time-table, maps and plan of attack. Wainwright was fascinated. He wrote back at once, offering to sponsor Len, who hadn't asked for any money, saying he would give him £1 for every Munro climbed, up to a maximum of £50, enclosing £25 in advance, and this was months before Len was due to start. In the event, Len climbed thirty-three mountains, but Wainwright paid him another £25 all the same, having had the fun of reading Len's accounts.

Their correspondence continued, swapping walking experiences, then in May 1965, Wainwright asked Len to be one of his four advance researchers for his proposed book on the Pennine Way. Each researcher was given a section and specific instructions and sent a cheque for their expenses. 'Payments need not be accounted for,' so the instructions said. 'If there is any balance it may be spent in riotous living with AW's compliments.' During the next two years, they were in constant contact, all to do with the Pennine Way, and the notes and letters flying between them is enormous, showing how detailed AW's preparations were. They are not of much interest biographically, but fascinating for any study of the history of the Pennine Way.

Pen-friends

A PICTORIAL GUIDE TO THE PENNINE WAY

Collaborators	*Sections*
Mr Len Chadwick, of Oldham	Edale to Todmorden–Halifax road
Mr Lawrence W. Smith, of Bradford	Todmorden–Halifax road to Malham Tarn
Mr Harry Appleyard, of Wigton	Tan Hill Inn to Cross Fell summit
Mr Cyril Moore, of Morecambe	Cross Fell summit to Kirk Yetholm

(A. Wainwright will do the middle section, Malham Tarn to Tan Hill Inn)

INSTRUCTIONS

A complete set of $2\frac{1}{2}''$ maps for your section is enclosed. On them, Mr Moore has indicated the course of the Pennine Way by a faint green line, according to the best information available to him. Also enclosed are the related $1''$ maps in the latest editions, which indicate the Pennine Way.

The line of the Way is to be checked carefully. Where there is no evidence on the ground (by signpost or distinct path), the approved route should be verified, if necessary, from other sources – by the various official publications on the subject, by local ramblers' associations or the local authority for the area, or by the farmers over whose ground the route passes. Doubts will arise in only a few places, as a complete right of way has now been established. Where a certain amount of discretion is left to the walker, such as in crossing a pathless moor, the best line should be worked out. Where there are 'official' variations, as with the start at Edale, all variations should be given the full treatment, as below.

The plan is to indicate on the $2\frac{1}{2}''$ maps the nature of the course to be followed. Where the way lies along a motor-road, an unbroken black line should be used ———; where the path is clear underfoot, a broken line –––––; where the path is intermittent, a line of alternate dots and dashes ⸱—⸱—⸱—; and where there is no path at all, a line of dots . . . . . These must be indicated neatly on the maps provided, in black waterproof Indian ink.

It is not intended in the book to give detail more than a hundred yards on each side of a well-defined path, but where there is discretion a wider area will need to be detailed. Objects of interest in the vicinity of the Way, say within a mile, such as Roman Camps, tumuli, good viewpoints, waterfalls, etc, will be mentioned and these should be listed separately in order of progress (south to north) and the items numbered to agree with numbers written on the $2\frac{1}{2}''$ maps at the appropriate places. Apart from the classification of the footpaths as mentioned in the previous paragraphs, and these reference numbers, no other markings should be made on the maps.

Please return the completed $2\frac{1}{2}''$ maps, the list of notes of interesting places, the $1''$ maps, and any correspondence collected on doubtful matters, by Christmas 1965. A. W. will then go over *all* the ground, a bit at a time, during 1966 and 1967. Publication date: Easter 1968.

> Although all collaborators have offered their services out of the
> goodness of their hearts, it is not intended that they shall suffer any
> expense, and a cheque is enclosed to cover travelling and subsistence
> expenses. Payments need not be accounted for; if there is any balance
> it may be spent in riotous living with A. W.'s compliments.

Len was a bit disappointed that the name of the book changed just
before the end, becoming the *Pennine Way Companion* not *The
Pictorial Guide to the Pennine Way*, as first planned. He and the other
three researchers were given personal acknowledgments in the
book when it was published in 1968.

Wainwright had to write to Len, whom he had not met, asking
what his job was, as he wanted to put that alongside his name. Len
turned out to be a short-hand typist, working in the office of a
cotton importers in Manchester. Over the next twenty years, the
letters between them continued, but became sadder as bits of Len's
life trickled out, in turn losing his job and then his home. Wainwright in his letters tried to cheer him up, offering help and
advice, hoping at one time to find him a job as a Youth Hostel
warden. Len then had a stroke and died alone, in a home in
Oldham in 1987, aged seventy-two.

They never did meet, and Wainwright knew very little about
him personally as their letters were mainly to do with walking.
Donald Haigh, a friend of Len's, was left all his Wainwright
correspondence. 'Len was a small man, very untidy in appearance,
rather eccentric in manner, a bachelor, always short of money, but
he never sponged off anyone, living very simply. He was always
badly paid, as a male typist, but he lived rent free in a working
men's club, working occasionally in the bar in lieu of rent. When
the club closed, he lost his home. He was also made redundant. He
got very down in the dumps, but never asked anyone for money.
He wrote poems and songs all his life, but no one ever took any
notice of them, or him, very much. Wainwright was always very
kind to him when it mattered.'

*

Margaret Ainley wrote to him from Brighouse in Yorkshire in March 1971, telling him about one of his walks she had done. His reply, care of the Westmorland Gazette address, appeared on the surface fairly gruff and curt, moaning that he was exhausted. 'I'm getting old, that's the trouble. How I wish tempus wouldn't fugit so much.' But he thanked her for her update on Spout Force. 'I was still under the impression that you couldn't approach it without a machette and heavy armour'.

A few months later, she wrote again, with her account of another long walk, and added a postscript that she was pregnant. He thanked her for her thrilling news, and told her about the new book he was working on – about the Howgill Fells. The following year he was addressing her as 'Dear Margaret', although still not revealing his home address. When the baby was born, a girl called Catherine, he wrote at once. 'When she is old enough to have a rucksack of her very own, let me provide it.' Mrs Ainley wrote back to say that when Catherine was old enough to be given a rucksack, could she call and collect it? By return, AW sent the baby a rucksack, perhaps worried that one day some stranger might turn up on his doorstep. He hoped that Catherine 'could fit snugly inside it, until she is big enough to wear it'.

Catherine, while still a baby, was taken on her first climb, up Smearsett Scar in Ribblesdale, and the whole expedition reported to AW. He in turn tells the Ainley family about his Scottish expeditions, how he climbed two of the Munros, recommending villages and good digs, giving lots of personal details and personal opinions, such as his hatred of Clive Jenkins's voice, and generally writing like an old and very intimate friend. It was not until 1975 that he started putting his correct home address at the top of his letters. 'Write here if you prefer, but don't get too affectionate; my wife grabs the post first.'

He knew Mrs Ainley was a happily married woman (her husband Richard was employed by Nu-Swift manufacturers of fire extin-guishers), but there was the occasional saucy response.

38 Kendal Green,
Kendal,
21st November 1975

Dear Margaret,

Well, fancy you wishing I had called on you during my travels through Brighouse! You must have masochistic tendencies. No, the thought never once occurred to me. I wouldn't dream of making an unannounced appearance. I was never one for unexpected confrontations. Besides, what would your husband say, you entertaining royalty while he was slaving his guts out at Nu-Swift away in Elland? No, no, I was well content to sit in the bus and search the faces of the passers-by for someone, child or woman, who looked as though they might once have climbed to the uppermost inches of Smearsett Scar. But I saw no-one who looked, even remotely, as though they might have been inspired to undertake such an adventure. None of them even looked happy. You live in alien surroundings, love. Don't let your roots go too deep. There are better places than Brighouse. Couldn't Daddy persuade Nu-Swift to open a branch at Sty Head or Honister Pass?

I have drooled over your lovely transparencies and now return them for the family album, and I have taken to heart your regretful assertion that Lakeland means less to me than it did and Scotland more. Perhaps you are right. Lakeland is utterly lovely and charming, a heavenly paradise on earth – but oh the crowds! There is no fun in walking in procession, not even in delectable scenery. I remember Keswick when, even in summer, you saw only a few of like kin, fellwalkers out for a day's adventure on the hills; when the only place of refreshment after a hard day was a chip-shop. No, the old romantic atmosphere has quite gone. Only in the depth of winter do you get a reminder of things as they used to be, and only in winter can I be persuaded, these days, to re-visit the places that once I loved almost to distraction. You will see what I mean when at last you find yourselves in Torridon, or on Stac Polly, or by Loch Hourn. Then I think you might agree. Be quick and grow up, Cathy!

You must, I implore you, restrain your impulse to call at 38 K. G. Not only would you be disappointed because, having lived like a recluse for so long I have developed the eccentricities of one, but, more important, I have a wife who is also consumed with insatiable curiosity, not only about female callers but even about female correspondents. You see, I have a secret past, or so she suspects, and what is worse, I continue to enjoy a virility far beyond my years. You'd best leave me alone to get on with my writing.

  With very best wishes for a happy Christmas and new peaks in 1976,
  Yours sincerely (well, partly what)
  A. Wainwright

Catherine herself started writing letters to Wainwright in 1983, and he replied, saying he had gone off her mother, now that she had fallen in love with steam trains. In June 1986, Margaret congratulated him on his television series and he replied that 'everyone seems to have enjoyed it'. He also told her that he'd tried to get away from the pressures of fame by going on holiday to the north of Scotland, but that he was spotted six times – naming the exact places – and then returned to find a hundred fan letters waiting for him.

The letters between them lasted for twenty years, right up to 1990, and Margaret has now enough to fill a small book, yet they never met. 'I think the correspondence flourished because I never asked to meet him – though I did meet Betty after his death.' Catherine Ainley is now twenty-three, recently graduated and is working for the Church of England. And she still has the rucksack, now very worn.

Many other correspondents remained in regular touch for a similar time, without ever meeting Wainwright face to face. By keeping his home address secret for as long as possible, until he got the measure of his new correspondents, he usually managed to stop fans turning up on his doorstep, which is what he feared most. Valerie Malam of Shrewsbury, after several letters, and being allowed his home address, did make the occasional visit to Kendal Green in the hope of spotting him, but never managed it. 'Instead, we did a lap of honour round the Green, and I had to content myself by pinching a pebble from his drive.'

Beatrix Potter had a similar phobia about meeting her fans, dreading them turning up at her home in Sawrey. Wordsworth, on the other hand, as a Grand Old Man, enjoyed seeing how many worshippers had gathered at his garden gate at Rydal. About five hundred would come each summer, and the lucky ones were allowed a tour of his garden and a peep at Dorothy. The really lucky ones, if they chatted up his gardener, who was also his part-time barber, got a lock of Wordsworth's hair. Wainwright did at least reply to every letter, so the fans always got autographs, almost always written on an Animal Rescue notelet.

Several of his long-term correspondents were struggling amateur artists and writers, mostly trying to draw or write prettily about Lakeland, and to these he wrote long, helpful letters, often giving advice on their material and sometimes recommending them to Bill Mitchell, editor of *Cumbria*, which often led to their being published.

Chris Jesty had already published when he first wrote to Wainwright in 1973 from Wales, sending him a panorama view as seen from the summit of Snowdon, which he had published himself, asking him if the distant peaks of Lakeland were correctly identified. Wainwright wrote back an effusive letter, marvelling at Jesty's meticulous draughtsmanship and topographical knowledge. In this first letter, Wainwright addressed him as Chris, a sure sign of acceptance, though over the next seventeen years of regular letters, during which they did meet once, fleetingly, in Wales, Chris always addressed him as Mr Wainwright. 'I didn't know his christian name when I began writing to him, so I called him Mr Wainwright, and just continued. He never invited me to visit him at Kendal Green, though Betty did. I thought as the senior person, it was up to him to invite me. He never did, but that didn't worry me. I'm better in letters than in the flesh, and so was he.'

The contact between them was maps. Chris Jesty had once worked for the Ordnance Survey as a cartographer, but later, when he started publishing his own maps, he worked as a taxi driver. His speciality is panoramic maps from the tops of famous British mountains. Over the last twenty years, he has published ten in all but, so far, hasn't covered his expenses. However, Wainwright was fascinated by all his work and agreed to co-operate with him on a 'Guide to the View From Scafell Pike', two large fold-out sheets: this appeared in 1978. 'He put about 100 hours of work into his sketches, but would accept no money. It was very generous of him.'

Their lengthy and detailed correspondence was almost always about maps and map making, and very serious. Wainwright did try to introduce a personal note early on, making jocular remarks about a girl called Margot, when he noticed that Chris had dedicated his Snowdon map to someone called Margot, imagining her complaining and moaning while Chris was off up the mountains. This teasing went on for some time until Chris revealed she was not his girl friend – in fact, he didn't have a girl friend. 'You have no reason to feel sorry for Margot,' so he wrote to AW, 'as she is one of the happiest people I have met. Perhaps I should explain that I only knew her because we were living and working in the Summit Hotel at the same time. She was everything to me and I was nothing to her, which is not her fault.' An admission which doubtless took Wainwright back to his own youth and his passion for Betty Ditchfield.

In 1980, Chris suggested that he might be allowed to update and re-draw some of the pages of Wainwright's early guides, now that some details had changed, gates gone, rights of way in dispute, but Wainwright declined. 'I think not yet, and probably not until after my death, now surely imminent.' In 1989, he repeated the suggestion, but this time Wainwright boasted that at eighty-two he might have another twenty years in him 'during which time your revisions may themselves need revising'.

In 1984, Chris produced his first book, a guide to the Isle of Purbeck, with his own words and maps, and sent a copy to AW, hoping for some kind remarks. The letter back was in large handwriting – as AW's eyes were growing weaker – but his opinions were as strong as ever.

He congratulated Chris on getting the book into print, but said he was horrified to find that it was stapled.

This is a shocking mistake. A stapled binding means that the book cannot be opened flat. Stapled books are infuriating and I never buy them on principle. Black mark. Another criticism concerns the maps which are excellently drawn but should have been given a scale in miles instead of the ridiculous 1:25000, these references being unintelligible to everyone, including myself. You have been a bit too clever here, and your device will not be appreciated by walkers. The personal notes are poor, not well composed and largely irrelevent, and would have been better omitted. You must avoid using the word 'so'. It is no substitute for 'therefore'. I haven't read the text, still having no wish to visit the Isle of Purbeck, but did notice you have described it as one of the most beautiful places in Britain – a surprising statement from someone who knows Lakeland and North Wales. I give you 5 marks out of 10. No more. AW.

Chris was naturally very disappointed when he got that letter. 'But he had perhaps over-praised me in the past.' However, Wainwright did put some work his way, and Chris was commissioned to do some maps which were used in two of Wainwright's large format books published by Michael Joseph – *Wainwright's Favourite Lakeland Mountains*, and *Wainwright in the Limestone Dales*, both published in 1991. More recently, Michael Joseph used Chris Jesty, knowing how much AW had admired his work, to make some revisions to the *Pennine Way Companion* and *A Coast to Coast Walk*.

John Marsh, a local policeman in Kendal, was another person for whom Wainwright provided some work. 'I don't know how he found out about me, but I think my Superintendent at the time, Robert Walker, must have told him that my wife and I had two handicapped children. This was in 1973 and I was pretty depressed and in a low state. AW took a great interest in our children and their progress. In 1976 he paid me £400 to do some research for him on his book on Kendal in the nineteenth century. This was a tidy sum in 1976 as policeman's salaries were low. Local history had always been one of my hobbies, but there were other people who knew more about it than me. I researched two Westmorland books for him and helped with one on Furness. He was a heck of a taskmaster, finishing a drawing every day, seven days a week, and

I was expected to have the research notes ready for each one. It was good therapy for me, at a bad time, and the money helped my family.

'His kindness to me will never be forgotten and his regard and support for my son David, who was born deaf, was a great help over many years. What he wrote in his books about himself, saying he didn't like human beings, was manifestly untrue. It had its root in his own brand of self-deprecating humour which he used to feed to journalists he didn't like. He was a normal human being under that gruff façade.'

There are many other examples of Wainwright acting kindly towards people. He made friends with a group of blind climbers called the Milton Mountaineers, sending them a large cheque to pay for a celebration dinner. In 1980, he gave the proceeds – over £1000 – from the sale of his original drawings from *A Ribble Sketchbook* to the old Furthergate Congregational Church, Blackburn, to help them build a new church, even though he was no longer a churchgoer.

There was also an act of kindness done to Wainwright himself by a correspondent which, at the time, he was never aware of. This concerns his MBE in 1967 which as far as he knew came out of the blue. In *Ex-Fellwanderer*, published in 1987, he said it was only some time later he learned a bit more. 'The Town Clerk of Kendal told me in confidence that a Southport man had spent a day on Great Gable collecting signatures to a petition. I never knew his identity.'

Now it can be told. The man in question was Max Hargreave of Southport, a chartered accountant, who only took up walking at the age of fifty. He had been in correspondence with AW for some years, telling him how he had climbed all 214 of the Lakeland fells listed in AW's Pictorial Guides, twice, with his dog Meg. 'She is rather conceited and swanks around with a medallion on a little chain round her neck which reads "Twice Climbed all 214 LD Mountains." ' AW then started writing letters to Meg, without knowing what Max had done.

Mr Hargreave died in 1993, aged eighty-four. According to his widow, it wasn't just on Great Gable he collected signatures but all over Lakeland – and he only had one refusal. 'From a man on the summit of Ill Bell who said he was pro-Wainwright but anti-honours.'

Some of Wainwright's friends and correspondents were of course professional writers in their own right, such as Molly Lefebure. Harry Griffin was an established journalist when he first met Wainwright in the late 1940s, but at that stage he hadn't had a book published. In 1957, when Wainwright's own Guides were beginning to do well, he offered to pay for publication of Harry's collected articles from the *Lancashire Evening Post*. 'He read my pieces on Lakeland every Friday and thought they were wonderful. He offered me £800 to get them published and said I didn't have to pay him back until the book began making money. It was very nice of him, but I refused. I suppose I didn't want charity. I wanted a proper publisher to do it. Eventually one came along and my first book was published in 1961.'

Harry went on to write twelve books about Lakeland and, as a journalist, reviewed every Wainwright book as it came out. One of them, Book 5 of the *Scottish Mountain Drawings*, is dedicated to Harry Griffin.

'I probably helped him a little, but he did me several favours as well. He drew a special Lakeland map for my first book, and let me use several of his drawings.' In Harry's second book, *In Mountain Lakeland*, he wrote a chapter on Wainwright, describing him as a 'tall, well-built, middle-aged man, spectacled, grey-haired, rather distinguished-looking, with a long-ranging stride that covers the ground slowly but surely'.

AW wrote to Harry afterwards, complaining about one word in his description. He would have preferred the word 'rather' to have been omitted.

Harry is extremely proud that he published a very early photograph of Wainwright. This was in his *A Lakeland Notebook*, 1975. 'It took me weeks of persuading before he agreed.'

He took part in the first television programme about AW for BBC North-East, the one in which Wainwright made a brief appearance at the end, and is still upset that most of his contribution was omitted. 'I was appalled. It was all eulogies without any balance whatsoever.'

Harry's criticism of Wainwright is as it always was – that his detailed Guides take the adventure out of walking. 'I'm against all guide books to the hills. They're unnecessary and over done. Some hills have got twenty books on them. A map is all you need. You can read Wainwright's Guide afterwards for pleasure, but people *will* walk with them, turning left at the tree, right at the wall, or, whatever, destroying the spirit of adventure. It's not Wainwright's fault, of course, that people use his books the wrong way. Sadly he made everything too easy for them. When I used to tell him this he said, "It's not my fault, I didn't expect them to sell so many!"

'He could be a difficult man to others but to me he was a kindly, generous friend possessed of awe-inspiring industry, single mindedness and a real love of the hills.'

Ron Scholes, a retired primary school headmaster from Staffordshire, came into Wainwright's life quite late, beginning a correspondence at the end of the 1970s which went on for many years, during which he met AW several times, once actually staying overnight at Kendal Green – a rare honour. This personal contact came about after he had given an illustrated lecture in Kendal, the proceeds going to Animal Rescue. Their mutual passion was not maps but animals and long-distance walks, including one from Land's End to Cape Wrath which Ron spent most of his spare time doing and AW liked to hear about. In 1984, AW agreed to draw some sketches for a book Ron was working on about Wales. He completed ten drawings, which Ron still has, but the book was not finished.

'The bad news is that I have clearly come to the end of the road as far as close pen work is concerned,' so AW wrote to Ron in April 1984. 'After a frustrating three weeks struggling to hand write captions, being unable to see properly what I was doing, with my writing constantly straying from the pencil guide lines, I had to give up.'

In August the same year, he wrote – in large handwriting on A3 paper – to tell Ron he had tried medical help. 'I saw two specialists, and neither gave me any hope of a cure. The trouble is not cataract, as I thought, but damaged retina at the back of the eyeballs. A symptom of old age, they say. Latterly, as an experiment, I have been trying to draw maps, and find it impossible. Not only cannot I see what I am doing but am getting blind spots as I work. I am afraid I will not be able to do the Welsh maps for you and am sorry about this because I would have liked to help.' Tempus, as he had sadly remarked to Margaret Ainley, was on the fugit.

CHAPTER TWENTY-SEVEN

Last Years, 1987–91

Despite his failing eyesight, Wainwright could still get some pleasure out of watching Blackburn Rovers. He went to see them in early 1987, on one of his regular twice-season visits, staying as ever with Doris Snape. He was eighty by then, but had got himself to Blackburn on his own, and to the match.

On the way to Ewood Park, working his way through the crowds (such as they were, as Rovers were then in the old Second Division, and about to play Barnsley) he was spotted by Clifford Singleton. He had not seen Wainwright in person for forty-six years, since he had been a boy in the Blackburn Treasurer's office and Wainwright had been one of the seniors. 'He was wearing old clothes and what looked like hiking boots, and he seemed to be wandering a bit. I introduced myself, and he said he remembered me, so we went into the ground together and watched the game, sitting in the A stand. He couldn't make out the players, because of his eyes, but he could tell by the noise what must be happening.'

Afterwards, Clifford took him into the Board Room. 'You must have some influence here,' commented Wainwright, unaware that Mr Singleton had gone on from their youthful office days together and had become Blackburn's Chief Executive and Town Clerk, a position he had only recently given up. Wainwright was introduced to various local dignities, as the eminent author and television star, and was able to see enough to point out to Clifford that he, Wainwright, was the only person in the Board Room wearing a cap.

Clifford gave him a lift in his car after the match, dropping him off at the end of a road where Doris was living. Wainwright later wrote him a typewritten thank you letter, squeezing it on to an Animal Rescue notelet, saying what a privilege it had been to be taken into the Board Room. 'It occurred to me afterwards it might have been appropriate to the circumstances if you had introduced me as the man who (with Fred Haslam) started the Rovers Supporters Club in 1939.'

His failing eye sight did not seem at first to affect his typing, which is how he wrote all his Michael Joseph books, nor his capacity to write long formal letters, most of which he enjoyed composing, even a marathon series of letters to the Inland Revenue. This particular correspondence clearly gave him some sort of pleasure because afterwards he arranged and edited all the documents into a special folder, added explanatory notes, and headed it: 'THE INLAND REVENUE Versus WAINWRIGHT. A DOSSIER ON THE ANTICS OF THE TAX OFFICE. A BLACK COMEDY'.

It began in March 1988 when, out of the blue, a Tax Inspector wrote to say that Wainwright's tax affairs were being investigated. 'The letter contained an inference,' so AW noted, 'that I was suspected of evading or avoiding payment of tax due from me.' This is what really annoyed him, and made him spring to his typewriter, knowing that he had not only paid full tax on all his received income over the last thirty years as a published author, but that he had never once submitted claims for travelling expenses, stationery, postage, etc, which must have amounted to at least £10,000.

The Tax Inspector's suspicions stemmed from the fact that Wainwright had become known publicly as a best-selling author, as the book pages in the newspapers revealed, and a TV performer, but that his actual declared income seemed relatively small. In the year 1987–88 he had received only £19,173 in royalties from the Westmorland Gazette, plus £8,427 from Michael Joseph. That was what had apparently sparked off their interest.

On investigation, they found that most of the Wainwright

royalties had been going elsewhere, under a clause which appeared in most of his contracts saying: 'I hereby renounce all legal rights to the royalties from this book and leave their distribution to the discretion of the publishers.'

They then discovered that these royalties had been going to two charities, the Wainwright Animal Trust and Animal Rescue, Cumbria, the Treasurer of which that year happened to be Mrs Betty Wainwright. Hence their worries. Hence their intention to investigate all his financial affairs over the last six years. They wanted full details, suggesting he should appoint his solicitor to answer their questions. AW refused to use legal help, determined to fight them personally and directly.

After a year of letters and documents flying back and forward, a head-to-head meeting took place at 38 Kendal Green, on 14 March 1989 between Wainwright and the Inspector. 'I had formed an image of him as a little bald-headed man with a pince-nez,' wrote AW, 'but he turned out to be a strapping young fellow with a beard and a friendly disposition.'

AW argued in the meeting that income tax should only be on income received, but the Inspector insisted that renounced royalties were nevertheless earned royalties, and AW could therefore be liable to pay unpaid tax on the last six years – which might well amount to over £100,000 . . .

To keep Wainwright's files open, back over the six years, the Inland Revenue then had to send out quickly an additional assessment for the years 1982 and 1983. When AW received them, he found they were demanding £65,000 – just for these two years. 'By imposing these assessments, they had committed their greatest blunder,' so AW wrote in his Black Comedy. 'In neither year had I signed contracts with renunciation clauses. From then on, they were on the defensive. I had them on the run . . .'

That was AW's opinion, but the letters and demands continued, plus telephone calls, until AW told the Inspector to 'reply in writing from now on, not by telephone or interview.' The BBC in Newcastle and Michael Joseph provided proof of where the royalties had gone, and the animals charities opened their books, but the additional assessment (which had been issued by another department, in Cumbernauld, Glasgow) remained, culminating in a threat of Court action, if he didn't pay up.

AW then threatened to sue the Inland Revenue for harrassment, accused them of overcharging him on past tax and warned the Inspector that he had a full dossier on the case, which he was going to make available to a publisher. Heavy threats from old AW, but at the same time, on his holiday in Scotland in May 1989, he sent the Inspector a picture postcard with the message: 'Even on holiday, in faraway Scotland, I am thinking of you. Wish you were here.'

Wainwright knew he personally had neither received nor spent the monies concerned, so his own virtue made him confident of victory, but he was still treading a dangerous path, quoting back to Inland Revenue officials their own rules, ridiculing their logic, sending them endless letters and queries. He had, of course, been trained in the minutiae of accountancy, and had won prizes, and was well experienced in the ways of bureaucracy as a Borough Treasurer, even though for the last thirty years he had scarcely bothered about money for himself or the details of his own contracts.

On 15 June 1989, the Inland Revenue admitted defeat. The Inspector who had begun the investigation wrote to tell him he had nothing to pay, and offered apologies for having irritated him. AW was hardly humble in his victory, giving him a lecture on his conduct.

38 Kendal Green, Kendal, 21st June 1989

Dear Sir,

Thank you for your letter of the 15th informing me that the Board of Inland Revenue had confirmed that the renunciation clauses in my contracts with publishers were valid and absolved me from any tax liability on the royalties thereby renounced.

The outcome was as I expected and never really in doubt. It is nice of you to express pleasure at the decision when you must have felt some disappointment at drawing a blank after spending a year of your life barking up the wrong trees and exploring blind alleys that led nowhere.

You will surely realise now that it would have been far better to have obtained the Board's opinion before starting an exercise that wasted so much of your time and the time of others. For my part I must say I found it galling to reflect that I was contributing to your salary, while you were seeking to prove or disprove that I was a villain.

Your difficulty was in failing to interpret correctly the word 're-nounce'. The word has no hidden or double meaning: it is exact, absolute and conclusive. When King Edward VIII renounced the throne there was no investigation into his intention, no doubt about his meaning. To renounce a thing is to give up all rights and entitlement to it.

Of course I appreciate that you were doing your duty as you saw it. In two respects, however, you exceeded your authority. You had no right to enquire how the publishers had distributed the renounced royalties, their discretion in this matter being absolute, and it was no business of yours to ascertain how the charities benefitting [sic] had spent the money they received.

You must now call off your Cumbernauld dogs, who are pursuing me with the ferocity of Rottweilers and threatening distraint or Court proceedings if I do not pay promptly the sums raised by your additional assessments. I have warned the Collector that unless he desists he will face a Court hearing for unlawfully demanding money with threats.

I will not embarrass you further by sending a presentation copy of the dossier I am compiling to the Board of Inland Revenue as I intended and will content myself by circulating it only amongst the people you have involved by your enquiries.

Now that this sorry saga has come to an abortive end I believe I can claim compensation for the disruption caused to my life over the past twelve months by your investigations, for the distress to my wife, for the harassment resulting from your Collector's unlawful demands and threats, and for the costs incurred by my solicitor in carrying out your instructions. I am prepared to settle this claim for a modest single payment of £5,000. Please make your cheque payable to Animal Rescue, Cumbria.

AW

Wainwright didn't get his compensation, not surprisingly, but he never heard again from the Collector of Taxes about their threat of court action. In what he called the Epilogue to his Dossier he wrote: 'It is perhaps premature to assume they have fled the country. They may, of course, simply be hiding under their desks.'

Oh, what fun he had had. In a way, it was a lease on life, getting Betty to dig out all the appropriate tax laws, keeping his brain ticking over, his pencil and mind sharp. Behind all the threats and fury, he had partly been teasing, putting on the outraged face: meaning it, but amusing himself at the same time.

At the end of *Ex-Fellwanderer*, having paraded various of his right wing views on crime and society, he included what appeared to be almost a recantation, saying that he wasn't 'crusty and intolerant', as some people had described him. They were just niggles, not meant to be a catalogue of criticisms and grumbles.

Don't get me wrong. I have no complaints, none at all. I have had a long and wonderful innings and enjoyed a remarkable immunity from unpleasant and unwelcome incidents. Events have always moved to my advantage. So much could have gone wrong but hasn't. I never had to go to be a soldier, which I would have hated. I never had to wear a uniform, which I would also have hated. I was never called upon to make speeches in public nor forced into the limelight; my role was that of a backroom boy, which suited me fine. I never went bald, which would have driven me into hiding: I see so many men who have lost their hair and seem not to care a damn, but to me it would have been a major tragedy. Most of all, I have enjoyed perfect health, despite smoking like a chimney since the age of sixteen. I have never had a serious illness, never had an accident, never had an operation. So, all told, I have enjoyed a charmed life. I have been well favoured. The gods smiled on me since the cradle. I have had more blessings than I could ever count.

Good to think that those thirty-seven years of unhappiness during his first marriage had now been forgotten. Interesting to see his pleasure in his fine head of grey hair, having been ridiculed for its carroty nature as a boy. And reassuring to see that his fading eyesight was not getting him down too much. All the same, the last page of the book seemed to be a farewell.

I can't expect to last much longer. My sisters and my brother have passed on, dying in the order in which they were born, all in their eighties. My turn next. I shall be sorry to go and leave behind a world I have enjoyed living in, a world of wonders, despoiled in parts by man but still a realm of infinite delight, free to all mankind equally.

This book is not a personal lament for the end of fellwalking and the end of active life, but a thanksgiving for the countless blessings that have been mine in the last eighty years. I don't know where I go from here. Nobody does. I fear a black void of nothingness, as it was before birth. We are promised God's heaven. I wish I could think so. It would be great, wouldn't it, to move on to a brand new life, with new eyes, in new territory. I would not feel a stranger in heaven, having for so many years lived in the earthly paradise of Lakeland. There may be hills there to climb. There may be an opportunity for a pictorial guidebook to heaven. I may be permitted to come down occasionally and flap my wings over Haystacks.

His sister Alice had died in 1971 aged seventy-seven and Annie in 1986 aged eighty-six. His brother Frank, who had managed to reduce his drinking in later life, had died in 1977 at the age of eighty.

Wainwright's first wife Ruth, whom he never met again after the day she walked out of the Kendal Green house, lived in Windermere for several years until struck down by rheumatoid arthritis. She died in a nursing home near Sedbergh, on 9 April 1985, aged seventy-five. Peter Wainwright scattered her ashes on Loughrigg Terrace, overlooking Grasmere and Rydal Water. 'It had been her favourite walk,' he says.

Peter got married in 1973 to Doreen Bell, a local girl from Staveley, in a simple register office ceremony. His mother was present, but he didn't invite his father. 'It would have upset my mother too much – but he probably wouldn't have come anyway. He gave me two drawings as a wedding present, and later the money for us to double-glaze our house. And he did pay for my mother's funeral.'

On his return from Bahrain, Peter had taken a job locally with Kentmere Boxes as an estimator and then as a salesman, but in 1988 he too began to develop rheumatoid arthritis. He retired from work on health grounds in 1989, aged fifty-six. There was no antagonism between him and his father, no rows or arguments, just very little contact after Peter had grown up and moved abroad, although Betty did her best to keep in touch. Wainwright never had had much time or interest in keeping up family connections.

He was more concerned, and as obsessed as ever, in finishing his books. In 1990, he was working on three books for Michael Joseph, each at different stages. They did not require the close work of his Guides, as he had given up drawing sketches and maps, but he was kept busy at his typewriter. He was also standing by to start another television series for the BBC, showing remarkable energy and optimism for someone of eighty-three.

At the age of seventy-nine, his vitality had finally lessened, and for a time he had started to fall asleep in the evenings. However, he recovered from this when it was discovered he had mild diabetes which was helped with medication. A lifetime of smoking did not seem to have affected him, or a passion for chips and sweet puddings. All that appeared seriously wrong were his eyes, which he had always feared would let him down. In that office story about the Beautiful Lady, the strange young man ended up blind.

'I think he was about seventy-six when he first realised his eyes were going,' says Betty.' He was holding a photograph of Morecambe Bay, trying to draw a panorama, when he said it was a bad photograph, all fuzzy. I looked at it and it was perfectly sharp. From then on we realised he couldn't see things clearly. When out walking, he could no longer see the horizon. He said it was like looking at the landscape through a lace curtain.

'In 1984, after the eye specialists said nothing could be done, he accepted the situation. He was always totally stoical. Never moaned. He moved on to large print books, but eventually he couldn't read those either. He still watched TV, but he'd lost all the details, and had to rely on the sound.'

In the summer of 1990, while visiting North Yorkshire for his illustrated book on the Limestone Dales, Betty was alarmed when he dropped his pipe in the car. 'I was driving, and Red was smoking as usual, when it suddenly fell from his mouth onto the floor. "Oh, you silly thing!" I started to say, but he was just sitting there, very ·still, not knowing what had happened. However, he soon recovered, lit his pipe again, and we continued driving, but it struck me then that he'd possibly had a minor stroke.'

In September 1990, still waiting to hear from the BBC about the dates for filming, he and Betty had a short holiday in Scotland in one of their favourite places, Plockton in Wester Ross, staying in a log cabin. 'He wasn't very well. He couldn't walk far and could hardly see. I had a feeling he was beginning to wear out.'

In October, filming at last began on what was to be the fourth Wainwright television series. 'We had waited for them to start for some months, but there were delays. I was very upset, especially when I heard they were doing some film with Chris Bonington. I said they couldn't expect an old man to do winter filming.' Richard Else says the delay was caused by problems raising money, nothing to do with the Bonington film.

Wainwright seemed fit enough to undertake the filming, and was looking forward to it. The new series was going to have a biographical content, taking him back to his roots, in and around Blackburn. They filmed him outside the house where he had been born in Audley Range, where he recalled being hidden in a drawer because of his red hair, in case neighbours might think he was illegitimate. They also filmed him outside a cinema he used to go to, around Darwen Tower and inside Ewood Park.

'AW had an amazing smile,' says Eric Robson, who again was doing the series with him, 'but it was always severely rationed. That day, standing with him in the middle of Ewood Park, he had the most radiant smile I'd ever seen on his face – even more wonderful than when he was standing admiring some marvellous view in Lakeland.'

Alas, after only three days of filming, Wainwright fell ill while sitting in a café, and was unable to continue, complaining of pains in his legs. He returned to Kendal and went into hospital. But he recovered and, after three weeks, was allowed home. He was soon strong enough to do some gentle typing and to receive visitors.

Visitors had, of course, never been a major feature of life at Kendal Green so he was not overwhelmed by their arrival now, but there always had been a couple of regulars, notably Percy Duff, his deputy in the Kendal Borough Treasurer's office, and later his successor. Over the years, Percy had become, for want of a better word, his best friend. Not exactly a crowded field. Betty once heard them arguing over something and Percy replying, 'Don't you fall out with me, Alf, I'm your only friend, remember.'

Calling him Alf, to his face, was a rare mark of intimacy, normally only heard from those had known him from his pre-war days in Blackburn. 'When I was his deputy,' says Percy, 'I couldn't tell him things straight to his face, as he was the boss, but afterwards I always did. I was about the only person who always answered him back. I'd had a broader experience of life than he had, been in the war, been abroad, had lots of interests. I used to tease him, when he went on about fellwalking, that he hadn't seen proper mountains, never having been to Switzerland. He liked a good joke. On my visits, he always asked if I had any new jokes for him. Nothing rude, mind you.' Any choice example, Percy?

'I remember one that made him laugh about two shepherds in Longsleddale. It was at the time we were going into the Common Market. A car pulls up beside these two shepherds, and a man leans out of a big smart Volkswagen and shouts, *"Spreken ze Deutsch?"* The two shepherds look blank. *"Parlez-vous français?"* asks the man. They still look blank. *"Parla italiano?"* Still they look blank, so the bloke in the car gets fed up and drives on. One of the shepherds turns to the other and says, "Now we're in the Common Market, don't you think we should learn a foreign language?" "Oh no," says the other shepherd. "Yon feller knew three – and look where it got him . . . ." Alf loved that joke.'

The other regular visitor was Andrew Nichol from the Westmorland Gazette, still making his twice-weekly calls. Even though AW's current publisher had become Michael Joseph, the Gazette of course owned the copyright in all his other books and there were constant marketing proposals and other topics to be discussed. Andrew also hoped there might be another WG book as *Ex-Fellwanderer* and *Fellwalking with a Camera* (1988) had both been published by them, despite the arrival of Michael Joseph.

On 10 December 1990, Andrew was summoned to come at 3.30 pm, not 2.30 as usual. 'I thought something was up. Since 1982, I had always called to see him at 2.30. He told me he was going to retire. It was the end. I could announce his retirement in the *Westmorland Gazette* newspaper, but he didn't want to see a reporter or talk to anyone. He didn't actually seem too unwell that day, so I suggested we should have some sort of dinner to mark his retirement.'

In his diary for that day, Andrew recorded the rest of their conversation: 'AW said all he wanted on his retirement was four cornettos, paid for by the Westmorland Gazette. "Then some time you and I will go to the Little Chef and I'll buy you a pancake." We discussed other matters, things we'd talked about before, but there was no pointing of the pipe, no leaning forward in his chair. He then reminisced about the old days, going out by car with the first of the Guides and selling two hundred on the first day, sale or return. He asked me how much my house was worth now.'

Next day, Nichol returned to Kendal Green, carrying Wainwright's retirement present from the Westmorland Gazette, a mark of gratitude for their twenty-seven years as his official publisher – or thirty-five years, if you go back to their connections as his printer – during which time they had sold almost two million copies of his books and generated some £5 million in sales income. 'I gave AW his four cornettos,' says Andrew. 'He took one, then Betty offered one to me, but AW said, "He's not having one, they're my presents, put the others in the fridge".'

A few days later, Andrew arrived in his car to pick up Wainwright for the return celebrations. 'Betty hadn't been told about the outing, so she started to rush around, saying she wasn't ready, but AW quipped he wasn't paying for her as well. Just the two of us were going.'

They drove to the Little Chef at Ings between Kendal and Windermere, where AW duly bought Andrew his pancake. 'As we came out, with me holding his elbow, he stopped at the bottom of the entrance ramp. "Did you enjoy that?" he asked. "Should we have another?" he asked. He was just joking. I think.'

On December 19, Wainwright gave his last television interview. Not to the BBC but to Eric Wallace of Border TV, his local independent company, based in Carlisle. Eric had almost been the first person to capture him on television in 1982 when he'd arrived to cover an Abbot Hall exhibition of Wainwright's work. Mary Burkett, then a director of Border TV, had hoped AW might agree to say a few words – but he didn't turn up. In July 1983, after the BBC's first programme, Eric Wallace did manage a few minutes with him, on camera, which was used in Border's Looka-round programme, during which AW said no, he didn't give interviews.

This time, however, he agreed to talk about his retirement from writing books, despite having said he wouldn't. 'I told him we wanted to do a five-minute piece for Lookaround on his retire-ment,' says Eric. 'He said he couldn't condense eighty-three years into five minutes, but when we got him started, he didn't stop talking, so we just let the camera run.'

He sat in his favourite armchair, dressed in a white Arran-style cardigan, his hair long and flowing, coughing rather worryingly from time to time, with Betty hovering in the background. He talked about his books, smiling wryly when he said they had been written for him to read in his old age, and now he couldn't read anything. 'I live in a world of mists, but by closing my eyes I can see a thousand walks as clearly as when I first walked them. Memory is going to be a big comfort to me.' (The interview was not shown until 27 January 1991, a week after his death, by which time Border had turned it into a half-hour programme.)

Wainwright spent Christmas quietly at home with Betty, sleeping much of the time. Since their marriage, twenty years earlier, Betty had spent part of each Christmas with one of her daughters. It had been arranged she would go and stay with Anne in Edinburgh, but she felt Red was too weak to be left. Instead, she met her daughter halfway, at Lockerbie, driving herself there for the afternoon, then coming home.

Two weeks after Christmas, on 6 January 1991, Wainwright woke up in bed saying he felt very ill. 'I tried to sit him up, but I couldn't, he was such a very heavy man. I realised he'd had heart failure. The arteries must have been blocked and he was getting very weak. I rang his doctor, who came straightaway, and immediately sent for an ambulance. He was rushed to the County Hospital in Kendal, the one I used to work in, and was put on oxygen.'

Betty moved into the hospital to be with him, sleeping overnight in an adjacent bungalow, kept for relatives of seriously ill patients. 'He never really recovered, though they had him on all sorts of drips and drugs. It was obvious his heart had packed up. He never properly spoke again and I think he was only half-conscious.'

His son Peter came to see him, sitting by the bed and holding his hand and telling him the latest football scores. 'He died to order, you might say,' says Peter. 'Slowly, just as he did everything. He could no longer walk, talk, or read his maps, so that was it. It was a shame he never lived to see Rovers come up into the First Division, which they did the next year. He would have liked to have seen that.'

Percy Duff also visited the hospital, and chatted away to him, not knowing how much he could understand. 'Although he appeared semi-conscious,' says Betty, 'I told Percy and Peter to be careful what they said. Hearing is always the last faculty to go.'

He took pleasure in being read to by Betty, even though he could make little response. Jenny Dereham couriered from London the first bound copy of his next Michael Joseph book, *Wainwright in the Limestone Dales*, which was not due to be published for several months. 'He wanted me to read the Introduction to him,' says Betty. 'I thought I might be tiring him, but he was squeezing my hand to tell me to go on. There were no last words. The last spoken words in hospital were his own words, me reading them to him.

'It was merciful that he was ill for such a short time. His heart had packed up. He would have been no good as an invalid. I couldn't possibly imagine Red being able to bear life in a wheelchair.'

Alfred Wainwright died on Sunday 20 January 1991, three days after his eighty-fourth birthday, at six o'clock in the evening. He went peacefully, knowing where his soul and his ashes were heading.

'All I ask for, at the end, is a last long resting place by the side of Innominate Tarn, on Haystacks,' so he wrote in 1966, 'where the water gently laps the gravelly shore and the heather blooms and Pillar and Gable keep unfailing watch. A quiet place, a lonely place. I shall go to it, for the last time, and be carried: someone who knew me in life will take me there and empty me out of a little box and leave me there alone. And if you, dear reader, should get a bit of grit in your boot as you are crossing Haystacks in the years to come, please treat it with respect. It might be me.'

CHAPTER TWENTY-EIGHT

After Words

Every national newsaper covered the news of Wainwright's death and the tributes were long and fulsome. In *The Times*, Ronald Faux wrote that he was 'a close companion whom I never met ... although he has died, the shadow remains and his books will stride on for generations of walkers who have not yet learned to toddle.' John Hillaby in the *Independent* predicted: 'There can never be another literary walker quite like Alfred Wainwright.'

The tabloids made much of the free half-pint at the Border Hotel in Kirk Yetholm for those finishing the Pennine Way, which would now presumably dry up. A party of twenty Japanese had recently just made it, flying from Tokyo especially to do the walk and collect their drink. It was estimated that Wainwright's gesture had cost him £15,000 since 1968 when beer was only 1/6 a pint. Now it was £1. 'The last cheque I got from him was for £500 last March,' so the landlord was quoted as saying. 'It has been just about spent, so he has died with a clean slate.' (In fact, Michael Joseph, his publishers, now pick up the tabs.)

Betty received calls from all over the country, asking about a memorial service, but she had decided the funeral would be totally private and there would no public service. Wainwright was cremated three days after he died, without any sort of church ceremony. Peter attended at the crematorium but was not able to manage the climb up Haystacks.

There were many enquiries about the final Haystacks climb but Betty sensibly refused to reveal any details. It took place two months later, on 22 March 1991. Betty and Percy Duff, both in their seventieth year, waited for signs of spring and better walking weather. Percy's sons, Paul and Michael, accompanied them as possible stretcher bearers, so Percy said, in case he collapsed. He had never been a keen fellwalker. One of the boys carried the casket of ashes. Percy took mint cake and sandwiches. They left Kendal at six in the morning, reached the old quarry on Honister Pass at seven – not the prettiest way to climb Haystacks, but by far the easiest – and were at the shores of Innominate Tarn at 8.30. The sun was out. Not another soul was in sight. Betty scattered the ashes near a cairn, they took photographs, and commenced the return walk. On the way down, they met the first people they had seen all morning, a party from a photographic club, carrying cameras and tripods and heading for Haystacks. Percy managed, but only just, not to tell them they had just missed a good photo opportunity.

In Wainwright's desk, after he had died, Betty found a wallet containing the photographs of five different women, plus Peter his son. There were two snaps of Betty, from their early, secret courting days, smiling at the camera. There was a photo of Ruth, his first wife, giving just a faint suggestion of a smile. There was one of Doris Snape, the widow of his old friend from Blackburn. The other two women were unknown to Betty. After exhaustive enquiries in Blackburn, it can be revealed that one of them is Betty Ditchfield, the passion of his office days in Blackburn, her hair parted in the middle, looking decidedly clever. But who is the fifth woman? So far, I have failed to identify her. She has been cut out from another snap. By the look of it she is a 1930s-style woman, hair parted to the side, standing, full length, holding a magazine or book. One of his Blackburn dream girls? Did she ever know of his interest? Was this interest ever consumated? Letters please. (*See* plate 29)

Betty also found an envelope addressed to herself – under her old name and address – marked 'To be opened only upon the death of Mr A. Wainwright'. In it she found a letter dated 14 October 1968, two years before they got married, at a time when their future together was still uncertain, although by that date their respective divorces had come through.

In the letter, AW said that he had made a new will that very day, thus revoking his previous will, dated 1 June 1956, in which he had left everything 'to my wife Ruth Wainwright'. In the new will, Ruth was left only £2 a week, his house and contents were to go to Peter, while all the rest of his estate and all income from his royalties were to go to Betty McNally. In this personal letter to Betty, which was typewritten, he asked her to do four things – maintain her own standard of life; give a correspondent from Halifax [now dead], whom he'd never met, £15 a year for a Lakeland holiday; keep up the beer money at Kirk Yetholm; and make anonymous donations to animal charities. The letter finished with a hand-written addition. 'Goodbye, love, and thanks for a thousand kindnesses. If there is another life, I will be waiting for you. Red.'

This caused great tears from Betty. In writing the letter that day, he had clearly felt they would never marry. When they eventually did, at the age of sixty-three, he promised her ten good years. In the event, they had almost twenty-one good and happy years together.

There was a later will, in 1970, on their marriage, in which Peter was no longer to receive the house, which was to go instead to Betty. Peter was to receive only £1,000, plus his father's books. On his death, it was discovered that an even later change to the will had been made – and Peter had been left nothing at all.

'I wasn't surprised,' says Peter today, sitting in his house in Staveley, his joints swollen with arthritis. His wife Doreen has also been seriously ill, suffering from depression. They have no children. 'That was just like him, to leave me nothing, yet he knew I was crippled and would never work again. Betty didn't get much either, when you think about it, mainly just the house, but she did give me his Russian pocket watch.'

The lack of contact between AW and Peter, despite the pride and pleasure he took in him when young, appears to have been partly caused by AW's feeling that he was 'her son', so that when the divorce came through, he no longer felt responsible. He also didn't believe in inherited wealth, not to humans anyway.

Did you like him? 'Yes, but we were never close,' says Peter. 'After he retired, he was more talkative, he had mellowed. I suppose I'm like him. I prefer my peace and quiet and not being bothered, but I'm not as bad as he was. I wouldn't say he was eccentric. Just obsessive.'

Were you proud of him? 'Yes, up to a point. I was proud but I considered the human cost to family relationships was too great.'

Wainwright's will, when it was published in November 1991, revealed he had left estate valued at £234,316, which included his house plus some savings. Betty had been left everything. She had expected there to be legacies to others.

'We were happy to live a simple life,' she says. 'My first husband was quite well off, but he lived a rich life, and spent quite a bit. Red and I preferred high thinking and low living.'

She expected to be able to live comfortably from his pension as a retired Borough Treasurer, which had been around £10,000 a year, plus some of her own invested savings. 'When he was alive, we lived quite easily on £20,000 a year, which seemed perfectly adequate. Red worked out that I would have most of that to live on which I agreed was more than enough.'

However, the moment AW died, his municipal pension stopped completely – because she had married him *after* he had retired. If they had married while he was still working, she would have got a good proportion of his pension for the rest of her life. It was typical of him, say both Betty and Peter, not to have kept a better eye on his own affairs, even though he was a trained accountant, supposedly used to reading the small print. There was once a fire in Kendal Green, and they made a claim for some carpets, but had got nothing because AW still had the house valued at £2,500 when it was by then worth £100,000.

For the first couple of years after his death, Betty had to live very carefully on a small income, despite the fact that during their life together, from the time they met properly in 1965, they had given away almost one million pounds to animal charities. 'It was his money, not mine, to do what he liked with, though I suppose he would not have written as much without my help, as chauffeur and researcher, but I agreed entirely with all his donations.'

Betty sold the Kendal Green house six months after he died, never having liked it much anyway, and moved to a bungalow in a village not far away. The Michael Joseph contracts with Wainwright had stated: 'I hereby renounce all legal rights to the royalties from this book and leave their distribution to the discretion of the publishers.' The publishers, in response to Betty's request, now divert some of the royalties to her.

In 1992, after nearly seven years' negotiations with the Westmorland Gazette, Michael Joseph took control of all the Wainwright books, including the Pictorial Guides. AW had not only known that these negotiations were in hand, but was very much in favour of the switch, repeatedly urging Jenny Dereham to get a move on. They started re-publishing the best-known ones under their own imprint in April 1992. About 25,000 copies of the seven Pictorial Guides are sold each year.

They published, posthumously, the two other illustrated books he had been working on – *Wainwright's Favourite Lakeland Mountains* (1991) and *Wainwright in the Valleys of Lakeland* (1992) plus *Memoirs of a Fellwanderer* in 1993 (a compilation of his two earlier books, *Fellwanderer* and *Ex-Fellwanderer*) and a recreation of one of his pre-war walks, *Wainwright's Tour in the Lake District: Whitsuntide 1931*, which came out in 1993. Frederick Warne, now owned by Penguin, keep Beatrix Potter's books alive and well, ever thinking up new ways to exploit her name, and in a similar fashion, Michael Joseph, also owned by Penguin, look after Wainwright.

Betty keeps a sharp eye on the Wainwright merchandising, the rights of which legally Michael Joseph now own, although they keep her informed when they allow the Wainwright name and logo to appear on T-shirts (which she does not like), on Kendal mint cake and on Wainwright boots made by K Shoes. The latter two products are at least produced in Kendal, and seem to me perfectly harmless, but many Wainwright devotees do not agree, maintaining old AW would turn in his grave to find his name being commercialised in such a way. New merchandising offers come in all the time, and most are refused.

One of the most surprising aspects of Wainwright devotion has been amongst collectors. Copies of all his old books are in great demand by those trying to acquire everything he ever published. First editions of the first five Pictorial Guides, with Henry Marshall's name as publisher, sell for around £150. A copy of *Westmorland Heritage*, which was limited to 1,000 copies in the first instance, has sold for £400. Original drawings, which in the 1980s he himself was selling for £10 each (all proceeds to charity), now appear in catalogues at £450.

The most valuable Wainwright book would probably be the one millionth copy of the Pictorial Guides, the one which he specially signed – that is, if it had ever appeared on the market in the first place. Amongst his possessions after his death, Betty found several copies of first editions of the guidebooks, cut up by him in order to save him re-drawing certain views and maps for use in later books. These copies he marked in green ink, rather alarmingly, with the one word 'MUTILATED'. There was also a copy of Book Six, the North Western Fells, not marked as 'mutilated', but it has one page missing – the page on which his name was signed in handwriting. Betty thinks this is the missing one millionth copy. If so, Andrew Nichol's suspicions were probably correct. AW sneaked back to the Keswick book shop, bought that copy as he couldn't face any publicity or fuss, then tore out the the vital page, destroying the evidence for ever.

Since his death, there has been great discussion, and great disagreements, over creating suitable monuments to his memory. Purists say his books are enough, let there be nothing else. But many Wainwright lovers feel there should be other more concrete commemorations and Betty, his widow, and Percy Duff, his old friend and one of the main keepers of the Wainwright flame, have been canvassed by many interested parties putting forward their own ideas.

There is a plaque in Blackburn on the house where he was born, at 331 Audley Range, put up by the local Civic Society in

1991, and the present owner of 38 Kendal Green is considering putting up his own plaque to mark AW's forty-two years of occupation. At the beginning of his Coast to Coast Walk at St Bees, there is a plaque which marks his creation of the walk. Apart from those, the most notable memorial is a commemorative window and tablet at Buttermere church, looking out towards Haystacks. This was organised by the vicar, Canon Michael Braithwaite, and a parishioner, Alan Johnson, with Betty's agreement, although there are those who say there shouldn't be anything inside a church as AW was not religious. It is a very discreet and attractive memorial (*see* plate 37). In 1994 plans were proposed, and some money raised, for a cairn or memorial on Orrest Head, but planning problems have caused this project to collapse.

There was a suggestion put forward by an official of Allerdale Council to re-name Innominate Tarn as Wainwright Tarn. I thought it was a nice idea, as Wainwright had always loved maps, and he might have been amused to think his name was on one for ever, but there were cries of shock and horror from several quarters, saying it was sacrilege, you can't change Lakeland names and, anyway, AW would never have indulged in such vanity. Clever clogs pointed out that Innominate means no-name, and has been acquired through usage only, and anyway there have been precedents, such as Birkett Fell which was named after the famous judge who helped save Ullswater from Manchester Water Works, and Robinson which was named after Richard Robinson, a local estate owner. (As AW said in Book Six, it could have been worse – 'It might have been a Smith or a Jones or a Wainwright.') Betty was not keen at first on the idea of Wainwright Tarn, but was persuaded and gave her approval for the approaches to be made. The Ordnance Survey was approached, and eventually said yes, they would put any change on future maps. So, all seemed set, until at the last moment it was discovered that Innominate Tarn is not actually in Allerdale. It's just over the boundary in Copeland District. Oops. Since then, silence.

Towards the end of his life, Wainwright agreed on a memorial display to be set up in his name at Brantwood on Coniston, the home of Ruskin. It was the idea of Bruce Hanson, the curator, who managed to collect several Wainwright related items, including an old printing press, some original pages, drawings and first editions, as well as one of his pipes, a jacket, a pair of socks, and a pair of spectacles. The Wainwright Room was opened in 1989 and drew many visitors. After his death, however, Betty had second thoughts. She decided she would like the display transferred to the Kendal Museum – on to local ground where he had lived all his Lakeland life, and where he had spent many years as Hon. Curator. 'I was sorry to see the display go,' says Bruce Hanson, 'but I recognize that Kendal was his spiritual home.'

The Kendal Museum is now the main pilgrimage centre for Wainwright fans where they can see his writing desk, pens, socks, inks, pipes, specs, rucksack, patched jacket and also an excellent selection of thirty-six original pages for the Pictorial Guides. The full impact is perhaps slightly spoiled by the exhibits being spread around the museum rather than in one concentrated display, and by the fact that the Kendal Museum, in Station Road, has not quite got the pulling power of Abbot Hall.

The memorial Wainwright was proudest of was Kapellan, the headquarters of Animal Rescue, Cumbria. I went to visit it one fine day in early summer, to see where all the Wainwright money had gone, what sixty books and forty years of obsessive writing and drawing and television series had produced. It's about five miles outside Kendal, a large bungalow in its own grounds, with a lush three-acre field affording splendid views of the Howgills and the Whinfell range. They bought the property for £62,000 and opened it as an animal shelter in 1984. In its early days they had problems finding a suitable resident manager, despite the comfortable and spacious accommodation, the pretty setting, the attractive way of life, and got through three different managers in four years, receiving some bad publicity on the way. (The *News of the World* did a story about 'three sacked managers'.) Now they have settled down happily with John Estensen as manager, aided by his wife

Dorothy. He used to be a policeman, then a trainer of gun dogs, while his wife ran a cattery.

Kapellan normally houses between thirty and forty cats and up to eighteen dogs. Half of them are unclaimed strays, usually passed on to them by local council wardens. The others come through a variety of sources. Some come through vets who, having been asked to put down an animal, discover the animal is too fit and healthy to die; in these cases, the vets usually discover the owners have become bored with looking after the animal. Others arrive at Kapellan having been owned by the sick and the elderly who, although still loving them dearly, are unable to care for them any more. All newcomers are checked by a vet, inoculated, then given individual accommodation and individual attention. On aver-age, their stay at Kapellan is two weeks before a new home is found. Animal Rescue has a regular advertisement in the *Westmor-land Gazette*, appealing for homes for their animals.

Not everyone who turns up, wanting a cat or a dog, is given one. That way a poor animal could end up where it began, with an unsuitable, uncaring owner. John Estensen cross-examines every prospective owner, asking them questions about their home life and their experience with animals. 'I used to go out and visit their homes, but now I can tell by talking to them. If in doubt, I say no. I say no to about two out of ten.' No fee is charged, but John never lets anyone go without getting a donation of around £25 for Animal Rescue. 'If they can't afford that, they can't afford to keep an animal. The other day I had a teacher who wanted to give a donation of £5 on a post-dated cheque. I said no.'

I went on a tour of the establishment, along with Betty. The bungalow itself is the manager's residence. In an adjoining garage and stable block there is a little office and an isolation room where the vet examines new animals. The cat quarters are round the back of the bungalow, custom built, amidst immaculate lawns. Each cat has a little wooden building to itself. Upstairs there is the sleeping quarters with a heater, floor rug and a glazed window. Downstairs is another room which has private access to a large exercise area at the rear, and a small patio complete with table and blanket at the front. I have seen humans living in less well-equipped accommodation. Admittedly, the scale is small, the rooms being animal size, but the space is generous, big enough for human children, and the facilities impressive.

The dogs live in a brand new building, just across the lawns, which at first I took for another bungalow as it is a full-size, proper house. It's called the Wainwright Shelter and cost £40,000 to build. Inside, there are individual kennels for eighteen dogs, each with their own exercise area. 'I did the basic drawings', said John, 'and suggested a cheap flat roof, like a hut, but AW wanted it to have a proper sloping roof. "We'll only do it once, so I want it done properly," he said. He saw the foundations, but he never lived to see it completed.'

Animal Rescue's annual report for 1993 showed that it found homes for 149 cats and 121 dogs. Annual income in 1992 was around £70,000 while annual expenditure was £33,000, thus leaving them a good annual profit. This is explained by the fact that they had £500,000 in the bank, in cash, and £100,000 in National Savings Income Bonds, which was giving them an investment income of around £50,000 a year.

If you tot up the total assets of Animal Rescue, with a property now worth around £200,000 plus the £600,000 in savings, and divide it by the number of animals they help every year, then each stray notionally represents around £3000. Unfair, perhaps to equate it like that, but it does seem a little, well, out of proportion, when you think of the stray humans who are in need across the planet.

I tried, gently, to put this point to John Estensen. 'The State provides for humans, not for animals. Man made animals dependent, because of their own selfishness, so we have to look after them. We need a large sum in the kitty so that we can continue to operate for ever, otherwise we could evaporate. We run it on commercial lines, but fortunately all our decisions don't have to be strictly commercial, as you can see by the quality of the new Wainwright kennels. It was his dream. I think it is a very fitting memorial to him.'

Wainwright did, of course, give some money to people, helping those in need, and just before he died he gave £10,000 to Kendal to set up an annual Special Achievement Award for a person doing most to help the town, but all the same, the major proportion of what in the end was a vast amount of money went to animals. Why didn't he help the environment? His money came from the Lakeland landscape; wouldn't it have been apt to give some of it back, the way Beatrix Potter did with the National Trust?

'Red disliked the Trust,' says Betty. 'It went back to some row he had with them, over a high-handed letter they wrote. We worked for Animal Rescue after we found a real local need. Homeless but healthy animals were being put down because they couldn't be housed properly. We had to do something.'

I'd gone to Kapellan ready to carp and criticise, feeling it was potty if not wicked for a man to give away a million pounds to animals yet leave nothing to people, let alone his only son, but I came away feeling slightly uplifted. Even amused. If someone has earned all their own money, by fair means not foul, and given pleasure to millions along the way, creating employment and income for others, a mini industry which will continue long after he has gone, then who are we to dictate how his money should be spent? The day was sunny, the pastures lush, the animals happy, the refuge clearly well run, which all helped to influence my mood – but it was the thought of Wainwright's happiness which really cheered me. Money had little part in his life. He wasn't interested in popular success or literary esteem, which anyway is an abstract notion, not something you can keep or hold. He wanted to have something solid for his life's work, an expression of his own private passion, something which would survive him and last for ever. I like to think he died happy, thinking of Kapellan, and probably smiling.

For millions of the rest of us, the books will of course be his main and lasting memorial. Wainwright prided himself on his drawings, knowing how long and meticulously he had worked on them, and his style though derivative is always distinctive. Yet his prose displays equal gifts, particularly in sections of *Fellwanderer*,

Ex-Fellwanderer and *Pennine Journey*, and in many of his letters. He was always slightly dismissive of his literary skills, saying he was merely filling up gaps between the drawings. Perhaps with more encouragement in his earlier days he might have written more general non-fiction, maybe even a novel, and emerged as another J. B. Priestley.

I consider his seven Pictorial Guides to be his masterpieces, terms not usually attached to mere guide books, but of course these are not merely guide books, but philosophical strolls, personal outpourings of feelings and observations, written and drawn by a craftsman, conceived and created as a total work of art. It is inconceivable that anyone should attempt to climb and describe all 214 of those Lakeland fells in quite the same way, ever again. Certainly not by using public transport to reach them.

APPENDIX

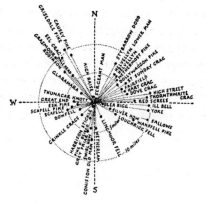

Bibliography

WAINWRIGHT'S BOOKS AND MAPS
Pictorial Guides to the Lakeland Fells
1. *Book One*: The Eastern Fells   1955
2. *Book Two*: The Far Eastern Fells   1957
3. *Book Three*: The Central Fells   1958
4. *Book Four*: The Southern Fells   1960
5. *Book Five*: The Northern Fells   1962
6. *Book Six*: The North Western Fells   1964
7. *Book Seven*: The Western Fells   1966

8. Fellwanderer: *The Story behind the Guidebooks*   1966
9. Pennine Way Companion   1968
10. A Lakeland Sketchbook   1969
11. Walks in Limestone Country   1970
12. A Second Lakeland Sketchbook   1970
13. A Third Lakeland Sketchbook   1971
14. Walks on the Howgill Fells   1972
15. A Fourth Lakeland Sketchbook   1972
16. A Coast to Coast Walk: *St Bees Head to Robin Hood's Bay*   1973
17. A Fifth Lakeland Sketchbook   1973
18. The Outlying Fells of Lakeland   1974

Scottish Mountain Drawings
19. *Volume One*: The Northern Highlands   1974
20. *Volume Two*: The North-Western Highlands   1976
21. *Volume Three*: The Western Highlands   1976
22. *Volume Four*: The Central Highlands   1977
23. *Volume Five*: The Eastern Highlands   1978
24. *Volume Six*: The Islands   1979

25. Westmorland Heritage 1974
26. A Dales Sketchbook 1976
27. Kendal in the Nineteenth Century 1977
28. A Second Dales Sketchbook 1978
29. A Furness Sketchbook 1978
30. Walks from Ratty 1978
31. A Second Furness Sketchbook 1979
32. Three Westmorland Rivers 1979
33. A Lune Sketchbook 1980
34. A Ribble Sketchbook 1980
35. An Eden Sketchbook 1980

Lakeland Mountain Drawings
36. *Volume One* 1980
37. *Volume Two* 1981
38. *Volume Three* 1982
39. *Volume Four* 1983
40. *Volume Five* 1984

41. Welsh Mountain Drawings 1981
42. A Bowland Sketchbook 1981
43. A North Wales Sketchbook 1982
44. A Wyre Sketchbook 1982
45. A South Wales Sketchbook 1983
46. A Peak District Sketchbook 1984
47. Wainwright in Lakeland 1983
48. Old Roads of Eastern Lakeland 1985
49. Ex-Fellwanderer 1987
50. Fellwalking with a Camera 1988

51. Fellwalking with Wainwright 1984
    with photographs by Derry Brabbs
52. Wainwright on the Pennine Way 1985
    with photographs by Derry Brabbs
53. A Pennine Journey 1986
54. Wainwright's Coast to Coast Walk 1987
    with photographs by Derry Brabbs

55. Wainwright in Scotland   1988
    with photographs by Derry Brabbs
56. Wainwright on the Lakeland Mountain Passes   1989
    with photographs by Derry Brabbs
57. Wainwright in the Limestone Dales   1991
    with photographs by Ed Geldard
58. Wainwright's Favourite Lakeland Mountains   1991
    with photographs by Derry Brabbs
59. Wainwright in the Valleys of Lakeland   1992
    with photographs by Derry Brabbs

60. Ordnance Survey Outdoor Leisure Series 1:25 000,
    Map 33 – Coast to Coast Walk: St Bees Head to Keld   1994
61. Ordnance Survey Outdoor Leisure Series 1:25 000,
    Map 34 – Coast to Coast Walk: Keld to Robin Hood's
    Bay   1994

NOTES ON PUBLISHERS: The first fifty books (1–50) were originally published by the Westmorland Gazette, except for: Books 1–5 which had the name Henry Marshall as publisher until 1963 when Westmorland Gazette took them over; No. 30 published by the Ravenglass and Eskdale Railway Co; No 47 published by Abbot Hall. Books 51–59 were first published by Michael Joseph, who now also publish all the books previously published by the Westmorland Gazette. Maps 60 and 61 published by Ordnance Survey in conjunction with Michael Joseph.

OTHER WAINWRIGHT WORKS
Map of Westmorland 1974
Map of Cumbria 1980

WAINWRIGHT ILLUSTRATIONS IN OTHER PUBLICATIONS
Inside the Real Lakeland by A. H. Griffin, Guardian Press, Preston, 1961
Annual Accounts of Southern Lakes and Lune Water Board, 1963–73
Scratch and Co by Molly Lefebure, Gollancz, 1968
The Hunting of Wilberforce Pike by Molly Lefebure, Gollancz, 1970
The Plague Dogs, novel by Richard Adams, Allen Lane, 1977
Guide to the View from Scafell Pike, Chris Jesty Panoramas, 1978
Climbing at Wasdale Before the First World War by George Sansom, Castle Cary Press, 1982

BOOKS ABOUT WAINWRIGHT OR DERIVED FROM HIS WORKS
A Companion to Wainwright's Pictorial Guide to the Lakeland Fells compiled by Joan Newsome, Michael Joseph, 1992
After You, Mr Wainwright by W. R. Mitchell, Castleberg, 1992
Memoirs of a Fellwanderer, Michael Joseph, 1993
Wainwright's Tour in the Lake District: Whitsuntide, 1931, with photographs by Ed Geldard, Michael Joseph, 1993
The Official Wainwright Gazetteer, compiled by Peter Linney, Michael Joseph, 1993
The Walker's Log Book, Volumes One and Two, Michael Joseph, 1993
For Those Who Love the Hills, quotations from Wainwright's Pictorial Guides to the Lakeland Fells, compiled by William F. Dyer, Michael Joseph, 1994

COLLECTING WAINWRIGHT BOOKS

Expect to pay the following prices (1995) for First Editions: *The Pictorial Guides to the Lakeland Fells*, Book 1–5, published by Henry Marshall: £100–£150

Later editions, also published by Henry Marshall: £15–£50

First editions published by the Westmorland Gazette: £15–£50

Fellwanderer, first edition, published by Westmorland Gazette, 1966: £30–£50

Westmorland Heritage, Westmorland Gazette, 1974, signed limited edition of 1,000: £300–£400

Kendal in the Nineteenth Century: Westmorland Gazette, 1977: £75–£100

Wainwright in Lakeland, published by Abbot Hall, 1983, signed limited edition of 1,000: £300–£450

Any Westmorland Gazette first edition: £30–£75

Any signed edition – Westmorland Gazette books £60; Michael Joseph £30

Original drawings: £300–£450

Book dealers who usually carry a stock of Wainwright early editions:

Hollett and Son, 6 Finkle Street, Sedbergh, Cumbria, LA10 5BZ. Tel. 015396 20298

Kirkland Books, 68 Kirkland, Kendal, Cumbria, LA9 5AP. Tel. 01539 740 841

Page 6 Books, 18 Underwood Close, Parkside, Stafford, ST16 1TB. Tel. 01785 41153

Carnforth Bookshop, 38 Market Street, Carnforth, Lancashire, LA5 9JX. Tel. 01524 734588

WAINWRIGHT VIDEOS

Five videos, based on the BBC TV series, produced by Striding Edge Presentation. Available in bookshops, price £12.99 each, or write to Crag House Farm, Wasdale, Cumbria, CA19 1UT.

WAINWRIGHT MERCHANDISING

Wainwright Kendal Mint Cake – made by Wilson of Kendal. In 1994 they sold 14,000 boxes, price £1.50. In 1995 they also brought out a small bar, price 50p. Yum yum.

Wainwright Boots – made by K Shoes of Kendal. In 1994 they sold 10,000 pairs of the Wainwright Master Fellwalker Boot, price £89.95. In 1995 they also brought out a Wainwright Lady Fellwalker Boot, price £89.95. Hurry, hurry.

THE WAINWRIGHT TRAIL

Blackburn

Birth place: 331 Audley Range, Blackburn. Plaque outside.

Other Wainwright homes in Blackburn: 1 Hamer Avenue and 90 Shadsworth Road.

Town Hall Information: 01254 585934

Blackburn Tourist Office: 01254 53277

Ewood Park, home of Blackburn Rovers: 01254 698888

Kendal

First home: 19 Castle Grove.

Main home: 38 Kendal Green.

Kendal Museum: Station Road, 01539 721374. Recreated AW office, original pages, memorabilia on show.

Buttermere

St James's Church: memorial window.

Haystacks: ashes scattered beside Innominate Tarn.

Index